THE COMMERCIALIZED CRAFTS OF THAILAND

ConsumAsiaN Book Series
edited by
Brian Moeran and Lise Skov

The ConsumAsiaN book series examines the way in which things and ideas about things are consumed in Asia, the role of consumption in the formation of attitudes, experiences, lifestyles and social relations, and the way in which consumption relates to the broader cultures and societies of which it is a part. The series consists of both single-authored monographs and edited selections of essays, and is interdisciplinary in approach. While seeking to map current and recent consumer trends in various aspects of Asian cultures, the series pays special attention to the interactions and influences among the countries concerned, as well as to the region as a whole in a global context. The volumes in the series apply up-to-date theoretical arguments frequently developed in Europe and America to non-western societies – both in order to analyse how consumption practices in Asia compare to those found elsewhere, and to develop new theories that match a specific Asian context.

Women, Media and Consumption in Japan
Edited by Lise Skov and Brian Moeran
Published 1995

A Japanese Advertising Agency
An Anthropology of Media and Markets
Brian Moeran
Published 1996

Contemporary Japan and Popular Culture
Edited by John Whittier Treat
Published 1996

Packaged Japaneseness
Weddings, Business and Brides
Ofra Goldstein-Gidoni
Published 1997

Australia and Asia
Cultural Transactions
Edited by Maryanne Dever
Published 1997

Asian Department Stores
Edited by Kerrie L. MacPherson
Published 1998

Staging Hong Kong (*1998*)
Gender and Performance in Transition
Rozanna Lilley
Published 1998

Consuming Ethnicity and Nationalism
Edited by Kosaku Yoshino
Published 1999

The Commercialized Crafts of Thailand
Hill Tribes and Lowland Villages
Erik Cohen
Published 2000

THE COMMERCIALIZED CRAFTS OF THAILAND

Hill Tribes and Lowland Villages

collected articles

Erik Cohen

CURZON

First published in 2000
by Curzon Press
Richmond, Surrey
http://www.curzonpress.co.uk

© 2000 Erik Cohen

Typeset in Times by LaserScript Ltd, Mitcham
Printed and bound in Great Britain by
Biddles Ltd, Guildford and King's Lynn

British Library Cataloguing in Publication Data
A catalogue record for this book is available from the British Library

ISBN 0-7007-0662-2

ISBN 0-7007-1196-1

CONTENTS

ACKNOWLEDGEMENTS

Chapter 2 – Previously published in *Journal of the Siam Society*, 77(1), 1989, 69–82.

Chapter 3 – Previously published in the *Journal of the National Research Council of Thailand* 15(1), 1983, Part II, 69 82.

Chapter 4 – Previously published in *Studies in Popular Culture*, 11(2), 1988, 49–59.

Chapter 5 – Previously published in *Res*, No. 14, 1987, 27 45; copyright by President and Fellows of Harvard College.

Chapter 6 – Previously published in: D.Eban, E. Cohen and B. Danet (eds.): *Art as a Means of Communication in Pre-Literate Societies*, Proceedings of the Wright International Symposium on Primitive and Pre-Columbian Art Israel Museum, Jerusalem, 1990, 51–95.

Chapter 7 Previously published in *Visual Anthropology*, 9, 1996, 25–40.

Chapter 8 – Previously published in *Tourism Management*, 16(3), 1995, 225–235, copyright 1995 with permission from Elsevier Science.

Chapter 9 – Previously published in *Annals of Tourism Research*, 20(1), 1993, 138–163, copyright 1993 with permission from Elsevier Science.

Chapter 10 – Previously published in M. Howard, W. Wattanapum, A. Gordon (eds.): *Traditional Thai Arts in Contemporary Perspective,* Studies in Contemporary Thailand (Erik Cohen ed.), No. 7, Bangkok: White Lotus, 1998, 149–174.

LIST OF ILLUSTRATIONS

LIST OF ILLUSTRATIONS

ix

LIST OF ILLUSTRATIONS

xi

Note: All photos by author if not indicated otherwise.

LIST OF TABLES

THE STUDY OF THE COMMERCIALIZED CRAFTS OF THAILAND

Approach, Background and Principal Conclusions

Thai arts and crafts have attracted considerable international attention in recent decades; in response a voluminous literature on the amazing variety of Thai arts and crafts has recently emerged. However, as rich as this literature is, it relates predominantly to 'traditional' Thai arts and crafts – whether to those created by the masters of the past, or to those still made by traditional artisans in contemporary Thailand (for example, Leesuwan 1981, *Sawaddi* 1982, Warren and Tettoni 1994). Much of this literature is ahistorical, sometimes even purposely seeking to obliterate the difference between past and present arts and craft products (Warren and Tettoni 1994). This is particularly the case with touristic publications, which seek deliberately to create the impression that Thai arts and crafts still maintain their authenticity and viability, while passing silently over the decline and transformations which modern influences imparted to them. Even serious students of Thai culture have usually preferred to devote their attention to the renown crafts of former times (for example, Wenk 1980, Gittinger and Lefferts 1992), rather than to the study of more recent developments, probably because they saw in those developments – and particularly in commercialization – an unretrievable debasement or corruption of Thai crafts, not worthy of serious attention. Consequently, only few researchers conducted any systematic work on recent developments in Thai arts and crafts (but see Mabry and Mabry 1981; Parnwell and Khamanarong 1990); particularly absent are specific studies of their commercialization.

Seeking to deal with this deficiency I have in the course of the last two decades conducted a series of studies on the commercialization of the crafts of two major population groups of Thailand: the hill tribes and the lowland villagers. This volume brings together my articles based on these studies. In this introduction I shall outline my conceptual approach and provide the necessary background information; I shall also present the principal conclusions which emerge from the material presented in the body of the book.

The over-arching concern of my studies was the analysis of the process of commercialization of the folk crafts in Thailand: the conditions of its emergence, the parties involved in its development, the changes in the processes and organization of production which accompany it, the channels through which commercialized craft products are marketed, the nature of the audiences which they reach, and the transformations in appearance and meaning which the products undergo as a result of their commercialization. Each chapter of this book is in a sense monographic, dealing with a specific issue in a particular context; but virtually all of them relate to one or another of these principal aspects of the process of commercialization; though they have not been originally written with a broad comparative context in mind, they can still be analyzed comparatively, to show the divergent trends of change in the commercialized crafts of the two populations under study. These trends will be outlined in the concluding section of this introduction.

The Studies

The book brings together two groups of articles based on materials from studies conducted under very different circumstances and during different periods of time.

The study of the commercialization of hill tribe crafts grew out of my initial research on the penetration of tourism into the hill tribe regions of Thailand (Cohen 1996: 29–148), begun in 1977. In the course of fieldwork, conducted in the mountainous trekking area of northern Thailand, I became aware of the significance of craft sales to tourists, passing through tribal villages, as a source of income for the tribals (Cohen 1979).

My interest gradually shifted from tribal tourism to tribal art, especially as in the late 1970s and early 1980s the tourist market in Thailand became flooded by great quantities of Hmong crafts, produced by the huge number of refugees interned in camps in Thailand, after their escape from communist-dominated Laos. Though I visited several refugee camps, my study focussed on the activities of the relief organizations, located mainly in Chiang Mai and Bangkok, which sponsored and marketed the craft production of the refugees, rather than on the producers themselves.

With the gradual resettlement of the refugees in third countries in the 1980s and the repatriation of those who remained behind in the 1990s, the scope of tribal crafts produced for the market in Thailand decreased substantially; even though some crafts are still produced in the tribal villages of Thailand, the production process and the products underwent considerable routinization: few if any changes took place in recent years in the organization of production or in the form and style of the tribal products. In contrast to the commercialized crafts of the lowland villages, commercial hill tribe crafts are presently in a state of stagnation. The articles in the first part of the book relate to the period of their florescence, up to the mid-1980s.

In the course of the 1990s I turned to the study of the commercialization of the crafts of lowland villagers. The focus of this study differed significantly from that of the preceding one: I studied the artisans and traders in the villages themselves, rather than the wider marketing frameworks. Upon surveying a large number of villages throughout Thailand, I settled on a series of case studies of several 'craft villages' in northern Thailand and on one in its northeast, in which various types of commercial crafts are produced. Four of these case studies are included in the second part of this book (Chs.9–12). In contrast to the study of the hill tribe crafts, where a cyclical process of commercialization, from inception to stagnation, was investigated, in the case studies of lowland villages, I could document only some temporal segments of the process, although I followed it in some villages for up to eight years, since the process started years before I initiated my study and is still going on. However, I concluded my study during a significant turning point in the Thai economy, the financial crisis of 1997/8, which has also significantly affected craft production. The crisis constitutes an interlude in the process of commercialization, but there is little doubt that, once the crisis is overcome, the process will proceed further, possibly along new lines.

Conceptual Approach and Research Problems

In the popular consciousness of the West, the people of the Third and especially the Fourth World, namely the tribal and ethnic minorities incorporated in the Third world states (Graburn (ed.) 1976), are often conceived in terms of an ahistorical Other: mirror images of the modern world, simple, authentic and unchanging, at least until their penetration by modern global forces of change; these forces are seen as inevitably detrimental and destructive of the lives and cultures of these

3

people. As a corollary, the commercialization of the arts and crafts of Third and Fourth world people, involving their re-orientation from a predominantly local, internal audience to some new external and often foreign audiences, tends to be seen as leading to an irretrievable decline and debasement of the 'authentic', vital and unchanging traditions of the past. The sense of discontinuity between an ahistoric, isolated past of these societies and their incorporation into global history, inherent in this image, leads to the view that arts and crafts produced in the wake of contact between a local culture and the economic and acculturative forces of the West are necessarily 'unauthentic', meaningless to the locals and even to their producers. Terms, such as 'tourist arts' or even the more derisive 'airport art' (Graburn 1967) symbolize this attitude (Cohen 1992c:3).

However, this image is historically wrong, and leads to unwarranted theoretical and empirical claims; by discarding a priori the commercialized arts and crafts emerging from the inter-penetration of local and global cultural trends, a serious analysis of the nature and meaning of commercialized cultural products is precluded.

It should be noted indeed that even in the past most Third and Fourth world people were not isolated from external influences. Their arts and crafts were throughout history influenced by the styles, designs, materials and techniques of other cultures and societies, even as they influenced them. It is true, however, that in recent times such influences have been extraordinarily intrusive and often destructive at least in the short run.

It should also be noted that Third and Fourth world societies have not necessarily been autarkic: even though their artisans produced primarily for local consumption, some products, especially the more refined ones, were consumed by the local or national elites or even entered the routes of international trade (Bowie 1993b:187–189).

It follows from the preceding discussion that commercialization and other processes brought about by modern global forces do not constitute a unique gradient in the history of Third and Fourth world arts and crafts, but are only another stage in their historical process of change. A corollary of this observation is that there does not exist an ahistorical point of departure at which local arts and crafts were pure and uncontaminated by outside influences, from which a study of their change in modern times could depart. Rather, a historical 'base-line' has to be chosen to which the present state of the arts and crafts could be related and compared; a convenient base line is the state of the arts and crafts of the people under study in the period immediately

4

preceding commercialization. But, as anyone who peruses Southeast Asia travel accounts from the nineteenth or early twentieth century would immediately realize, the costumes and the other arts and crafts of the people of Thailand, were at those earlier times often markedly different from those at such a base-line; the latter are hence not any more or less 'authentic' from those which preceded or followed them.

When modern, global forces impinge upon the arts and crafts of Third and Fourth world people, their impact is not simply uni-linear: they do not undergo an undifferentiated transition from 'traditional' to 'modern' (Cohen, 1992c:5). Rather the processes of change are extraordinarily complex and varied. Different models have therefore been proposed which sought to take account of this complexity and variability, while introducing some theory-related order into the multiplicity of concrete phenomena of change. Graburn (1976b,1984) proposed models for the classification and evolution of tourist arts. Shiloah and Cohen (1983) proposed a model for the study of change in folk music, based on the variables which I used in my earlier work on change in commercialized hill tribe crafts (Ch.3). These models conceptualize various types of change in folk-arts, which are generated by the intersection between the defining variables of the models (Cohen 1992c:5–7). However, for present purposes it suffices to specify only those variables which are frequently used throughout this book to characterize particular processes of change in commercialized crafts. Since I refer only occasionally to the specific types of change, conceptualized by these authors, I shall not present them systematically in this introduction.

This book focuses on processes of stylistic change in arts and crafts under conditions of commercialization; four principal variables will be applied to the analysis of these processes:

(1) Perpetuation vs. Innovation: this variable refers to the extent to which an art or craft changes under conditions of commercialization: in particular, whether artisans tend merely to reproduce the stylistic elements prevalent at the 'base-line' (perpetuation) or tend to introduce new elements into their work (innovation).

(2) Orthogenesis vs. Heterogenesis: this variable, adapted from the work of Redfield and Singer (1969) on the cultural role of cities, refers to the nature of stylistic innovations: whether artisans merely continue to adapt or elaborate stylistic elements inherent in the style at the base-line (orthogenesis) or tend to introduce radically new stylistic elements, unrelated to the style of the base-line, or to the artisans' broader cultural traditions (heterogenesis).

5

(3) Internal vs. External Audience: this variable, adapted from Graburn (1976b), relates to the intended audience of commercialized products: whether this audience shares the cultural background of the artisans (internal public) or whether it is unfamiliar with it (external public).

(4) Spontaneous vs. sponsored production: this variable relates to the source of the initiative of commercialization: whether the artisans commercialized their products on their own initiative (spontaneous) or whether the initiative came from an external agent such as a governmental agency, relief or other non-governmental organization, or private entrepreneur, who ordered, promoted or marketed the products.

The four variables are here presented in dichotomous terms merely for the sake of clarity; the terms used represent polar points of essentially continuous variables; thus, there are many kinds of external publics, differing in the extent of their familiarity or identification with the cultural background of the artisans; and there are various configurations of spontaneity and sponsorship in the commercialization of different kinds of arts and crafts.

The principal research problem dealt with in various ways in the articles collected in this book regards the relationship between marketing and stylistic change, under diverse conditions of commercialization of craft products. In particular, how and to what extent various kinds of external audiences reached by expanding marketing channels, bring about the gradual heterogeneization of local production; and whether and to what extent the intervention of sponsoring agencies helps safeguard the survival of indigenous styles despite commercialization.

A second major problem relates to the motivation of the producers and the meaning of their products to them under conditions of commercialization; in particular, whether economic considerations become so predominant that the cultural meaning of the products becomes irrelevant to them; or whether even in cases of extreme heterogeneization, their work is still meaningful to them, albeit in a novel sense. This is closely related to the question of whether, and in what sense commercialized craft products, even the heterogenetic ones, are still in some sense 'authentic' in the eyes of producers, sponsors or clients.

A third major problem concerns the various technological and organizational changes accompanying the different processes of commercialization, which both influence, and are influenced by, the stylistic transformations which the craft products undergo: The introduction and dissemination of new techniques, implements or machinery, and of new, often industrially produced raw materials; changes in the scope, composition and skills of the labor force; changes in the scale of production, in the division of labor and in the organization and management of production, promotion and marketing. The most significant question here is whether, with the rise in the scale of production, a transition to industrial forms of organization takes place.

A fourth problem relates to the distribution of the benefits of craft production between artisans, workshop-owners, and middlemen or other intermediaries in the marketing channels. The question of interest here is, what is the share of total benefits accruing to the original producers, and how does it compare to alternative sources of income. This leads to the last major problem of my studies: what is the long-term viability of the commercialized crafts? Will they be able to survive under prevailing conditions on the national, and especially international crafts market, in a modernizing, expanding economy, which – at least until the financial crisis of 1997–98 – offered attractive alternatives to craft employment, especially to the younger generation of craft-producing communities; and will they be able to weather the financial crisis itself.

'Court Arts' and 'Folk Crafts' in Thailand

Old Siam, like other pre-modern Southeast Asian kingdoms, was endowed with a rich and varied artistic tradition. The splendor of the Siamese court and of the adjacent royal Buddhist temples was created by superb artisans. Many of those, however, were not indigenous; rather, they were often captives resettled by the rulers from outlying conquered territories, mostly onto areas close to the royal capital, to produce the luxurious goods demanded by the court. Smaller potentates within the Siamese 'galactic polity' (Tambiah 1976:102–131) followed the example of the paramount rulers on a lower scale. Thus, many of the 'craft villages' of northern Thailand, which endowed the region with its reputation for fine arts and crafts, were inhabited by 'ethnic minorities brought into the Chiang Mai Valley [by the rulers of Chiang Mai] as war captives sometime during the 19th century' (Bowie 1993a:148). These were often slaves of the court, who had to supply it with fine art and craft products. The rulers also extracted additional

7

craft products as tribute from the rural population over which they ruled (Bowie 1993a:148–9).

In pre-modern times craft skills were widely diffused; ordinary villagers were capable of making by themselves many objects for daily use. But, contrary to the widely held image of the rural 'subsistence economy', Thai villages were not completely autarkic. Particular villages and whole regions specialized in crafts demanding special skills, such as various weaving and silver-smithing techniques. Their craft output was traded on local or even international markets (Bowie 1993b). Indeed, the commercialization of Thai crafts in recent decades often began in villages in which such special skills survived up to the contemporary period.

With some simplification we may claim that Siamese arts and crafts fell into two partly overlapping domains, distinguished by the qualities of their materials and craftsmanship, their distributive channels and their principal audiences: 'court arts' and 'folk crafts'.

The court arts were made of rare and expensive materials by highly skilled artisans for royal, aristocratic or sacerdotal patrons; they served as decorative status symbols or for the ceremonial or cultic needs of palace and temple (Warren and Tettoni 1994:9–64). Prominent court arts were gold and silversmithing (Nildej 1986, Warren and Tettoni 1994:15–17, Shitamara 1991) mother of pearl inlay (Wenk 1980, Leesuwan 1981:36–43, *Heritage* B.E. 2532), nielloware (Leesuwan 1981:44–50, Clark 1991, Pandit 1991), lacquerware (Leesuwan 1981:52–60, Wright 1978), and silk and brocade weaving (S. Brown 1979, I. Brown 1980, Arin 1992, Conway 1992, Bowrie 1993b).

Siamese 'folk crafts', made of commonly available, more ordinary materials were less refined (though often exquisitely made) and served primarily the practical purposes of household and field, or the requirements of festive occasions (Warren and Tettoni 1994:65–88).

The variety of Siamese folk crafts was very great indeed; here I shall list only some principal kinds of these crafts, within each of which many specializations can be distinguished: basketry and mat-making (Chudhavipata 1986/7, Angsanakul 1997, Sukphisit 1997), pottery (Graham 1954 [1920], Leesuwan 1981:1–9, Parnwell and Khamanarong 1990:20–22, Katz 1991), woodwork (*Holiday Time in Thailand* 1978, Warren and Tettoni 1994, passim), bamboo work (Warren and Tettoni 1994: 67,69), iron smithing (Sukphisit 1993), metal and bronze casting (Bekker 1978, *Lookeast* 1988), brassware making (Larnlua 1990, Parnwell and Khamanarong 1990:19–20, Sukphisit 1991b), candle making (Kanwerayotin 1988), stone cutting (Savanya 1992) and many types of weaving with vegetable fibres (Conway 1992, *Thai Life* 1994, Warren and Tettoni 1994:89–105).

The articles collected in this volume deal only with the commercialization of hill tribe and lowland folk crafts; they are not concerned with the refined court arts, even though some of these also underwent a process of commercialization, much of it under the sponsorship of the Queen's SUPPORT Foundation (SUPPORT 1985, 1992).

Decline and Resurgence of Thai Arts and Crafts

Old Siam has been imagined in the popular Western consciousness as an enchanted Oriental kingdom, rich in sumptuous ceremonies and ornate arts and crafts. Traces of this image still survive, notwithstanding the far-reaching technological, economic and cultural transformations which Thailand underwent in the last one hundred and fifty years. Moreover, the image is still unabashedly promoted by the Thai tourist establishment, especially the Tourism Authority of Thailand (TAT), as for example, in its current 'Amazing Thailand' campaign (Thanya 1997). The glaring contrast between the touristic image so promoted and the everyday reality marks virtually every domain of Thai life: the glowing descriptions of the Thai landscape contrast with the rapid destruction of the environment, the exotic image of the hill tribes contrasts with their actual deculturation and marginalization (Cohen 1996:145–148), and the glorification of Thai cultural traditions contrasts with their concomitant transformation, impoverishment and even extinction in social practice, as life styles change under the impact of forces of cultural globalization, penetrating through the mass media into ever more remote and previously isolated groups and regions of the country.

Thai arts and crafts are similarly celebrated in richly illustrated books and articles, which seek to promote an impression of continuing and vital artistic creativity while disregarding the threat of extinction faced by many of these arts and crafts as demand for them on part of its former internal audience declined over the last decades, and in many instances all but disappeared. The older elites, which have been the principal patrons of the 'court arts', insofar as they kept their social positions, adopted novel, modern status symbols; and the villagers, the users of 'folk crafts', increasingly substituted industrial for craft products, in the field, the household and in their personal attire.

The decline of craft production was particularly severe in the central region, the plains close to the capital Bangkok; it was less pervasive in

the outlying parts of the northern, northeastern and southern regions. In some of the more isolated areas of these regions 'craftsmen continued to produce the items needed in their daily life . . . using the same techniques and designs as their ancestors have done' (Warren and Tettoni 1994:7). This is especially true for the hill tribes of the north and some other isolated ethnic groups, like the Phu Tai (Lohitkul 1990) in the northeast of the country. But even in many lowland villages the skills of craft production were often preserved, although they may have lost much of their vitality; their preservation sometimes depended on a single person, who came to play later on a leading role in the revival of the craft – eventually to be declared a 'national artist', as was, for example, Saengda Bansidh, a famous northern Thai weaver (Samosorn 1989). Many of the crafts which survived the decline were given a new lease on life by commercialization, often through the intervention by some sponsoring agency, for new external audiences. This is the main theme running through the articles collected in this book. However, the conditions and the dynamics of commercialization of hill tribe crafts differed in significant respects from those characteristic of the crafts of the lowland villages. A brief background on these two populations and on their crafts will facilitate an understanding of these differences.

The Hill Tribes and Their Crafts[1]

The term 'hill tribes' has been employed by foreign travellers and researchers to designate the highland people of northern Thailand (and of other mainland Southeast Asian countries): it corresponds to the French 'montagnards' or the Thai 'chao khao'. 'Hill tribes' is a vague and controversial term (Cohen 1992d) engendering an unwarranted image of the highlanders as internally cohesive and externally bounded groups; recently, indeed, researchers have sought more adequate and less 'loaded' terms to designate these peoples (cf. McCaskill 1997). I use the term here mainly because the crafts of these people have been generally known as 'hill tribe crafts'.

In the 1960s, when the Tribal Research Institute was established in Chiang Mai, six groups have been officially designated as 'hill tribes': the Karen, Hmong (Meo), Mien (Yao), Lahu, Lisu and Akha; to these were later added three more groups: the Htin, Khamu and Lawa (Lu'a) (Kunstadter 1983, Lewis and Lewis 1984). Some tribal groups, such as the Hmong (Ch.2), are further divided into sub-groups, whose names derive mostly from the color of the costume of their womenfolk. The distribution of the tribal population residing in villages in Thailand in the mid-1970s, immediately preceding the inception of my field work, and in 1996, is presented in Table 1.1. The table does not include the tribal refugees from Laos, who were from the mid-1970s interned in refugee camps in Northeastern Thailand, and whose numbers reached up to 40–45,000 in the early 1980s; by far the largest group among these refugees were the Hmong (Ch.2), but there were also smaller numbers of Mien and Htin. The Karen refugees from the fighting in Burma (Raksakul 1995), presently interned in camps along the Burmese border, are also not included in the table.

Most of the tribal groups in the highlands of Thailand are not indigenous, but migrated into the country at an accelerating rate in the course of the last century (Lewis and Lewis 1984:9). In the past, they moved in with a complete disregard of international boundaries, in search of suitable forest land, on which to practice their shifting (or 'swiddening') agriculture (Kunstadter and Chapman 1978): they cut and burned the trees to create fields on which to cultivate mountain rice, corn and various other subsistence crops. The Hmong, Lisu and Mien also grew opium poppies, as their principal cash crop (Geddes 1970, Tapp 1986:19–28). As the fields surrounding their settlements became exhausted, they moved further on towards the south along the mountain ranges and into ever lower elevations, until some groups, especially the Karen, reached the valleys and partly intermingled with the lowland peasant population (Hamilton 1976). Swiddening of virgin forests has by now virtually stopped, partly due to their growing

Hill Tribe	mid-1970s[**]	1996[***]
Karen	184,648	402,095
Hmong (Meo)	37,301	126,147
Mien (Yao)	22,652	47,305
Lahu	22,584	78,842
Lisu	12,542	31,536
Akha	13,566	48,468
Htin	19,398	32,755
Khamu	6,315	10,153
Lawa (Lu'a)	11,250	15,711
Total	330,256	793,012

Table 1.1 The Hill Tribe Population of Thailand, mid-1970 and 1996[*]

*Does not include the tribal refugees from Laos and Burma
**Source*: Kunstader 1983:17
***Source*: Kampe 1997:22–23

scarcity and partly to the efforts of the authorities to settle the tribal people and interdict their further migration. In the last two decades, the in-migration of tribal groups diminished, but a trickle continues to enter the country up to the present, settling in highland villages.

The spectacular growth in the number of hill people in Thailand between the mid-1970s and 1996, does thus not derive from in-migration, but is principally due to the rapid rate of reproduction (and possibly also to some under-estimation of the tribal population in the 1970s).

Most hill tribe villages maintained a considerable degree of isolation and independence from lowland society well into the 1960s and 1970s, when lowland population pressures, economic development and governmental action began to penetrate the highlands with growing intensity (Bhruksasri 1989, Vienne 1989). Communist-inspired in-surgency (Ch.2), destruction of the forest cover and opium production were the principal factors which induced the Thai authorities to attempt to incorporate the hill tribes into the Thai state. They aimed to incorporate and 'Thaify' the growing tribal population, which suffers from an uncertain and vague status in Thai society (Cohen 1992d). These efforts brought basic health and welfare services, as well as schools to the villages, but also led to a progressive deculturation, marginalization and even pauperization of the tribal people, as they entered Thai society at its lowest rungs.

Ironically, as these processes progressed, the hill tribe people became, from the 1970s onward, an ever more popular attraction of ethnic tourism; they were promoted in the tourist literature, and perceived by the mostly young tourists, as 'primitive and remote' natives (Cohen 1996:31–66), even as they gradually lost their remoteness and their cultural identity. Perched on their mountain tops, tribal villages became the goal of ever more popular trekking trips of youthful tourists; while with the improvement of the road system in the north, the lower lying, more accessible villages were visited by parties of sedate, motorized excursionists (Cohen 1996:67–86). The highly diversified languages, customs and material culture of the tribal people (McKinnon and Bhruksasri (eds.) 1983, Lewis and Lewis 1984, Kanomi 1991), which contrasted sharply with the relative homogeneity of lowland society, and especially the colorful, richly ornamented costumes of their women, were a major factor enhancing their attractiveness to tourists. While the visitors purchased few of their costumes, the various embroidered, woven or batiked pieces of cloth, smoking pipes and other trinkets which the hill tribe people soon began to offer to the passing visitors, became in some villages the principal source of income from tourism (Cohen 1996:113–144). Thus started a spontaneous commercialization of tribal crafts in some of the more popular tribal villages on trekking and even more on motorized tours. Among these, the Hmong village of Doi Pui (Cohen 1996:123–131) on the mountain overlooking the city of Chiang Mai, stood out as the principal market for tribal wares from the 1970s onwards; resembling the dynamics of lowland craft markets (Chs.9–10), the Hmong in Doi Pui initially sold mainly their own products, moving gradually to trade in other tribal wares, especially in those of the Hmong refugees from Laos, and later on to clothing, crafts and souvenirs from diverse other sources, including some from India and Nepal. The Hmong from that village are also the principal tribal stall-keepers on the night bazaar in Chiang Mai, which is oriented mainly to foreign and domestic tourists. In the 1990s, crafts produced by tribal artisans in Thailand constituted only a fraction of the wares carried by the tribal vendors on both markets.

The spontaneous production of tribal crafts for sale to tourists was altogether of a limited scope. However, even as tourism began to penetrate the highlands in the 1970s, several, mostly foreign, non-governmental organizations (NGOs) began to sponsor the commercialization of tribal crafts independently of tourism development in the region (Ch.3). Their activities were at the outset focussed primarily on the resettlement areas for tribal people, created by the authorities on the northern lowlands in response to the communist-inspired tribal uprising in the highland border areas, in which the Hmong played a leading role (Ch.2). However, the NGOs later on also reached out to the more accessible tribal areas which were not affected by the insurgency, especially those in which they sought to develop new sources of income, as a substitute for the cultivation of opium. These sponsoring organizations helped to develop new products, which would sell on the urban tourist and the export markets. Some production and marketing networks which were developed by the NGOs in the 1970s and 1980s remain up to the present the principal outlet for the crafts of tribal villagers, insofar as they still continue to engage in their production.

With the arrival of the tribal refugees from Laos in great numbers from the mid-1970s onwards, the supply of tribal products on the crafts market increased dramatically. In particular, Hmong refugee textile products flooded the market in the late 1970s and the early 1980s, selling at much lower prices than the products of the hill tribe people from the highlands of northern Thailand. The refugee products also became the principal tribal items exported by the foreign NGOs. In Ch.2, which opens the first part of this book, I have outlined at length the recent history of the Hmong refugees and its impact upon their commercialized crafts.

The Hmong refugees gradually departed from Thailand in the course of the 1980s and 1990s, either for resettlement in third countries or for repatriation to Laos; their departure left a lacuna on the tribal crafts market, which was not filled by the tribal villagers from Thailand up to the present. Local tribal craft production has lost much of its vitality over the years, as the Hmong and other tribal groups turned to newer pursuits, like commercial truck-gardening. The dwindling production is highly routinized, with no significant innovations. In that the dynamics of the commercialized tribal crafts in Thailand resembles that common among other Third and Fourth world ethnic groups: their crafts tend to stagnate after a period of effervescence at an early stage of commercialization (Cohen 1992c: 19–20). At present, the major tourist-oriented craft markets in Thailand, like the popular night bazaar of Chiang Mai, feature only few local tribal products, while most such crafts, both old and new, are imported from other Asian countries, and especially from Laos, Burma and China.

Lowland Craft Villages

Before the Thai countryside was penetrated by industrial goods, a great variety of arts and crafts were practiced in virtually every village. Some villages specialized in particular crafts, either because they had access to a rare or particularly suitable raw material or owing to the special skills of their inhabitants, which were transmitted from generation to generation. Though craft production contracted significantly with the monetarization of the rural economy and the substitution of industrial goods for crafts, members of the older generation in many villages preserved, or at least remembered, some of their traditional skills even though they ceased practicing them. In some, mostly outlying, villages, craft production continued uninterrupted up to recent times, even though its scale contracted. Localities in which craft production was continuous, revived or newly introduced as a principal or significant supplementary activity became known as 'craft villages' (Gallagher 1973). Most of the renowned craft villages are found in the northern region, particularly in the area surrounding its principal city, Chiang Mai, the former capital of the Lān Nā kingdom (Penth 1994, *Sawaddi* 1985), such as the 'umbrella village' of Bo Sang (Herring 1985) or the 'pottery village' of Muang Koong (King 1988); however, owing to rapid recent urbanization some of the craft villages of the past, like the 'silver village' of Wualai became urban neighborhoods of the city of Chiang Mai. Others lost their distinct character in recent decades, either because the craft which distinguished them became industrialized, or because their very success as a tourist attraction engendered a far-reaching heterogeneization of craft products offered on their markets and in their shops. A good example is the so-called silk village of Sankhampaeng (Bowie 1993b:188–189), which is presently the site of the Shinawatra silk factory, while its shops offer such a variety of products that a visitor could not gauge from them its past role as a center of silk-weaving in the north (Ch.8).

Various crafts are also produced in many villages in northeastern Thailand (a region know as 'Isan'), in the south and even in some villages of the more developed and modernized central region of the country. Among the better known 'craft villages' in Isan are the pottery village of Dan Kwien (Ch.9) and the *mudmee* (knot-dyed) silk weaving villages in the *amphoe* (district) of Chonnabot (*Thai Life* 1994:88). *Mudmee* silk is also produced in several Cambodian minority villages of southern Isan (*Thai Life* 1994:86 88). Another minority, the Phu Tai (Lohitkul 1990) who immigrated from Laos into Isan in the past, are weavers of fine silk cloth.

Some southern crafts are also highly esteemed for their quality, especially silk weavings (Peetathawatchai B.E. 2519), *yan lipao* basketry (Townsend 1985, Supho 1989) and *nang talung* shadow puppets (Smithies and Kerdchouay 1975, Teerakhamsri 1996).

Lowland craft villages are visited primarily by domestic tourists, middlemen and shop keepers. As touring by motorcar in search of antiques (Sukphisit 1991a) or handicrafts became popular among the Thai middle-class, villagers began to put up craft stalls along roads adjoining their settlements, creating elongated 'ribbons' (Ch.8), which in some instances grew into crafts markets (Ch.9–10).

Foreigners rarely visit lowland 'craft villages', except some renown ones in the north; lowland life and lowland ethnic minorities are not touristically marked and are much less displayed in tourist-oriented books and promotional material than the hill tribes. There is no widely disseminated touristic image of lowland peasant life and of lowland ethnic minorities, which could serve as a reference point to gauge the degree of 'authenticity' of commercialized crafts, offered in urban tourist markets and in tourist shops. Indeed, for many foreign tourists, the 'authenticity' of a lowland craft object seems to be a much less salient consideration in purchasing decisions than it is in the case of hill tribe crafts. Such considerations are even less salient for customers of Thai export crafts, who constitute a major and expanding segment of the market for lowlander products. People in far-away European countries, in the US, Australia or Japan, may even be completely unaware of the provenance of the craft object which they purchase as a decoration or as a functional object. It follows that the preservation of some marks of 'authenticity' will be a less important consideration in the commercialization of lowland than of hill tribe crafts; therefore there will be fewer constraints on the heterogeneization of lowland crafts than of those of the hill tribes.

In contrast to the hill tribe crafts, lowland crafts did not become commercialized as a consequence of dramatic political events. Their commercialization progressed gradually along several routes. In some instances it was sponsored by the Thai Queen and her SUPPORT Foundation (SUPPORT 1985, 1992), with the principal aim of creating a supplementary source of livelihood for villagers, whose income from agricultural pursuits was deteriorating (Ch.11); in others it was sponsored by outside entrepreneurs (Ch.9); and in still others, commercialization was a spontaneous response of local artisans to market demand (Ch.10). In the second part of this book the differential dynamics of four kinds of commercialized crafts, pottery, woodcarving, weaving and basketry will be examined. The principal findings of both studies – that of the commercialization of hill tribe crafts and that of the crafts of lowlanders, will be summed up in the concluding section of these chapter.

Principal Conclusions

The articles collected in this volume are based on studies conducted during different periods of time and with diverse objectives in mind; it is therefore not easy to tease out from the variety of research concerns and empirical findings any general conclusions. If I still endeavor to do that, it is not for the formalistic reason to endow this volume with an appearance of unity, but rather because some general trends, relating to the principal research problems listed above, can be discerned in the diversity of specific findings.

The most general conclusion relates to the over-all differences between the dynamics of commercialization of hill tribe and lowland crafts. The Thai hill tribes and the tribal refugees from Laos had, for diverse reasons, less direct access to the craft markets than the lowland

16

villagers. The commercialization of their crafts was therefore predominantly initiated and facilitated through sponsoring foreign and domestic relief organizations and other NGOs. Production of hill tribe, primarily refugee, crafts peaked in the late 1970s and early 1980s. When the refugees left and the NGOs reduced or ceased their activities in Thailand, hill tribe crafts stagnated and lost their leading role in the touristic crafts market. The decline of demand from abroad, owing to a waning interest and growing apathy towards 'ethnic art' in Western societies, led to a fall in exports of tribal crafts by the remaining sponsoring foundations and other non-profit organizations.

The commercialized tribal crafts, being ethnically 'marked', preserved throughout the period their orthogenetic character; in contrast to lowland crafts, the feed-back of the market, mediated primarily through the NGOs, influenced the materials, forms and functions of the tribal products and the outlay and elaboration, as well as the colors and color combinations, of their designs – but did not lead to the introduction of stylistic elements extraneous to tribal culture. Tribal crafts remained recognizably 'tribal' – they did not undergo 'heterogeneization'. Moreover, the single important stylistic change in tribal crafts observed during the period, the emergence of representational designs (Chs.6–7), was largely a spontaneous development among the Hmong refugees, even though it was assisted by foreigners. Representational designs did not exist previously in the traditions of the Thai or Laotian Hmong – in that sense they were a heterogenetic innovation; however, this heterogeneity differed significantly from that found in lowland crafts – it expressed the refugees' nostalgic longings for a lost past and broadcasted to the world their present dire predicament. In contrast, the heterogenetic lowland crafts did not in themselves contain any significant new messages.

The tribal crafts underwent commercialization in wake of the turmoil which external events, related to the second Indochina War, wrought in their lives (Ch.2); at the 'baseline', the period preceding their commercialization, the crafts still manifested considerable vitality. In contrast, the Thai lowland crafts suffered an extended period of decline under the impact of penetration of industrial goods ever deeper into the rural hinterland; at the 'baseline', lowland crafts were still regularly produced for an internal public mostly in the more remote and inaccessible areas. The processes of commercialization of lowland crafts were more varied and complex than those characteristic of hill tribe crafts.

The degree of vitality at the 'baseline' constituted an important pre-condition of successful commercialization: the considerable vitality of hill tribe crafts, particularly among the Hmong refugees from Laos, facilitated the re-orientation of highly skilled artisans to the production of high-quality products for the new markets, without the need for a considerable investment in their re-training. In the case of lowland villages, insofar as the local craft was already in decline at the baseline, successful commercialization often depended on its revitalization, as in the case of Ban Namon (Ch.11), where local women had to be taught to produce their 'traditional' weavings. Where such revitalization did not take place, the craft continued to decline, like the basketware of Ban Pha Bong (Ch.11). Where the craft was still vital like the pottery of Dan Kwien (Ch.9) commercialization proceeded smoothly. (Ban Thawai wood carving (Ch.10) is a special case – its carvers were initially not locally trained, but acquired their skills in the city of Chiang Mai).

The sources of initiative of commercialization differed widely. Among the hill tribes there was a fairly sharp difference between the highland hill tribe villages and the tribal resettlement areas or refugee camps. Among the former, commercialization proceeded mainly through contact with foreign trekkers or tourists on tours, and remained relatively limited in scope. Among the latter, commercialization was primarily sponsored by relief agencies and other NGOs, which opened new, tourist and export markets for their products; however, these organizations insisted, to a varying extent, upon the preservation of the orthogenetic styles of hill tribe products (Ch.3); hence, the only heterogenetic products were the spontaneously produced representational textiles of the Hmong refugees from Laos.

In lowland villages, where local crafts were still vital, commercialization proceeded, usually on a limited scale, spontaneously, through contact with domestic tourists, middlemen and shop-keepers, rather than foreign tourists (Ch.8). The needs and preferences of these local publics differed considerably from those of foreign tourists visiting hill tribe settlements: the latter sought 'authentic' crafts or at least ethnically 'marked' ones; while domestic tourists also often purchase trinkets and other 'marked' souvenirs, many seek functional or decorative objects, whose provenance is not uppermost in their mind. Hill tribes therefore tended to produce an often exaggeratedly marked 'tourist art'. Spontaneously commercialized lowlander crafts, in comparison, do not have to be marked – but the relative cultural proximity between producer and consumer may preclude their far-reaching heterogeneization in response to market demand. Such heterogeneization occurs with the expansion into the foreign tourist and especially the export markets.

In two of the four villages which served as case studies, Ban Thawai (Ch.10) and Ban Pha Bong (Ch.12), commercialization proceeded spontaneously – but while the artisans in the former mastered the skills necessary to respond to the new demands of the tourist and export markets, the latter did not; as a consequence, Ban Thawai carving underwent considerable heterogeneization and prospered economically, while Ban Pha Bong basketware declined. In the other two case studies, Ban Namon (Ch.11) and Dan Kwien (Ch.9), commercialization was sponsored by outside agents – the Queen and her SUPPORT Foundation (SUPPORT 1985, 1992) in the former case, outsider private entrepreneurs in the latter.

The consequences of sponsored commercialization of lowland crafts depended largely, as they did in the case of the hill tribes, upon the relative emphasis of the sponsoring agent on the preservation of 'traditional' styles as against the adaptation of the products to changing market demand. The Queen and her foundation, though seeking primarily to create a supplementary source of income for rural artisans, put considerable emphasis on the preservation and revival of 'traditional' styles, and on the promotion of fine craftsmanship through training programs. The policy of the foundation was basically conservative: it encouraged the production of refined, high-quality wares to be marketed to the well-to-do foreign tourists and members of the Thai elite through the foundation's Chitralada shops (Hoagland 1985, Yawaprapas 1996), located in the royal palace, in luxurious hotels and in airports. Its policy thus encouraged primarily orthogenetic changes, though it was not averse from introducing styles of one region of the country into another (Ch.11). In contrast to the relief agencies which promoted hill tribe crafts, however, the hand of the Queen's foundation rested lightly on the craft villages which it sponsored: most products of Ban Namon, save the most refined ones, were privately marketed.

The sponsorship of commercialization by outsider entrepreneurs was less constrained by considerations of preservation of local stylistic elements, and has therefore encouraged the growing heterogeneization of local wares, as exemplified by the changes in Dan Kwien pottery (Ch.11). In general, it seems safe to conclude that institutional sponsorship, rather than outside sponsorship of commercialization by itself, is conducive to the preservation of stylistic orthogeneity, sometimes possibly at the cost of market expansion; private sponsorship, as private enterprise in general, is more conducive to the heterogeneization of local craft production.

My principal finding regarding stylistic changes in commercialized crafts is that these changes are closely associated with market expansion, through new marketing channels by which new and increasingly remote publics are reached. Graburn's original dichotomic distinction between the internal and the external publics (Graburn 1976b) proved insufficient: several kinds of external publics, such as domestic tourists, foreign tourists and customers abroad, reached through export channels, have to be distinguished. The domestic public in Thailand, contrary to the emphasis in most studies of 'tourist art', appears to be an important, and in many instances principal audience for commercialized craft products; its importance rose with the emergence of the new Thai urban middle classes, with a taste for 'traditional' craft products (Chs. 8 and 11). The impact of this audience appears to have been conservative; it encouraged primarily orthogenetic changes. Foreign tourists engendered more pressures towards heterogeneity, for in the case of lowland crafts they seem to prefer objects which are useful, decorative or otherwise suit their life style, while being less concerned with their 'authenticity' or 'markedness'. However, my findings strongly indicate, that the export markets engender the strongest pressures toward 'heterogeneization': foreign importers frequently demand that local craft products be standardized according to their precise specifications; these are based on considerations regarding the tastes and preferences of a foreign public which is not acquainted with Thai culture and is often unconcerned with the provenance of the objects it acquires. In such cases local artisans in fact become a cheap, skilled labor force working for foreign entrepreneurs, who supply them with models of products, completely unrelated to the artisans' cultural background, and order their reproduction in great quantities. Involvement with exports makes possible the large-scale expansion of local craft production; but it also leads to radical 'heterogeneization' and to a total absence of any relationship between the cultural background of the artisans and their craft-products (Chs. 9–10). Involvement with expanding markets, and particularly with exports, leads to an increase in the cultural and spatial distance between the original producer and the ultimate consumer of crafts, and thereby to a growing dependence of producers on unfamiliar and changing market forces, and consumer tastes and preferences. They therefore may become victims of the fluctuations of demand for local crafts on a world market; the current handicraft squeeze experienced by some craft producing villages (Chs. 9 and 12), is partly a consequence of such fluctuations, brought about by the recent flooding of the world crafts market by cheap products from countries with a large, underemployed labor force.

The far-reaching 'heterogeneization' of craft products under conditions of advanced commercialization, raises the problem of the motivation of the artisans and the meaning of their work for them. There is little doubt that economic motives are in general the dominant, and sometimes only, incentives for craft production among both the hill tribe as well as the lowland artisans. While a few major entrepreneurs discovered that craft production can become a source of considerable profits, for most artisans, it is a supplementary or surrogate source of livelihood either because, as in the case of hill tribe refugees, their traditional economic basis has bee destroyed, or because, as in the case of lowland villagers, it does not suffice any more to support their growing needs.

This does not mean, however, that stylistic changes or even 'heterogeneization' necessarily make craft production meaningless for the artisans. Indeed, refugee hill tribe women enjoyed their freedom of invention, made possible by the new materials and colors which became accessible in the refugee camps (Ch. 3); and lowland artisans, such as the skilled potters of Dan Kwien, take pride in their skill to reproduce any model supplied to them by a client (Ch. 9). Artisans, unlike ethnographers, museum curators and many tourists, are not necessarily keen on the 'authenticity' of their products.

Moreover, 'authenticity' is not a fixed cultural mark (Cohen, 1988a); new designs and objects, even such introduced by external agents or entrepreneurs, may over time become part of a local cultural tradition, and be perceived by the customers, and by the producers themselves, to be 'authentic' local products; lightly colored Dan Kwien 'garden furniture' (Ch. 9) may well over time be so perceived, even though the local village potters do not have gardens attached to their dwellings.

The commercialized production of crafts on a growing and in some instances massive scale, led to various technological and organizational innovations, especially in the lowland villages, rather than the hill tribes. Substitution of industrial for natural materials has in many instances begun at the baseline, prior to commercialization, which only provided an additional impetus to the process. Mechanical tools and machinery were introduced, particularly to accelerate the early stages of production, for example in woodcarving and pottery production (Chs. 9–10). In some instances, a greater functional or even spatial division of labor was observed, as, for example between the carving and the finishing of wooden objects (Ch. 10). However, no major organizational changes have taken place; even in the large workshops of Dan Kwien, which employed up to one hundred workers (Ch. 9): there was no transition from craft to industrialized organization in the villages studied. Craft production did not undergo industrialization.

The principal process of structural change, noted especially in Ban Thawai (Ch. 10), but also found to some extent elsewhere, is a process I called 'disassociation': the gradual break-up of the 'traditional' spatial, cultural and social nexus of craft production and its disjunction into separate, only loosely connected components. As Bowie (1993b) pointed out with regard to northern Thai weaving, even in pre-modern Thailand the process of production was not always fully integrated in such a nexus; but, whatever the local situation may have been at the baseline, there is no doubt that commercialization encouraged a growing disassociation between such components of the process as the spatial origins of raw materials, the cultural origins of the techniques and styles of production, the different stages of production and marketing, and the cultural backgrounds of the producers and consumers of craft products. It should be noted that disassociation ultimately leads to 'de-placement': what used to be a locally and culturally identifiable craft, loses its roots, and remains connected to its place merely for historical reasons; in fact it could be produced anywhere, even though promoters and advertisers may extol its alleged local identity.

Finally, I turn to the question of the distribution of benefits from commercialized craft production. No systematic economic study on the topic has been conducted and hence only some very general conclusions can be drawn from my findings. Artisans were mostly renumerated by NGOs, workshop owners and shop-keepers at a per piece basis, rather than by fixed wages. This system makes it difficult to evaluate their average income for a full working day, especially where artisans worked at home. According to my estimate, the incomes of most artisans were, in absolute terms, low: tribal refugee women in the late 1970s and early 1980s usually earned less than $1.00 a day; and most lowland villagers, whether working at home or in workshops, earned in the 1990s on the average approximately $4.00 a day. It should be noted, however, that the refugees received their basic food supplies and services from the U.N. High Commissioner for Refugees; while the returns of lowland artisans were at least equal and mostly higher, than the wages which agricultural and other unskilled laborers received in their villages or nearby towns. Highly skilled artisans earned several times higher returns than their less skilled colleagues. Auxiliary personnel in workshops, mostly young girls, earned about half the average daily income. My findings strongly indicate that, the later the stage of the production and marketing process, the greater its relative profitability. The first stages, the making of 'raw' craft products – a carving, a pot or a basket – are the least profitable in terms of financial returns on time and materials invested. The relative returns of the finishing stages, such as the painting and ornamentation of carvings, pots or baskets, are much higher. Owners of craft workshops therefore tend to shift from the production of 'raw' objects to their finishing, leaving the former work to less skillful artisans (Ch. 10). Moreover, marketing of crafts appears to be generally more profitable than their production; producers therefore tend to become stall and shop-owners selling their own craft products, and increasingly those of other producers and other localities. As a consequence, the craft ribbons and markets of craft villages undergo a process of increasing heterogeneization. Finally, the mark-up imposed by traders on craft products tends to increase, the higher their position along the marketing chain: middlemen who buy the wares directly from the producers usually set lower mark-ups on the wares than shop-keepers in the cities; while importers in foreign countries impose the highest mark-ups, reaching sometimes up to several hundred percent. Obviously, the expenses, investments and possibly also the risks related to the craft business also tend to increase along the marketing chain. It nevertheless seems fairly certain that the profits of urban shop-keepers and foreign importers per craft item sold, tend to be the highest in the chain. In any case, the prices which the ultimate consumer of an imported Thai craft product pays in his or her country tends to be higher by the order of ten relative to the price received by the original producer.

Craft production is not perceived by the artisans as a particularly attractive or lucrative occupation, particularly not by the younger generation in craft villages. Thailand enjoyed for the last three decades an almost continuous boom, which brought it to the verge of becoming a NIC (Jansen, 1991; Kulick and Wilson, 1996; Pongpaichit and Baker 1996). The boom created new employment opportunities, both in the major urban centers as well as in the provinces. Industrial enterprises, sometimes located in new industrial parks outside major regional cities, attracted the rural labor force away from craft production. The younger generation in many craft villages – including some of those in my study – sought employment in new, urban occupations, despising work in crafts. Owners of workshops were therefore forced to offer higher

23

wages to artisans and auxiliary personnel, to countervail the attraction of new occupations. The economic crisis of 1997 reversed this situation to some extent; the crisis led to a sharp economic downturn in Thailand (Siamwalla 1997), to the closure of financial institutions and businesses, and to a growing urban unemployment, which in 1998 rose to well over two million. As growing numbers of unemployed urban migrants begin to return to their villages, some may engage in crafts production as a temporary expedient, even while domestic demand for crafts diminishes, as the urban middle classes experience the crunch of the crisis in sharply reduced disposable incomes. However, with the drastic fall in the exchange value of the Thai currency, which in 1998 stabilized around at a rate of about 60 percent lower than before the crisis (at around 40 baht for one US$ as against 25 baht previously), the competitiveness of Thai crafts on the world market improved considerably. Insofar as the baht prices of crafts will remain stable, a growing reorientation of craft production to the foreign tourist, and especially the export market, will be necessary to keep up even the level of production preceding the crisis. It is questionable, however, whether under the present depressed conditions the necessary entrepreneurship will emerge to create the mechanisms for such a reorientation of production in the craft villages, the great majority of which have not been involved with exports, and many of which did not produce primarily even for the foreign tourist market. However, if such a reorientation could be effected, it would considerably affect the nature of craft production and the products themselves: since larger enterprises will be better able to exploit the new opportunities, they may prosper, while smaller producers may become dependent upon these enterprises for their survival; and since the products will have to be adapted to the tastes and preferences of ever more remote publics, they will become increasingly heterogenized.

Note

1 The literature on the hill tribes of Thailand is extensive. The earliest comprehensive surveys are by Seidenfaden (1967) and Young (1962). Major collections of articles about the hill tribes are Walker (ed.) 1975, Kunstadter and Chapman (eds.) 1978, McKinnon and Bhruksasri (eds.) 1983, and McKinnon and Vienne (eds.) 1989. There exist monographs on almost all the tribal groups. The major works on tribal crafts are: Campbell et al. 1978, Lewis and Lewis 1984, and Kanomi 1991; there exist monographic studies on the crafts of several tribal groups, especially the Hmong and the Yao (Ch. 2–3).

Part I

Hill Tribe Crafts

2

INTERNATIONAL POLITICS AND THE TRANSFORMATION OF FOLK CRAFTS

The Hmong of Thailand and Laos[1]

Introduction

The commercialization of the folk crafts of the Fourth World people (Graburn (ed.) 1976), the usually small and remote tribes and ethnic groups in developing or even developed countries, has been frequently described in the ethnographic and anthropological literature. This literature, however, has dealt predominantly with the immediate factors affecting the processes of transformation of folk crafts as they become oriented towards an 'external public' (Graburn 1976b:8). It is by now well established that these processes are closely related to tourism in a wider sense. However, though the spontaneous arrival of ethnic tourists (Keyes and van den Berghe (eds.) 1984) in a tribal area may lead to the gradual commercialization of the local crafts (e.g. Elkan 1958), such direct tourism seems to be responsible for only a fraction of the total volume of commercialized folk products. Much more important is what Aspelin (1977) termed 'indirect tourism' – the sponsored production of folk crafts for a wider tourist market, through the intermediacy of a variety of external agents, such as patrons, traders, trading companies, missionaries, governmental agencies and non-governmental organizations (NGOs). These agents initiate, encourage, and direct the production of crafts, and promote them on domestic or even international markets (see e.g. Graburn (ed.) 1976; *Cultural Survival Quarterly* 1982). Though the products may be eventually bought by tourists, the latter are not in direct contact with the producers themselves, and may be only dimly aware of their identity and culture.

The extensive literature on this variety of commercialization is primarily concerned with the kind of intermediaries, their policies and effects on the crafts. It does not usually pay much attention to the wider, political events and the sociopolitical context which affected the lives of ethnic and tribal groups in the first place, and thereby made them accessible to outside agents, and responsive to their demands and initiatives. The political factor in the commercialization of folk crafts thus remains unexplicated, and its influence insufficiently understood.

In this chapter I shall note the impact of the wider, particularly international political factors on the commercialization and transformation of the crafts of one ethnic group, the Hmong in Thailand and Laos.

Specifically, I shall show the variety of ways in which the Second Indochina War and its repercussions upon Thailand and Laos affected the crafts of the Hmong. I shall show how the disturbance and eventual destruction of the 'traditional' tribal life of the Hmong of Thailand, and especially of Laos, through insurgency, war and flight, wrought havoc in the Hmong economy, and made the Hmong accessible to the outer world and receptive to craft production for the market as an important supplementary source of livelihood. I shall describe the mechanisms which emerged, as a consequence of the political events, to guide the production of Hmong crafts, and to promote and market them. I shall point out the transformations which the Hmong textile crafts underwent under the impact of these developments and indicate the significance of the commercialized textiles themselves for the Hmong people – particularly for their 'external identity,' namely their identity in the eyes of the world into which they were precipitately catapulted by historical events over which they had no control.

The Hmong

The Hmong (called Meo by the Thais) are one of the four principal dialect groups of the Miao people (Enwall 1995: 20–22). The Miao are one of the bigger minority nationalities of China (Savina 1930; Yin 1989:338–47), inhabiting the mountainous areas of southwestern China, particularly the provinces of Guizhou, Yunnan, Guangxi, Hubei and Sichuan (Enwall, 1995:13). The Hmong are the only branch of the Miao which spread into Southeast Asia in significant numbers, inhabiting the northern regions of Burma (Diran 1997:42–53), Thailand (Bernatzik 1947, Geddes 1976, Cooper 1978a, 1978b, 1984, Tapp 1986, 1989, Cooper et al 1991), Laos (Lemoine 1972b, Yang Dao 1976, Hamilton-Merritt 1993), and Vietnam (Roux 1954, Schliesinger 1998: 80–85) (see maps in Lemoine 1972a, Enwall 1995:12).

In the early 1990s the Miao population of China was about 7.3 million. There are about 90,000 Hmong in Thailand, 250,000 in Laos and only about 10,000 in Burma. The possibly somewhat exaggerated estimate of their numbers in Vietnam is 558,000 (Schliesinger 1998:80).

The Hmong were in the past remote from the centers of political power, and lowland rulers maintained only a tenuous hold over them. Their independence of spirit and resistance to outside control led to occasional armed conflicts with the lowland rulers. Nevertheless, during hundreds of years of contact and conflict with the Chinese, the Hmong acquired various elements of Chinese culture. Together with the Mien (Yao) people, the Hmong are sometimes classified as the 'sinicized' hill people of Thailand (e.g., Walker (ed.) 1975:19ff), but they are less sinicized than the former.

The Hmong are one of several highland groups who over the centuries moved down from the Asian continent through China into Southeast Asia. They penetrated Laos and Thailand in about the middle of the nineteenth century settling on the higher altitudes, well away from the lowland population. They practiced shifting agriculture, based on swiddening (slash-and-burn) of primary jungle (Kunstadler et al. (eds.) 1978), and the planting of their staple product, brown mountain rice, as well as vegetables, and – in recent decades – opium (McCoy 1972, Geddes 1970, Tapp 1986, 1989:16–20). They exchanged opium and some other products with lowlanders, through itinerant traders. The village constitutes the basic political unit of Hmong society, although occasionally, particularly in periods of emergency and strife, Hmong leaders with an extensive following emerged.

Although the Hmong have a long history of contact with lowlanders, in China as well as in Laos and Thailand, the Hmong have striven throughout the centuries to keep themselves apart and maintain their distinct way of life. However, they were not completely isolated from their surroundings; they have selectively absorbed elements from neighboring lowland and tribal cultures, such as the Chinese and the Mien (Yao). Theirs, therefore, is not a completely closed indigenous culture, but one which developed through contact and exchange with surrounding cultures.

The Hmong of Thailand and Laos are divided into several major subdivisions, most of whose names are derived from the colors of the women's skirt. The two main subdivisions are the White Hmong and the Blue (or Green) Hmong[2] (Lemoine 1972b; Chindarsi 1976; Geddes 1976). They are further divided into about twelve exogamous clans; members of several clans usually reside in the same village (Lemoine 1972b: 184–192).

The Hmong engaged in a wide variety of crafts, especially silver smithing and the production of embroidered, appliqued and batiked textiles. Both men and women wore richly ornamented costumes (Bernatzik 1947, passim; Lemoine 1972b:114–21; Campbell et al. 1978, passim; Lewis and Lewis 1984: 100–133; *Hmong Art* 1986; Kanomi 1991). Square embroidered or appliqued pieces, generally known as *pa ndau* (more correctly spelled *paj ntaub*; see Dewhurst 1985: 15), were used as gifts in rites of passage, such as births, marriages and funerals (Fig. 2.1).

The relative isolation of the Hmong in their own world was rudely disturbed by the Second Indochina War and its repercussions, which came in the wake of earlier sporadic attempts of national and colonial governments to penetrate the highlands of continental Southeast Asia and impose their rule upon the tribal populations. While those earlier attempts still left Hmong society on the whole intact, the events of the Second Indochina War wrought drastic changes in the lives of many Hmong communities in Thailand, and completely transformed those of the Hmong of Laos. These developments, in turn, had a decisive impact on the commercialization and transformation of the Hmong textile crafts.

Three principal periods can be distinguished in the recent history of the Hmong of Thailand and Laos; each of these had a particular impact on Hmong commercialized crafts:

First, the period of insurgency, war, and removal of the Hmong from their villages in Thailand and Laos and their resettlement or flight.

Second, the period of the sojourn of the Hmong from Laos in refugee camps in Thailand. Third, the period of the resettlement of the Hmong from Laos in third countries, principally the United States.

Each of these periods had a distinctive impact on the commercialization and transformation of Hmong crafts.

The Inception: Insurgency and War

In the course of the 1950s the Thai government initiated the first sporadic steps intended to incorporate the hill tribe area of northern Thailand – heretofore virtually outside direct governmental control – into the Thai state. Three types of considerations purportedly induced the Thai authorities to make that effort: the alleged destruction of the forests by the swiddening agricultural techniques of the hill tribes; their production of opium; and considerations of national security, which became ever more paramount with the widening of the Indochina conflict (Marks 1973, 1994, Hearn 1974). In the process, attempts were made to impose various restrictive measures, often in a drastic manner, upon the tribal population.

By the 1960s the Hmong, who, living at the highest altitudes, were among the last hill people to be reached by the arms of government, accumulated sufficient grievances to be ready to offer armed resistance to governmental penetration (Hearn 1974:40ff.). In 1967, with Chinese, and later Pathet Lao (and, by extension, Viet Minh) assistance, a small-scale but fierce Hmong insurgency began in Nan Province of northern Thailand (Lindsay 1969, Marks 1973:932, 1994:107 9).

In the course of their initial, heavy-handed response to the insurgency, the Thai armed forces killed a considerable number of Hmong tribesmen, and napalmed or otherwise destroyed many Hmong villages (Lindsay 1969:82). The government also intensified an earlier-conceived resettlement program, according to which tribal people were removed from sensitive highland areas and resettled in lowland villages, often composed of households arbitrarily assembled from several tribal groups. Thus thousands of Hmong and other tribal people in fact became internal refugees (Thomson 1968a, 1968b, 1968c; Luche 1969:5–7; Abrams 1970; Charasdamrong 1971; Bhanthumnavin 1972; Hearn 1974; Marks 1994:103–8). It was in the areas of Hmong insurgency and in the Hmong resettlement villages that the commercialization and eventual transformation of Hmong textile crafts in Thailand was initiated by outside sponsoring agents. Later on, and independently of this process, commercialization also began sponta neously in some other Hmong villages, such as Meo Doi Pui (Cohen 1979: 14–20), which were not involved in the insurgency. Some of these were exposed to the penetration of tourism.

As the Thai authorities realized that the use of brute force would neither overcome the insurgency nor safeguard the loyalty of the tribal people, activities intended to improve their welfare and gain their trust were initiated (Kerdphol 1976, 1986). A crucial role in this process was played by the Border Patrol Police (BPP), a paramilitary organization combining security and civic functions (Lobe and Morell 1978). In an effort to create supplementary sources of livelihood for the tribal people, the Border Crafts of Thailand (BCT) was founded by the BPP as early as 1965. This enterprise, intended to collect and market tribal craft products, was designed to become part of a multi-pronged security effort in the tribal areas. From rather limited beginnings (Luche 1969: 5–7), the BCT eventually became one of the major channels through which the craft products of the resettled tribal people and particularly the Hmong and Mien were commercialized. Several foreigners, especially Christian missionaries working with the resettled population, also contributed to the commercialization of the tribal crafts; some of these eventually played a major role in the establishment and direction of other non-profit enterprises and NGOs, through which Hmong tribal craft products were marketed (see Ch. 3). The principal commercialized product were textiles, but some jewelry and basketry were also made for sale.

While sporadic commercialization of crafts took place in some original Hmong villages located in 'sensitive' security areas, it was in the resettlement villages that it expanded in scope and grew in economic significance. Craft production constituted an important source of supplementary income in the first years of resettlement, when the traditional economy of the tribal people was seriously disrupted by their removal from the highlands, and had not yet adapted to the new circumstances. However, the development of a market for these products proved difficult. The promoters of commercialization attempted initially to sell to outsiders the clothes and jewelry which the Hmong produced and used themselves; these were purchased by a few foreigners, especially volunteers, residing in Thailand, but did not prove marketable in significant quantities. In the course of a trial-and-error process, products especially intended for the market were developed; these differed in a variety of ways from those in use by the Hmong themselves. Traditional tribal designs were simplified, so that their production would take less time than that of traditionally executed designs; new products, adapted to the foreigners' and, later on, tourists' demand for souvenirs and utilitarian objects were developed, such as small, embroidered, appliqued and batiked 'patches' and squares of varying sizes based on the original *pa ndau,* which could be used as decorations on Western-type clothes or as wall-hangings. Material, colors and color combinations were gradually adapted to the tastes and demands of the external public, according to the feedback from the market reaching the marketing agents, and, through these, the producers (Ch. 3).

The market, however, remained limited for several years, since the Thai people themselves showed little if any interest in tribal products, and the marketing agencies were slow in developing export channels. Nevertheless, this initial period of commercialization is important in that in its course the prototype of many Hmong products and their designs were first developed; these were later on produced in much greater quantities in the refugee camps for the Hmong from Laos.

Figure 2.1 Old Hmong Square (*pa ndau*) from Laos (author's collection).

Approximately at the same time as the Hmong insurgency in Thailand, the Second Indochina War disturbed and eventually destroyed the accustomed way of life (Barney 1967) of the Hmong in Laos (Vang 1979; Yang Dao 1982; Hamilton-Merritt 1993). Laotian Hmong were mobilized by the French in their fight against the Vietnemese already in the 1950s. In the 1960s growing numbers of Hmong fought on the side of the French, and later the Royal Lao government, against the Pathet Lao insurgency (Yang Dao 1982: 7–8, 156 ff; Chagnon and Rumpf 1983a); subsequently they found themselves aligned with the Americans, who succeeded the French in the direction of the war against communism. The CIA eventually organized and equipped a 'secret' Hmong army, under the Hmong general Vang Pao (Warner 1996), which eventually numbered about 15,000 soldiers (Abrams 1974:24). The Hmong highlands soon turned into battlefields. As the forces supported by the Americans in the course of the early 1970s gradually lost ground to the communist insurgents, the Hmong aligned with the Americans and their dependents found themselves exposed to harsh Pathet Lao and Vietnemese reprisals (Gunn 1983; 324–5). In many war-ravaged areas, the Hmong were decimated. Others escaped from the highlands into the as yet 'safe' lower plains (Everingham and Burgess 1973; Ronk 1973). Eventually, up to 150,000 Hmong (one half of the total Hmong population) were thus displaced and became internal refugees in Laos (Abrams 1971a, 1971b, Everingham and Burgess 1973: 3). In their flight from the advancing Pathet Lao, many of these refugees eventually reached the capital Vientiane, whence they crossed the Mekong river into Thailand after the communist takeover of Laos in 1975. Great numbers of Hmong also entered Thailand at other crossing points. Others, however, continued to resist the Pathet Lao even after the communist takeover. Their rebellion was suppressed only by 1977–8 in a combined Pathet Lao and Vietnamese offensive, which involved '. . . the systematic destruction of villages and the massacre of the inhabitants' (Gunn 1983: 325). The Vietnamese were accused of seeking to 'exterminate the Hmong completely' (Gunn 1983: 325; see also Pringle 1979, and Yang Dao 1982: 17). Struggling to crush the Hmong resistance, the Vietnamese and the Lao armies took drastic action against the Hmong and apparently even used poison gas ('Yellow Rain') against them (Chagnon and Rumpf 1983b; Hamilton-Merritt 1980, 1982), thus evoking accusations of genocide (Pringle 1979). There is conflicting evidence as to the fate of the Hmong who remained in Laos after the communist takeover (compare, e.g., Chagnon and Rumpf 1983b with Chauvet 1984a), but there is little doubt that altogether hundreds of thousands of Hmong perished in the war and its aftermath. Many of those surviving fled into Thailand, often along dangerous escape routes from their mountain redoubts in Laos to, and across the Mekong river (Hamilton-Merritt 1993: 3–18); altogether, the number of Hmong refugees to Thailand surpassed the 100,000 mark (Yang Dao 1982: 18). A small number of those continued to fight a guerrilla war against the communist regime, departing on combat missions from the Thai refugee camps along the Laotian border (Chauvet 1984a). Most of the refugees, however, settled down to a quiet and bleak existence in several refugee camps (Long 1993, Donnelly 1994), hoping against hope that they would eventually be able to return to their homeland and highland villages. They were encouraged in this hope, and asked to stay in the refugee camps, by General Vang Pao (Sricharatchanya and Atkinson 1979; Walker and Moffat 1986: 54). However, as time passed, a growing number of the Hmong refugees asked to be resettled in third countries and particularly in the United States.

As in Thailand, the commercialization of the crafts of the Hmong of Laos also began among those groups who were affected by the war. Individuals working with the Hmong, and in particular foreign missionaries, seeking to help the displaced tribal people, began to sell small quantities of Hmong textiles from Laos to friends and acquaintances in Bangkok. American military personnel stationed in Laos also occasionally purchased Hmong products as souvenirs to bring home. According to one source, in the early 1970s '. . . [Hmong] women now in need of money began to sell textile pieces on the streets and in the market places of Laotian urban centers. Visitors from the West, and even Laotians, were their customers' (Dewhurst et al. 1983:19). In Vientiane, Hmong hawkers used to sell their wares in front of hotels where foreigners were staying. All these, however, were apparently sporadic activities, involving only small quantities of products. As interest in Hmong crafts grew and the market expanded, an enterprising Laotian woman opened a workshop in Vientiane, employing Hmong women, where Hmong textiles, already adapted to the demands of the external public, were produced. The workshop is said to have employed up to 100 women, but this may well be an exaggeration. The Laotian woman sold her wares not only locally, but also in Europe and Japan. After her flight to Thailand, she continued to supply Third World shops in those countries with hill tribe crafts, and eventually opened several shops in luxurious locations in Bangkok.

While the textiles of the internal Hmong refugees in Thailand were commercialized before those of the Laotian Hmong, the commercialization of the latter was the crucial event in the process of commercialization of Hmong textiles as a whole. Among the various Hmong commercialized products the most prominent place was taken by those developed from the square textile piece, *pa ndau,* which has been primarily of ceremonial use in Hmong culture. Whereas other traditional Hmong textiles could not be easily adapted to the life-styles of a potential external Western public, the *pa ndau* proved a handy souvenir, which could be used as a hanging or tablecloth (Figs 2.2 and 2.3). Known as a 'square,' it came to be specifically produced for the market by the Hmong while they were still in Laos. In the massive expansion of Hmong textile production in the refugee camps in Thailand and later in the United States, the 'squares' and patches of varying sizes and intended for different uses continued to be the most popular and well-known Hmong product (*TTC* [1978]: 26–31, *Cama-crafts* 1984; Chapter 3).

The Refugee Camps

As the Laotian refugees, among whom the Hmong constituted the principal group, crossed into Thailand, in one large wave (about 30,000) in 1975 and in smaller waves afterwards, they were settled in a

Figure 2.2 Commercial Hmong Square from Refugee Camp.

Figure 2.3 Commercial Hmong Square from Refugee Camp (author's collection).

string of refugee camps along the Thai-Laotian border (see map in Hafner 1985: 89). Their numbers peaked at about 60,000 in the late 1970s. The Hmong were at first dispersed among six camps, but as the Thai authorities implemented their policy to consolidate the camps and reduce their numbers (Hafner 1985: 84–5), the Hmong were eventually concentrated in one major camp, Ban Vinai in Loei province in northeastern Thailand (Dewhurst 1985; Long 1993; Fig. 2.4)).[3] The total number of refugees in this camp, by official count, fluctuated over the years between 40–45,000; the great majority were Hmong (Walker and Moffat 1986: 54). This number does not include a few thousand illegal Hmong refugees who were smuggled into the camp (Preechakul 1987). The relatively constant size of the refugee population, however, belies the perpetual movement of individual refugees, as some were transferred to transit camps and eventually left for resettlement in third countries, while others entered the camp. Many, however, have been stuck in the camps for more than a decade. Most were eventually resettled, mainly in the United States; the remainder were repatriated to Laos in the 1990s.

The basic necessities of the refugees were taken care of by the UN High Commissioner for Refugees. Additional assistance in the areas of education, health and welfare was provided by several international NGOs. While the refugees were formally confined to the camps, surveillance by the authorities was lenient; they were, however, not permitted to work outside the camp. In order to prevent refugees from enjoying a higher standard of living than the surrounding northern Thai villagers, salaries for those employed by the NGOs within the camps have in the 1980s been restricted by the Thai authorities to 300 baht (about US $15.00) a month (Hafner 1985).

The rudimentary nature of the U.N. support and the limitations on employment enhanced the importance of craft production as a significant source of supplementary income (Cohen 1982; Fig. 2.4). Highly skilled, often destitute and with plenty of free time at their disposal, the tribal refugees, especially the women, provided an enormous potential labor force for craft production; however, since they were restricted to the camps, their products could only be sold through non-profit organizations or private middlemen who had gained access to the camps (Cohen, 1982).

Even before the refugees were settled in orderly camps, foreign relief workers and local intermediaries – most of them themselves Hmong from resettlement villages in Thailand – began to purchase and to market the refugees' craft products. As life in the camps became

37

Figure 2.4 Hmong Woman Embroidering in Refugee Camp Ban Vinai (1984).

routinized in the late 1970s, several foreign religious and humanitarian NGOs started orderly projects intended to further the production and marketing of refugee crafts.[4] The primary target customers of the Hmong products were at first expatriates living in Thailand who were reached by means of the monthly Hill Tribes Sales on the premises of the International School in Bangkok. Later on, other outlets were developed: hill tribe craft shops, such as Thai Tribal Crafts in Chiang Mai, were oriented to foreign tourists, and increasingly also to exports. Indeed, the export of refugee crafts through non-profit channels, particularly to Europe, gradually became the principal outlet of several NGOs which marketed the crafts.

The NGOs faced several major policy dilemmas as they engaged in the promotion of Hmong crafts. Although there were important nuances in the manner in which each NGO sought to resolve these dilemmas, some major trends can be observed.

The first and most important dilemma related to the preservation of the Hmong material traditions versus the marketability of their products. The primary interest, indeed *raison d'être,* of the NGOs was to promote the welfare of the refugees; since wholly 'authentic' and unadulterated tribal products are not marketable in quantities, the NGOs had to compromise 'authenticity' to achieve marketability. However, this was done selectively, so that, while the functions, forms, colors and materials were innovative, the designs and techniques of production used were on the whole preserved. This was achieved by letting the Hmong women choose their own designs on the commercial products, within the constraints set by the NGOs' production policy. With time, the NGOs developed the practice of handing, or selling, to the producers 'kits' of materials, comprising cloth and threads in desired color-combinations, and receiving from them products ornamented with the women's 'traditional' designs, chosen according to their own predilection and taste. It is indeed astonishing how persistently traditional designs penetrated the Hmong commercialized products (compare Fig. 2.5 and Fig 2.6).

The preservation of the traditional designs in commercialized products, thus, metonymically, safeguarded their 'authenticity' for the consumers (Cohen 1988a). However, while the NGOs helped to conserve, within the existing market constraints, the Hmong textile traditions, the Hmong spontaneously introduced their own innovations into the commercialized products. The most important of these is the emergence of representational motifs, which were unknown in the textiles of the Hmong of Laos prior to their flight to Thailand and confinement to the refugee camps.[5] While contact with news media, in particular illustrated books and magazines, and Chinese pattern books may have induced this radical innovation in Hmong designs, for our purposes its importance lies in its thematics. In addition to purely decorative representations of plants and animals, two themes stand out particularly in these products: the pictorial representation of Hmong customs and feasts prior to the war and the flight (Plates 1–2), and the experiences of the war and the flight themselves (Figs. 2.7–2.9; Ch. 6–7; cf. Withington 1987). In an important sense, these Hmong textiles carried a message, through which the displaced Hmongs presented to the wider world outside the camps the glory and joys of their past, and

Figure 2.5 Old Hmong Square (*pa ndau*) with Meander Design (author's collection).

Figure 2.6 Commercial Hmong Letter-Holder with Meander Design (author's collection).

the hardships and tragedy of their recent historical experiences. The personalized character of these representational designs is accentuated by the fact that some of these products were signed by the producers – while, at least as long as they stayed in Thailand, the Hmong refugees never signed their ornamental designs. Some producers of textiles with representational motifs even stated the place and date of their production (e.g. Fig. 2.10).

The second major dilemma faced by the NGOs marketing the refugees' products has been that of quality versus quantity. Lacking experience in business and seeking to help as many refugees as possible, individuals assisting the refugees and managers of the NGOs at first bought up whatever products they were offered, and sought to sell them to whoever would buy them. They realized soon, however, that this purely altruistic approach left them with great quantities of unsold products. Following this realization, the problem of quality control became one of the chief concerns of the managers of the NGOs. Indeed, the relative success which the Hmong textiles for a while enjoyed on the market is to a large extent attributable to the rigorous standards of quality which the managers imposed upon the producers. The NGOs in several camps also offered special courses for those Hmong women whose skills did not meet these standards. The producers whose products were rejected could always attempt to sell them to local intermediaries, at much lower prices. Since, however, the market was able to absorb only limited quantities, and the women had virtually no alternative sources of income, most preferred to adhere to the standards demanded by the NGOs, and to put in more time and thus make more money. The NGOs on their part were careful not to set their standards too high so that they would become unattainable to most women. While some NGOs were more exacting in their demands than others, none concentrated on the production of 'masterpieces' by the few top producers, to the detriment of the provision of employment to less skilled workers. Indeed, as the best workers gradually left the camps for resettlement in third countries, the NGOs were gradually forced to compromise their standards. In 1988 the products marketed by the largest of the long-established NGOs were of considerably lower quality than those marketed in the late 1970s.

The third dilemma faced by the NGOs has been that of variety versus standardization. The attractiveness of Hmong commercialized crafts largely depended on their rich variety. However, the conditions of the crafts market engendered pressures for standardization. The longer the chain of intermediaries between the producer and the ultimate

41

Figure 2.7 Commercial Hmong Batiked Square with Scene from the War in Laos (author's collection).

Figure 2.8 Commercial Hmong Embroidered Square, Depicting the Flight from Laos Over the Mekong River (author's collection).

42

consumers, the stronger these pressures became. Once an NGO turned from the domestic to the export market to sell Hmong craft products, these pressures became decisive. Wholesale importers in Europe, the United States and Japan stipulated not only the precise sizes and forms of the products which they ordered, but also the colors, color combinations and even the designs. The tendency to standardization was further reinforced by the publication of catalogues listing and illustrating the NGOs' products (for example, *TTC* [1978], *Camacrafts* 1984). Even though the illustrations were meant as mere examples, customers tended to order those designs which they saw in the catalogue, to the detriment of variety and change. The principal NGO active in the camps has in fact eventually formalized the range of Hmong designs which it offered, by numbering them serially, so that desired designs can be ordered simply by their number (Ch. 5, Fig. 5.10).

While craft production for the market began in the refugee camps on a small scale in a haphazard, trial-and-error fashion, it gradually became a well-organized, large-scale industry. This achievement, however, though providing a large number of Hmong women with an important supplementary source of income and conserving some of the traditional Hmong designs, had also its more problematic aspects: it hampered creativity and change, took away some of the spontaneous enjoyment of making handicrafts and led to a petrification of this home industry, thereby also detracting from its inherent aesthetic interest. Indeed, perhaps paradoxically, while much of the production sold to local intermediaries was often inferior in quality to that marketed through the NGOs, this segment of the market was nevertheless more dynamic and innovative than that of the NGOs. This is true even for some products decorated with Hmong ornamental designs, but it is especially true for the products carrying representational designs, which were marketed almost wholly outside the NGO marketing channels.

Resettlement in the United States

From the late 1970s onwards, the United States admitted growing numbers of Hmong refugees, resettling them in various localities, and particularly in Minnesota, Michigan, California and Rhode Island (Catlin and Beck 1981; Dunnigan 1982; Downing and Olney (eds.) 1982; Scott 1982; Hendricks et al. (eds.) 1986; Chan (ed.) 1994, Donnelly 1994). Altogether, about 100,000 Hmong refugees have immigrated to the United States.

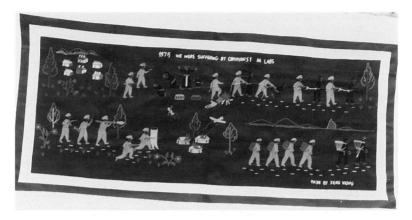

Figure 2.9 Commercial Hmong Embroidered Runner with Serial Scenes from the War in Laos; Signed by Producer (author's collection).

The precipitate resettlement of a Southeast Asian highland tribal people from the restricted and sheltered life of refugee camps into the urban centers of a modern large-scale industrial society led to serious disorientation and culture shock, as they were in the words of one observer 'transported into what seemed centuries away form their mountain homeland' (Thompson 1986: 46; cf. also Viviano 1986: 48). The most salient and dramatic manifestation of the distress experienced by the resettled Hmong is the still largely unexplained phenomenon of 'sudden death in sleep' (Marshall 1981; Lemoine and Mounge 1983). The Hmong in the U.S. also suffered serious problems in the areas of integration and employment. For a mostly illiterate people, the learning of a new and unfamiliar language, English, presented serious difficulties, despite much effort to adapt its study to the Hmong context, in both the camps in Thailand and in the U.S. (cf. Downing and Olney (eds.) 1982). Unable to find work, many Hmong fell back upon welfare, which, owing to state welfare regulations, was also not always readily forthcoming (Viviano 1986: 47; cf. also Freeman et al. 1985).

Under these circumstances, the Hmong textile products appeared to offer a promising source of support to the destitute and often helpless new immigrants. Indeed, the American public 'discovered' the Hmong textile crafts soon upon the refugees' arrival. Their unaccustomed designs and colors made them a popular item in bazaars and craft shops (Lacey 1982, *New York Times* 1984). With the help of volunteer

Figure 2.10 Detail of Commercial Hmong Bedspread with Inscription Stating the Identity of Producer and Date and Place of Production.

American women, cooperative workshops for the production of Hmong textiles were established (Godfrey 1982, *New York Times* 1984; Barry 1985; Donnelly 1986). It was felt that the Hmong, unacquainted with the American market conditions, so vastly different from those they experienced in the refugee camps in Thailand, needed assistance in the production, promotion and marketing of their products. As Americans recognized the uniqueness of Hmong culture, they also initiated projects to preserve the Hmong folkways (*New York Times* 1985). Numerous exhibitions of Hmong commercialized textiles of both an academic and a commercial character were held, and catalogues and other publications on Hmong textiles in the U.S. proliferated (*Textile Art* 1981; *Flower Clothes* 1981; Finch 1982; Henninger and Hoelterhoff 1982; White 1982a and 1982b; Dewhurst and MacDowell (eds.) 1983; Rush 1983; Randall (ed.) 1984). By all indications, the Hmong in America appeared in the early 1980s on the way to become a minority with a distinctive identity, thanks to their handicrafts, which were simultaneously also becoming an important source of their livelihood.

The Hmong on their part did not have to struggle much to adapt their products to the American market, since the commercialized textiles produced in the refugee camps had already been so adapted.

Much of their production followed closely the designs introduced in the camps; indeed, it is often difficult to distinguish pieces produced in the camps from those produced in the U.S. Nevertheless, some interesting innovations, influenced by the American setting, can be observed. These can be described in terms of two opposing tendencies: growing Laotization on the one hand, and growing individuation on the other.

The Hmong are only one of several ethnic refugee groups from Laos resettled in the U.S. The others were lowland Laos and another hill tribe, the Mien. As is common in such situations, the Americans do not always distinguish between these groups, often labeling them collectively as 'Laotian refugees' (*New York Times* 1981; Barry 1985). Apparently responding to this identification, some Hmong women began to integrate Laotian national symbols, especially the three-headed elephant, into their products (Dewhurst and MacDowell 1983:57,71).

The second tendency, growing individuation, appears to be much stronger than that of Laotization. Freed from the restrictive control of the NGOs in the camps, and exposed to a highly competitive environment, the Hmong women proceeded to spectacularize their work significantly beyond what was common in the camps (see, for example, the illustrations of Hmong textiles produced in the U.S. in Dewhurst and MacDowell (eds.) 1983). In the exhibition catalogues, items were listed under the name of their individual producers. The women also began to sign products with ornamental designs (Dewhurst and MacDowell (eds.) 1983: 37, 47), rather like Western artists, a custom which was rare in the refugee camps. Hmong commercial textiles appeared on the way to become art products, rather like Eskimo soapstone sculptures (Graburn 1976a).

However, the Hmong commercialized textiles in the U.S. failed to develop in the indicated direction, or to become a continuous and viable business proposition. For, soon after production for the market began, serious difficulties arose, and put the whole enterprise in jeopardy. At the bottom of the crisis is the problem of prices and profits. In the sheltered environment of the refugee camps, the Hmong women could devote themselves to the production of labor-intensive textiles, often earning less then one U.S. dollar a day. With minimal wages in the U.S. several dollars an hour, the production of textiles, which often yielded the producers only about 30 cents an hour (*New York Times* 1984), proved highly unprofitable. Many Hmong women therefore stopped producing for the market. Older women, who cannot find other employment, tended to remain in the field, while the younger ones turned to other occupations. Exacerbating the problem has been the fact that the refugees in the camps in Thailand continued to produce huge quantities of textiles, sending them for sale to their relatives in the U.S., where they were often sold at lower prices than those fetched by the products made in the U.S. itself (*New York Times* 1984). Some Hmong women have therefore found it more profitable to become intermediaries for refugee products rather than to produce crafts themselves. This predilection, indeed, provoked a serious conflict between the American volunteer advisers and the Hmong women in one of the major producers' cooperatives (Donnelly 1986:167), thus impeding the consolidation of the enterprise. It appears, therefore, that the long-term chances of survival of the Hmong textile crafts on the American scene are slim indeed; without a concentrated effort at their preservation, which might involve subsidies from external sources, the Hmong textiles may either disappear or become a degenerate shadow of their earlier self – as did many folk craft products in other highly industrialized countries. The explosion of Hmong textiles on the world scene, which initially received its impetus from the repercussions of the Second Indochina War, may thus eventually be extinguished by the hard economic facts facing those victims of that war who have been resettled in the modern West.

Conclusions

Political events and folk crafts appear too remote from one another to serve as a topic for research, and hence their relationship has rarely, if ever, been made the subject of express consideration. And yet, a close relation appears to exist between them, at least in some significant instances: major political events on the international scene have frequently had drastic effects on hitherto cut-off and remote people, who have previously had little opportunity or motivation to sell their craft products on the wider national or international market – indeed, they may have been completely unaware of the possibility for the commercialization of their crafts. Once caught in the events, displaced or otherwise drawn into national and international struggles and wars, their economy transformed or shattered, their life-ways and customs in jeopardy, the traditional crafts of these people may become an important, even if only subsidiary, means of livelihood and a vehicle of communication to the wider world, whose salience for the affected people has suddenly been significantly increased. In the process, however, their crafts also become transformed, the precise nature of the transformation depending on the channels through which their products are marketed.

The case of the Hmong, whether internal refugees in Thailand, refugees from Laos in Thailand, or resettled immigrants to the United States, illustrates the multiple effects of dramatic international political events on the transformation of folk crafts. Specifically, we have seen how the early efforts to help the displaced Thai and Laotian Hmong gave the first spontaneous, and often only tentative, impetus to the production of craft items, which could be marketed to an external public; how the intervention of NGOs enrouted the development of the commercialized crafts along some major lines, which eventuated in the conservation of basic Hmong designs on marketable products, but also in a gradual stifling of creativity and innovation, and the standardization of an ever greater volume of production for an expanding market; and, eventually, how the apparent promise of a new flourishing of Hmong crafts in the U.S. was frustrated by the hard economic facts of the American market.

However, besides this major line of development, largely influenced by the policies of the NGOs, another, minor but significant process of spontaneous innovation took place: namely, the emergence of representational motifs on Hmong products. This process was more directly related to the tragedies of recent Hmong history than the transformation of the traditional ornamental designs on other commercialized products.

In their representation of the recent Hmong experience of war and flight, and in their idealized pictorial reconstruction of Hmong life in the periods preceding these events, the Hmong women expressed their anguish, longings and distress, and communicated them to the wide and unknown world into which they were precipitately catapulted (Withington 1987; Chs. 6 and 7).

The particular development of Hmong textile crafts should be compared with similar developments in other parts of the world, where ethnic groups experienced major cataclysmic events in recent decades. The impact of such events on small and marginal ethnic groups is a subject which has been given growing attention by anthropologists.[6] However, the cultural expressions given to the events and experiences remain practically unexplored. Here an important link could be established between the study of ethnic arts and crafts and research on precipitate social change among the people of the Fourth World.

Notes

1 This chapter summarized one aspect of a longitudinal study of the commercialization of the crafts of the hill tribes of northern Thailand, conducted by the author mainly between 1977 and 1983; after that date, a brief yearly survey of new developments has been conducted. This study was supported by the Harry S. Truman Research Institute for the Advancement of Peace at the Hebrew University of Jerusalem, whose support is herewith gratefully acknowledged.
2 Most authors translate the self-appellation of this subdivision, Hmong Njua, as 'Blue Hmong.' Lemoine (1972b), however, prefers 'Green' Hmong (Hmong Vert). The confusion stems from the fact that there is no distinction between our blue and green in Hmong color classification (cf. Lemoine 1972b: 116 pp.).
3 For a description of Ban Vinai, see Hafner 1985: 87–91, Long 1993.
4 On the activities of the several NGOs active in the camps, and the differences in their approach to the commercialization of tribal crafts, see Ch. 3.
5 On the stages of development of Hmong representational art, see Ch. 6.
6 See, for example, the two issues of the *Cultural Survival Quarterly* (1987) on Militarization and Indigenous Peoples.

3

THE DYNAMICS OF HMONG AND MIEN COMMERCIALIZED ARTS[1]

Introduction

This chapter analyses the differential dynamics of change in the folk arts, particularly textiles, of two hill tribe people in Thailand, the Hmong (Meo) and the Mien (Yao). These changes occurred as a consequence of the commercialization of their arts, which accompanied the economic and political incorporation of these people into the wider national and even international frameworks. Whereas 'traditionally', i.e. in the period prior to incorporation, folk art objects were produced in relatively small quantities for an internal audience – i.e. for use by the producer, members of his or her household or community, or other members of his culture – they came to be produced in ever larger quantities for an external audience (Graburn 1976b), which, in the case of the Hmong and Mien, consisted primarily of tourists, both foreign and Thai, expatriates, and, through exports, members of remote western societies.

The differential dynamics of Hmong and Mien arts, under conditions of commercialization, can be fruitfully analyzed in terms of a typology based on four principal variables (ch. Shiloah and Cohen 1983):

1. Perpetuation vs. Innovation in artistic productions. This variable relates to the extent to which the tribal artisan merely reproduces existent art objects or introduces artistic innovations.

2. Orthogeneity vs. Heterogeneity of the process of artistic change. This variable has been adopted from the work of Redfield and Singer (1969) and refers to the extent to which the tribal style is merely replicated, further developed or elaborated under the new conditions (orthogeneity) or combined with extraneous elements to create a new, original artistic style (heterogeneity).

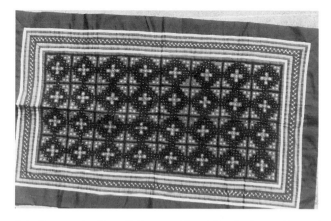

Figure 3.1 Hmong Appliqued Square, Nam Yao Refugee Camp (author's collection).

3. Internal vs. External Audience. This variable, adopted from Graburn (1976b) relates to the intended audience of the work: the internal audience is that of the artisan's tribal group; while the external audience ranges from other tribal groups to foreigners; in our context it embraces primarily Thais, foreign tourists, expatriates and other Westerners.

4. Spontaneous vs. Sponsored Production. This variable relates to the source of the initiative for new artistic production – whether it came from the tribal group itself (spontaneous) or from various kinds of outside agents (sponsored).

Each permutation of these variables represents a different type of dynamics of change in folk-arts. These range from 'traditional art' (spontaneous perpetuation of orthogenetic traditions for an internal public) through a variety of intermediary types, to 'fine art' (heterogenetic innovation for an external public, often sponsored by outside agents) (Shiloah and Cohen 1983). The chief empirical question for our analysis is: which types of dynamics are characteristic of the Hmong and Mien arts and which factors in their culture and circumstances of production helped to enroute them along these rather than other lines of development. I shall examine this question on data collected during several periods of field work in northern Thailand in the years 1977–1980.

The Hmong and Mien in Thailand

In the late 1970s the tribal population of northern Thailand fell into two distinct categories: tribal villagers and refugees from Laos.

1. Villagers: These comprised the bulk of the tribal population, amounting in 1979 to about a third of a million people. They live in the mountainous areas of northern and northwestern Thailand. The majority are dispersed in thousands of semi-permanent small villages on the slopes and ridges of jungle mountains. In the past they have been largely self-sufficient, engaging in swidden agriculture with dry mountain rice the chief staple food. In recent decades, however, they became increasingly incorporated into the national society. This led to a growing need for cash and hence the production of cash crops, of which opium was frequently the principal one. Tribal villages close to Thai settlements became gradually sedentarized and some turned to wet rice agriculture. Contact with lowlanders intensified, and processes of acculturation affected the traditional life styles. While an outlet was thereby provided for some of their tribal products, including arts and crafts, the latter often declined under the impact of industrial products introduced from the outside. In many cases, incorporation into the national society was accompanied by economic and cultural stress and impoverishment.

While the village Hmong and Mien were affected by these general processes, they appear to have suffered fewer disruptions and accommodated more successfully to the new circumstances than some of the other hill people like the Akha or Lahu. The Hmong (see Ch. 2) are the second largest tribal group in Thailand (after the Karen); they numbered at the time of research about 40,000 people, living in about 160 villages. Most Hmong villages were still located in remote and unaccessible areas; production of opium was still common and an important factor in their relative prosperity.

The Mien (Kandre 1967, Walker (ed) 1975:21–59, Shiratori (ed.) 1978, Lemoine 1983, Hubert 1985, Kacha-Ananda 1992) are a much smaller tribal group, the fourth by size (after the Karen, Hmong and Lahu); they numbered at the time of research about 24,000 people living in more than a hundred villages. Their villages were located in somewhat more accessible areas than those of the Hmong; and while some still produced opium, their relative wealth derived, in the main, from other agricultural activities, such as hog and cattle breeding, and from trade.

2. Refugees: While the tribal people entered Thailand from neighboring Burma and Laos for the last few centuries, the tribal

Figure 3.2 White Hmong Women's Dress, Chiang Kien Village.

refugees first arrived in great numbers from 1975 onwards, after the communist takeover in Laos, and were initially settled in six large camps along the border with Laos (Ch. 2). Their basic necessities were provided for by the UN High Commissioner for Refugees through the Thai Ministry of the Interior. They also received some help from various international relief organizations. They were not allowed to leave camp without permission; only a few engaged in gainful employment. Some have brought their wealth along from Laos, whereas others received remittances from their relatives in the West. The majority, however, were destitute and idle.

The Hmong constituted the bulk of the refugee population – their numbers in the camps reached up to 60,000 men, women and children in the late 1970s. The Mien were the second largest group of tribal refugees, numbering, in 1979, about 9,500; they hailed from the same regions of Laos as the Hmong refugees.

All the tribal groups in Thailand, including the Hmong and Mien, share some common social structural characteristics. For our purposes, it is enough to point out that the basic social unit is the individual household, commonly composed of a nuclear or a stem family. There is a traditional division of labor in the household, encompassing, among other things, art and craft production. The women are usually responsible for all clothing and textile work, while men do metal, wood, bamboo and basket work, and manufacture musical instruments and silver jewelry. Even after commercialization, art and craft products continued to be manufactured within the confines of the household by the traditional producers. Since the market demanded primarily various textile products, commercialization gave work mostly to women. This was particularly striking in the refugee camps, where women were often busily producing handicrafts while men sat around idly. Men, however, engaged in the sale of the products of their wives; among the refugees, a few had started to do simple embroidery.

Despite the social-structural similarities, the tribal groups manifest a surprising variety of cultural patterns. The Hmong and Mien, however, are culturally closer to one another than to the other tribal groups; they share common origins and a common cultural background. nevertheless, they differ markedly in their material culture and especially their art, notwithstanding some mutual borrowing of Mien patterns by the Hmong.

The Hmong of Thailand and Laos are further divided into several main sub-divisions which differ in dialect, house form and ritual, and are marked off by the colors and designs of their women's costumes: The Blue Hmong (Hmong Njua, also referred to as Green Hmong (see Lemoine 1972b), who are distinguished by the batiked blue skirt worn by their womenfolk, and the White Hmong (Hmong Doh), distinguished by the white skirt worn by women on festive occasions. Among the Hmong refugees from Laos, there is another distinct group, popularly referred to as the 'Striped Sleeve Hmong' (Hmong Kue Bang or Hmong Lam); it is probably a further sub-division of the White Hmong, distinguished by parallel colored stripes on the sleeves of the women's jackets. They lived in more remote areas of Laos than the other Hmong refugees and their crafts were simpler and less sophisticated than those of the others. Hence, while it was relatively easy to adapt the products of the latter to the emerging handicrafts

Figure 3.3 White Hmong Maze Pattern; Below: Appliqued Dress Collar, Above: Commercial Patch (author's collection).

market, the Striped Sleeve Hmong refugee women had to be retrained by the relief organizations in the camps in order to raise the quality of their work to the level demanded by the market.

The Hmong produce a wide variety of arts and crafts, outstanding among which are the different types of textile products. Traditionally, the Hmong spun and wove their own cloth; nowadays, however, they buy it mostly from other groups, particularly the Shan. The Blue Hmong, on high altitudes, however, still prepare their own hemp cloth for the richly ornamented women's batik skirts. They embellish their other clothes with bold applique and embroidery. The White Hmong practice reverse applique and embroidery, but do not batik their clothing. The women acquire their skills from a very early age. Though practically all women are capable of textile work, there exist considerable differences in individual skills and inventiveness, a factor of significance for the dynamics of change of their textiles in the process of commercialization.

The Hmong ornamental designs, particularly those on the festive costume are very complex, colorful and varied (Lewis and Lewis 1984: 100–133, *Hmong Art* 1986, Kanomi 1991: 159–192). Some of the applique and batik designs have names, but their original meanings seem to have been lost and they are, at present, devoid of any religious or magic significance. Some designs, particularly the embroidered ones, were borrowed from the Mien; even before their crafts have been commercialized, the Hmong women were quite free to vary and combine designs and even invent new ones, according to their taste and imagination (Campbell et al. 1978). They also combined freely the five basic colors used by the Hmong (red, gold, shocking pink, green, and blue) in their designs. This traditional artistic freedom is an important factor in explaining the astonishing proliferation of new variations and combinations of designs on commercialized Hmong products.

The Mien are one of the sub-divisions of the Yao people, most of whom inhabit the mountainous areas of southern China (Pan 1991:47–48). Their culture has been more heavily influenced by the Chinese than that of any other hill people in Thailand. They engage in two principal kinds of folk crafts, silver jewelry and embroidery, but they do not weave their own cloth (Lewis and Lewis 1984: 134–169, Kanomi 1991: 193–218, Goldman 1995). While some jewelry is produced for the market, embroideries are their most important commercialized products.

All Mien women traditionally prepared their own costume for daily wear as well as their festive and funerary clothing. The principal piece of their embroidered clothing are the women's trousers (Campbell et al. 1978: 116–7, Layton 1968, Lewis and Lewis 1984: 139–41, Goldman 1995: fig. 73–91), but their headdresses ('turbans') and particularly bridal veils (Fig. 3.17) are also richly ornamented. The Mien use over 100 five-colored designs (Butler-Diaz 1981) based on their mythology. These reflect significant Chinese influences. Unlike those of the Hmong, the Mien designs generally have some symbolic meanings, though Layton's (1968:27) claim that '... many of the customs, traditions and perhaps even the "Legend of the Mien" may be recorded in the embroidery on the clothing of Mien tribeswomen' is probably somewhat exaggerated. In any case, neither the designs nor any of the five basic colors in traditional use (red, yellow, dark-green, dark-blue, and white) are sacred. While women are free to choose a particular basic design on their costume and its color combinations

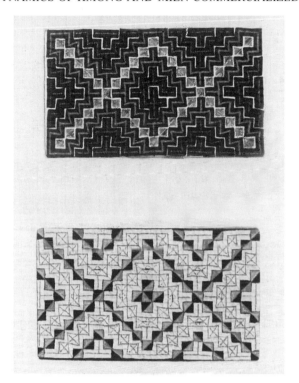

Figure 3.4 Master Designs for Hmong Commercial Designs (UNDPAC Program).

according to taste, the order of categories of designs on the trousers, headdresses and other objects is fixed by tradition. Altogether there exists among the Mien less license to combine, vary or invent designs than among the Hmong, a fact which is reflected in the smaller amount of spontaneous innovation in the designs on commercialized Mien products.

The Onset of Commercialization of Hmong and Mien Crafts.

The multifarious forces of incorporation have, to some extent, affected all the tribal people of northern Thailand. The folk arts of the various hill tribes, however, have become commercialized to a markedly unequal degree. The arts of the Hmong and Mien people stand out in that they have been more intensely commercialized, and more thoroughly changed, than those of the other tribal groups. Which factors favored their intensified introduction into the market? Their crafts are undoubtedly attractive to an external audience, colorful and varied. But so are the crafts of other hill people, like the Karen or the Lahu. It is also true that the Mien have been drawn into the market economy to a degree surpassing that found in other tribal groups. This fact could help to explain both their greater access to the arts market, as well as their stronger motivation to sell their art products. Among the Hmong, trading is also an expanding activity. While these factors undoubtedly contributed to the commercialization of Hmong and Mien arts, the decisive factor appears to lie in the political events which radically upset the traditional lifestyles of some of the village Hmong and Mien of Thailand, and, to a much more drastic extent, that of their co-tribals, the refugees from Laos: The Hmong uprising in the 1960s which led to the resettlement of Hmong and Mien villagers in the lowlands (Hearn 1974), and the arrival of large numbers of Hmong and a smaller number of Mien refugees from Laos in the middle 1970s (Ch. 2). Various government and private relief organizations initiated the commercialization of Hmong and Mien arts as a source of supplementary income for these people, whose accustomed way of life has been completely disrupted. Private middle-men, some of tribal origin, also helped to commercialize Hmong and Mien arts – particularly those of the refugees – by collecting or ordering them from tribal artisans and distributing them on the market.

In the case of the Hmong, another partly political factor also contributed to the commercialization of their arts: the opium problem. With US help, a special program was started by the UNPDAC (UN-Thai Program for Drug Abuse Control) to evolve alternative cash crops to replace opium in the tribal villages. The program developed an experimental crafts project, which was implemented in a few Hmong villages and was later on taken over by the Handicrafts Projects of the Hill Tribe Division of the Department of Welfare of the Thai Ministry of Interior.

The commercialization of Hmong and Mien arts has thus, on the whole, not been a spontaneous process, initiated by the tribal artisans, but one sponsored from the outside by a variety of agencies and private entrepreneurs. These had to master the tricky problem of developing a market for the tribal products and adapting these products to market demands, even as they endeavored not to destroy the tribal artistic traditions. These outsiders thus became an important factor in the process of artistic change and decisively influenced its dynamics.

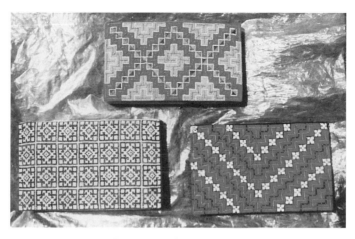

Figure 3.5 Hmong Lady Bags, Manufactured from Master Design (UNDPAC Program).

The production of Hmong and Mien crafts for the market tended to be concentrated in those localities where it has been initially sponsored from the outside. While in most of the more accessible tribal villages, and in particular the touristic ones, like Hmong Doi Pui (Cohen 1996: 123–131) and Mien Nong Wen, there was at least some sporadic production for sale, regular production for the market could be found only in villages maintaining a continuous contact with agencies or middlemen. Even this, however has declined significantly with the flooding of the market by Hmong and Mien refugee products; many resettled Mien villagers, for example, ceased producing for the market and some preferred to work as middlemen for refugee products, rather then producing themselves. Hmong and Mien refugee products came to dominate the market, not only of Hmong and Mien crafts, but of tribal crafts in general. Large numbers of Hmong and Mien refugee women in all camps engaged in production for the market. One or another relief organization was active in the promotion of handicrafts production in every refugee camp save in one, whose crafts were marketed only by private middlemen in large quantities. However, the refugees have stayed only temporarily in Thailand and as they gradually left for resettlement in Western countries, the massive infusion of tribal arts into the market ebbed off. As long as it lasted, it had decisively influenced the size and structure of the tribal crafts market; this, in turn, had an important influence on the dynamics of change in Hmong and

Yao crafts, since the need to find an outlet for the products of such a large number of producers, capable of devoting themselves full-time to the manufacture of handicrafts, had a marked effect on the types of products, their styles and quality.

The Role of External Agents in the Direction of the Process of Change in Hmong and Mien Crafts.

The artisans in hill tribe societies were traditionally craftsmen (and craft-women) rather than artists; the function of the produced object and the technical virtuosity of the producer were generally more important for its appreciation than its beauty (cf. Becker 1978). Though the artisans had considerable freedom to change and innovate, particularly among the Hmong, they worked within a tradition whose criteria of appreciation were well known to them and hence could anticipate the reaction of their audience. Though tribal styles changed over time, they did so slowly and imperceptibly.

Under conditions of commercialization, all these changed. With the transition to an external audience, the artisans' work came to be appreciated by the potential new clients more as a work of art than as a craft object; the criteria of appreciation of the new, external audience, however, were a complete mystery to the producers. In response to the new circumstances, the rate of change in tribal arts accelerated dramatically.

At first, such changes were sporadic and desultory, almost random attempts by the artisans to evolve products which would sell. Soon, however, outside agents stepped in to steer the adaptation of handicraft production to market demand. The resettled village Hmong and Mien, and even more the refugees, had little prior contact with a Western public, while the necessity to increase their production quickly left little time for slow, spontaneous experimentation. Changes in their crafts were often sponsored from the outside, and the outcome was a 'collective production' (Becker 1974), in a much more concrete and immediate sense than that which Becker had in mind. Hence, the changes which the commercialized Hmong and Mien crafts underwent did not initially reflect the spontaneous reaction of these people to the often drastic changes in their lives, as they did at a later stage (see Chs. 4–7); rather the changes were primarily sponsored by outside agents and reflected, to various degrees, the motives and intents of these agents.

The specific direction in which the work of a particular group of artisans – e.g. members of a village or inmates of a refugee camp –

Figure 3.6 White Hmong Woman's Headdress With 'Scroll' Design, Chiang Kien Village.

changed was, hence, the outcome of a collaborative effort of tribal producer and external agent, with the agent advising, proposing or conceiving new products or designs and sometimes even straightforwardly directing their execution, up to supplying the producer with a master design to be copied. While the extent to which change was a direct outcome of outside intervention differed from one agent to another, and is an important factor in the explanation of the differential dynamics of change, all regular production for the market was, at least to some degree, made according to specifications or instructions by outsiders. In giving these specifications or instructions, the various agencies and, to a lesser degree, private middlemen, were influenced by four basic considerations:

First, the urgent need to increase the market, so that a large number of resettled villagers, and, later, refugees from Laos could earn a basic income. A bigger market would also enhance the profits of the middlemen.

Second, the refugees, and the resettled villagers in the early stages of resettlement, had little if any opportunities for alternative employment; hence they were able and often prepared to invest considerable time into the manufacture of handicrafts, not only as a source of income, but also as a kind of 'occupational therapy.'

Third, the tribal people were, at least initially, completely unaware of the tastes and preferences of their new, external audiences – the tourists, expatriates and other foreigners who were the chief consumers of their products.

Fourth, the agencies and even the middlemen, desired to preserve tribal traditions and to prevent the destruction of tribal culture through commercialization.

These considerations created three types of dilemmas for the marketing agencies and middlemen:

1. Quality versus Quantity: the need to increase the size of the market creates a tendency to develop cheap, mass produced items, even at the expense of quality; while the availability of free time leads to an emphasis on labor-intensive, high-quality products, especially under conditions of a limited market.

2. Preservation versus Alteration: the need to adopt craft products to the tastes and preferences of an external public creates a tendency to introduce alterations into their form, style, function, colors and the materials from which they are manufactured; while the desire to preserve the producers' culture creates the opposite tendency to keep as closely as possible to the tradition.

3. Freedom versus Intervention: the need to increase the market for craft products and the lack of familiarity of the producers with the tastes and preferences of their new audience create a tendency for outsiders to intervene and direct them toward the production of more marketable items; while the desire to preserve the producers' traditions and individual creativity and to reinforce the 'therapeutic' aspects of crafts production create the opposite tendency, to permit the producers as much freedom as possible.

The various external agents differed in the specific ways in which they formulated their policies to face these dilemmas. Despite those differences, to which I shall yet return, some common tendencies can be discerned in the policies of most marketing agencies and even private intermediaries.

Figure 3.7 White Hmong Silver Coin Bag with 'Scroll' Pattern (author's collection).

On the whole, the external agents intervened to a considerable degree in tribal production; but only in rare cases did they deny the artisans' freedom completely; and they almost never sponsored the introduction of utterly foreign patterns or artistic styles into Hmong or Mien handicraft production. Neither did the Hmong or Mien people attempt to adopt such patterns or styles spontaneously. True, the Hmong frequently copied Mien designs and even produced embroidered Mien items such as shoulder bags, but such borrowing has also been common in the past. Both the sponsoring agents and the Hmong and Mien people thus preferred that their handicraft production remain in the orthogenetic tradition. Within that tradition, however, a great deal of innovation did take place, as agents and producers realized the market potential of different types of products. The point to note here is that the agents soon found out that the decisive factor influencing their customers' decision to buy tribal products was not so much their specific designs, but rather the quality of the materials and execution of the work, the intended function of the products and the colors and color combination used on the design. In these areas, indeed, considerable alterations were introduced. New kinds of materials, such as threads and textiles made of artificial fibers in color-fast dyes were substituted for the more traditional, often indigenously produced materials. It should be noted, however, that such substitution has merely reinforced an already existing trend; even before the commercialization of their crafts, both the Hmong and Mien have already used non-indigenous and even industrially produced materials for products intended for an internal audience. For example, the Blue Hmong substituted linen bought on the market for home-spun hemp for their batiked skirts; some even used printed, instead of batiked material. Indeed, in some villages, the Hmong women dress in printed skirts, while producing batiked ones for sale.

A major innovation were the new types of products, ornamented with embroidered, appliqued or batiked designs; prominent among these is Western apparel of various kinds, such as women's blouses and vests, tablecloths, bedspreads and a variety of decorative items, particularly ornamental 'patches' and 'squares' of various sizes. A wide range of new colors was introduced, far beyond the traditional Hmong or Mien palette; some agencies also instructed the artisans to reduce the number of colors in any one item from the traditional five to two, in combinations suiting the tastes of different kinds of modern customers. In some cases, new ranges of colors, such as pastels, completely foreign to the spirit of Hmong and Mien culture, were introduced. However, the new materials, and particularly the new colors, created expressive opportunities, unknown under the more limited circumstances of traditional production.

The external agents did not, on the whole, interfere with the designs embroidered or appliqued on the commercial products. They did, however, help the tribal women reduce the amount of labor invested in the products and thus increase production. Under traditional circumstances a woman could make, in her free time, one or at most a few elaborately ornamented objects a year. Under the new circumstances, she found herself in a quandary: though, particularly in the refugee camps, she had more free time, the ornamentation of the new products by the old, densely and painstakingly elaborated designs, would either so increase the price of the products that there would be no market for them, or so reduce the income of the artisan that it would not be worth

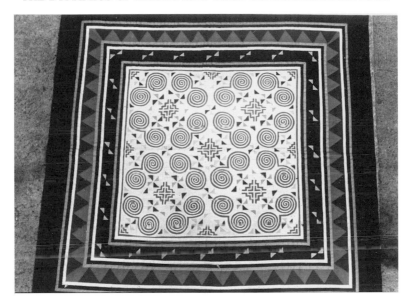

Figure 3.8 Hmong Appliqued Commercial 'Square,' Thai Tribal Crafts, Chiang Mai.

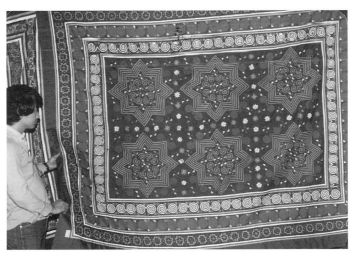

Figure 3.9 Hmong Appliqued Commercial Bedspread, Nam Yao Refugee Camp (Night Market, Chiang Mai).

her while to work for the market. The agents, and particularly the non-profit agencies, aimed at safeguarding the artisans a minimal income, without debasing the quality of their products and thereby destroying not only the culture, but also the market. The principal means used to preserve appeal while speeding up production was to make the designs larger and sparser: stitches, cross stitches and chain stitches became larger, designs bigger and more sparsely dispersed over the surface of the product. This can be seen by a comparison of the Hmong objects in Plate 3 and Fig. 3.1 (the coin bags in Plate 3 were made for internal use while the square in Fig. 3.1 was produced for the market).

However, the tendency to make the ornamentation larger and sparser, was countervailed by two other tendencies which preserved or even increased the appeal of the products for an external public: the further elaboration of traditional designs, which was mainly spontaneous and can be found particularly among the Hmong women (e.g. Figs. 3.13–15), and the deliberate rearrangement of designs over the surface to create an impression of ampleness, despite their sparseness, which was mainly sponsored by outsiders on Mien designs (e.g. Fig. 3.27). The products thereby became ever more remote in appearance from those produced for an internal audience, so that a clear separation took place between the two lines of production.

Under the prevailing conditions of a large labor pool with no alternative employment, all the efforts at safeguarding a minimal income for the producers could aim at only a modest goal. Indeed, even the non-profit agencies, whose main purpose was to enhance the tribal welfare, aimed at no more than a daily income of about 15–20 baht (US$ 0.75–1.00 at the rate prevailing at the time) for villager artisans, and even less for refugees. While the women working for the agencies often reached that income level, refugees working for private middle-men often made considerably less – sometimes only about 5 baht (US$ 0.25) and even 2–3 baht a day. When evaluating these results, one has to bear in mind that incomes of 15–20 baht a day were at the time not dramatically lower than those earned by tribal wage laborers in agricultural employment. Moreover, in the case of the tribal refugee artisans, who often earned the lowest rates, two additional circum-stances have to be taken into account: the fact that their most basic needs were taken care of by the UN relief agency; and the fact that they often had literally nothing else to do, so that handicraft work had for them taken on a therapeutic function, in addition to the purely economic one.

Figure 3.10 Hmong Embroidered Commercial Bedspread, Nam Yau Refugee Camp (detail) (author's collection).

The entrance of cheap and relatively high-quality refugee products into the tribal crafts market, however, had a detrimental effect on village Hmong and Mien production. Since they were unable to work at prices competitive with those of the refugees, and – in the case of the village Hmong – often unable to attain the quality of Hmong refugee work, the production of the villagers was seriously reduced. While some resettlement villagers continued to produce high quality work, others, particularly those close to the refugee camps, became intermediaries for the tribal refugees' production.

The easy availability of labor under conditions of a limited market, necessarily kept the earnings of refugee producers low and encouraged qualitative competition between producers: inventive individuals or those who were capable of producing work of a high quality were not only immediately rewarded by a marginally higher payment for their products, but were also assured of employment when the market declined and the less gifted artisans were laid off. Since originality, creativity and excellence in quality were generally rewarded, the Hmong and Mien commercialized crafts remained vital and dynamic, at least during the first few years after commercialization. While in some lines of production, such as that of small and cheap items produced in the thousands each month (e.g. Mien shoulder bags or small Hmong and Mien patches) standardization did necessarily set in, in the manufacture of bigger and more expensive items there was remarkably little repetition of designs, and innovations were constantly introduced, though their number has gradually declined.

One of the most interesting outcomes of this qualitative competition between producers – mainly refugees – was the constant innovation and variation of designs, their outlay and coloration. As one informant put it: "Owing to the large-scale production of tribal arts for the market, they presently undergo, in a single year, as much change as they did in a hundred years in the past." However, the pace of innovation has somewhat slowed down over the years. Indeed, after most refugees left Thailand in the course of the late 1980s and early 1990s, and the foreign relief organizations terminated their craft programs, the few Hmong and Mien products reaching the market became completely standardized.

We thus reach an interesting conclusion: if the Hmong and Mien arts had not been commercialized, they would probably have declined, owing to the dramatic circumstances in the life of these tribal people. Commercialization, however, led to a process of change and innovation, which breathed new life into their crafts. The impetus for the renewed activity, in the case of the Hmong and the Mien, however, did not come from within their cultures, as a spontaneous response to changed circumstances (as it did in some other Fourth World societies undergoing dramatic changes), but was externally sponsored by the various marketing agents. Still, the interference and direction of the external agents notwithstanding, the tribal artisans retained, in most cases, a considerable freedom to shape their products and especially to select the designs according to their imagination and creative power. In a sense, internal traditional, technical and cultural constraints on creativity were now weakened and gave place to external economic and organizational constraints. While the creative freedom of the artisans

Figure 3.11 Hmong Embroidered Commercial Square, CAMA (International School Sale, Bangkok).

Fig 3.12 Jacket Made from Hmong Appliqued Square, CAMA (International School Sale, Bangkok).

thus expanded, the direction in which their work changed came to be more and more determined by market demand, as mediated by the marketing agents, and was increasingly divested from the artisans' own culture. While variety proliferated, the artistic products lacked that expressive power and cultural significance which a purely spontaneous artistic revival would have generated.

Factors Engendering Variety in the Dynamics of Change of Hmong and Mien Crafts.

The preceding discussion established that the process of change of Hmong and Mien crafts was, on the whole, the result of a collaborative effort between tribal artisans and external agents. At the early stages of commercialization, both participants in the process were uncertain as to the direction in which tribal crafts should be developed for the market. There was a great deal of experimentation, accompanied at first by a marked decline in quality and the attempt to market simple, crude products, unattractive to the Western eye. With growing experience, however, the marketing agents developed more definite policies, and grasped the importance of quality control and enhanced attractiveness of the products for the development of a market. The external agents differed in the degree to which they have imposed their guidance upon the producers, but only one or two asked for exact compliance with precise specifications. However, they were the dominant factor in the relationship: Owing to their control over the access to the market, they wielded considerable influence not only over the economic, but also over the artistic side of tribal handicraft production. The commercialized crafts emerging under their guidance belong, predominately, to what we called the 'transitional' type (Shiloah and Cohen 1983), namely, primarily innovative, but well within the orthogenetic tradition, preserving some spontaneity despite external sponsoring, and absorbing selectively some heterogenetic elements.

   The dynamics of change of tribal arts, however, was not unilinear: not only was there considerable internal variety within the dominant type, but some other types of dynamics of change also emerged. We shall now review and illustrate these variations by examining three major variables: the cultural background of the producers, the policies of the external agents and the change in the clientele.

The Producers: both Hmong and Mien traditional arts are characterized by a remarkable richness and variety. Hmong traditional designs however were less formalized than those of the Mien. Consequently, as we shall see, their commercialized crafts were more amenable to change and manifested a greater variety than those of the Mien. Moreover, Hmong arts were from the outset more differentiated, owing to their division into sub-groups – such as the Blue, White, and Striped Sleeved Hmong – than those of the more homogeneous Mien. This circumstance added even more variety to commercialized Hmong arts.

70

Figure 3.13 Hmong Appliqued Commercial Cushion Cover (Sob Tuang Refugee Project).

Figure 3.14 Hmong Appliqued Commercial Square (Sob Tuang Refugee Project).

The Policies of the Marketing Agents: though most sponsoring agents resolved the three dilemmas of policy towards commercialized craft production listed above along essentially similar lines, there were nevertheless important variations among them in their relative emphases. It would be tedious to review the specific policies of each external agent but some of those whose policy deviated most from the dominant pattern will be briefly reviewed. Thus, CAMA (the relief arm of the Christian Missionary Alliance), working in two large refugee camps, emphasized primarily the production of as great a quantity of products as the market could bear, to safeguard employment for as large a number of tribal women as possible. In that it resembled the UNDPAC crafts program, which was active primarily in some Hmong villages. But the approach of the two agencies differed: CAMA advised the artisans to simplify and enlarge their designs, and adapt the colors of their products to the tastes of the modern mass consumers (Figs. 3.11 and 3.12). It thus lowered their price and increased their mass appeal, but also reduced their quality; nevertheless, artisans retained some freedom within the guidelines. The UNDPAC program choose a different approach: here the agency's own designer, an ethnic Thai, evolved a number of master patterns based on traditional Hmong designs (Fig. 3.4); the artisans were advised to replicate these precisely (Fig. 3.5). While the Hmong style was essentially conserved, and the quality of the products kept fairly high, the artisans' freedom was virtually eliminated – and their products were strictly standardized. The agency sought to resolve the dilemma of quantity versus quality by strict quality control and the introduction of simple, useful objects which were easy to make and had a large potential market.

Another agency, the THCF (Thai Hill Crafts Foundation) adopted a similar though somewhat less strict strategy, particularly in its work with resettled Mien villagers.

On the other end of the spectrum are agencies which encouraged the artisans to innovate freely, within very general guidelines concerning primarily the type and size of products and their color combinations. Representative of this approach was the Sob Tuang Refugee Project, which has first been associated with the YMCA and later with the British refugee relief organization Ockenden Venture. The project worked with Mien and Hmong refugees in the Sob Tuang refugee camp in Nan province. Its policy was intended to encourage creativity and to preserve higher quality products by marginally differential remuneration of artisans; while work of varying quality was acceptable, the better workers were given somewhat higher prices. As a consequence, an extraordinarily wide range of designs and of quality, and a strong tendency among artisans to innovate, leading them occasionally to the verge of heterogeneity, had emerged (Figs. 3.13–15 for Hmong and Figs. 3.22–24 for Mien work).

Figure 3.15 Hmong Appliqued Commercial Square (Sob Tuang Refugee Project).

The approaches of most other marketing agencies and private intermediaries fell in between these extremes, but were closer to the latter. It should be noted that no agent emphasized the uncompromised preservation of the traditional style at the expense of quantity of production, though the representatives of the various agencies had a differential regard for tradition and some clearly wanted to preserve it, if it would have been at all possible. The provision of employment, however, was the overriding consideration for all of them.

The various approaches of the external agents have, as we shall see, a significant impact on the differential enroutement of the stylistic dynamics of Hmong and Mien crafts.

Figure 3.16 Hmong Bedspread with Representational Design; Provenience Unknown (detail) (Night Market, Chiang Mai).

The Clientele: at an earlier stage, tribal crafts were sold primarily to expatriates and foreign tourists. Later on, a shift in the composition of the clientele had occurred: an expansion has taken place in both the domestic Thai market and the export market. This expansion has significantly increased the demand for Hmong and Mien products, but has also created, for different reasons, new pressures for standardization: the Thai customers were mostly young visitors to Chiang Mai, who either bought cheap Hmong and Mien products, such as shoulder bags, as souvenirs, or fashionable 'northern' clothes, such as dresses or jackets, ornamented by small embroidered or appliqued Hmong or Mien patches. The massive production of such items led quickly to standardization.

74

Figure 3.17 Antique Mien Bridal Veil (Mrs. Lewis's Collection, Chiang Mai).

Figure 3.18 Mien Commercial Square (Thai Tribal Crafts, Chiang Mai).

Exports led to standardization for a different reason: foreign importers usually gave detailed specifications on the exact size, materials, quality, colors and even designs of the products they ordered; these reflected the logistic, managerial and economic constraints of the market in which they operated, as well as the need to adapt the products for faraway mass-consumers, who were usually utterly unaware of the culture of the tribes or even of their existence. When semi-finished products such as small Hmong or Mien patches were intended as decorative elements on larger products, such as modern fashions (see Ch. 4), specifications became particularly precise.

Comparative Analysis of the Dynamics of Change in Hmong and Mien Crafts: Selected Case Studies.

I shall now illustrate the main directions of change in Hmong and Mien commercialized crafts by following the metamorphosis of a few concrete designs. The base- line of the comparative exercise will be the designs as produced for the internal tribal audience prior to commercialization. It will then be shown how these designs changed along varying routes of commercialization.

1. The Hmong: traditional Hmong embroidery and applique work featured a remarkable richness; and though some patterns such as the 'scroll' (Fig. 3.7), or the 'maze' ('*bouw chua*', see Cambell et al 1978:129) (Fig. 3.3) were fairly common, there existed a wide variety of rarely used ones and there was no traditionally imposed limit to variations (e.g. Plate 3 and Fig. 3.2). The base line from which the commercialization of Hmong crafts started was, then, an 'open' one. This openness made possible the enormous proliferation of variation in commercialized Hmong crafts, which became particularly prominent with the arrival of the refugees from Laos in the mid-1970's.

There are some differences in the extent to which village and refugee Hmong crafts changed with their commercialization: refugee crafts underwent, in general, more rapid and more pronounced changes. There were also differences in the extent of change according to whether commercialization was spontaneous or sponsored: change was more pronounced where commercialization was sponsored. Finally there were differences between commercialized crafts sponsored by different agents.

The spontaneously produced village Hmong crafts underwent the least amount of change: they tended toward 'orthogenetic perpetua-tion,' i.e. the replication of designs in traditional colors as

Figure 3.19 Mien Commercial Patch (Thai Hill Crafts Foundation, Bangkok).

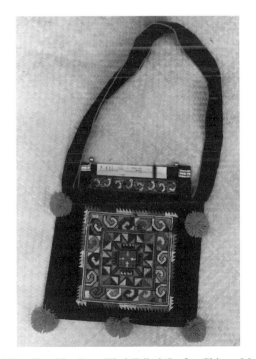

Figure 3.20 Mien Shoulder Bag (Thai Tribal Crafts, Chiang Mai).

commercialized products. This, however, was often accompanied by a marked decline of quality and carelessness in execution, which occasionally led to the production of cheap 'tourist art'; thus, the size of the cross stitches in the embroideries has been enlarged, the designs on the Blue Hmong batik were stained, etc. These phenomena could be, in particular, observed in such expressly touristic villages as Hmong Doi Pui (Cohen 1979). Interestingly, the locally produced items in that village changed little in style over the years, despite the fact that a large variety of other craft products, including those of Hmong refugees, were sold in the many tourist-oriented shops in the village. On the whole, however, the quantity of spontaneously produced village Hmong crafts has declined on the highly competitive tribal handicrafts market.

The major example of sponsored village Hmong handicraft production for the market is the UNDPAC crafts program. The manner in which the original 'maze' was stylized to suit Western tastes can be seen from a comparison of Figs. 3.3–5: Fig. 3.3 depicts the 'maze pattern' as traditionally executed; Fig. 3.4 features two master patterns, evolved by the program's Thai designer, based on the Hmong 'maze' design. Fig. 3.5 in turn, illustrates the precision with which the designs of the master pattern were copied onto actual commercialized products – in this case, lady bags. Though remaining within the orthogenetic Hmong tradition, the route of change taken by the commercialized arts of Hmong villagers as sponsored by the UNDPAC program are the best example of 'pseudo-ethnic' (Shiloah and Cohen 1983) craft in my study – an art form developed by outsiders and then marketed as if it were of tribal origin. Being extraneously determined, this route of change manifested altogether little, if any, dynamism.

Most Hmong refugee commercialized art products have been to some extent sponsored; the degree to which the external agent intervened in refugee production varied widely, however, and so did the expressive freedom of the artisans. Still, the artisans always retained at least some freedom to use creatively the new opportunities provided by their access to new materials and colors and by the partial breakdown of traditional guidelines for craft production. In conjunction with the extraordinary amount of time at the disposal of the artisans in the camps, these circumstances gave rise to a veritable avalanche of mostly orthogenetic innovations, their pace and variety largely depending on the extent to which the sponsoring agents directed or interfered with the artisans' work. While the variations between different refugee camps reflect to some extent the cultural differences between various Hmong groups from Laos, the major factor accounting

Figure 3.21 Mien Shoulder Bags (Night market, Chiang Mai).

Figure 3.22 Mien Cushion (Sob Tuang Refugee Project).

for variation were the influences emanating from the different external agents for whom the refugees worked.

I will illustrate these variations with the help of the metamorphose of a single design element – the well-known 'scroll' pattern commonly found on various Hmong objects such as headdresses (Fig. 3.7), 'sailor's collars' (Fig. 3.2), silver coin bags (Fig. 3.7), sashes, etc. In camp Nam Yao, in Nan Province, where private intermediaries rather than non-profit agencies were active, this design element was extensively used on Hmong products of varying kinds and sizes, from tiny 'patches' intended for the ornamentation of Thai or Western style dresses and costumes, to medium sized 'squares' intended for use as table cloths or wall hangings (Fig. 3.8) and large pieces used primarily as bedspreads (Figs. 3.9–10). This route of change manifested a considerable proliferation of new forms, under little outside guidance: hence, the items retained their multi-color quality and many of the colors and color combinations resembled those on Hmong items produced for an internal audience. The designs grew in size and were less carefully executed, but altogether remained closer to the orthogenetic tradition than those in camps where external interference was more pronounced. This can be seen by a comparison, on the one hand, with the products from the Nong Khai camp, marketed by CAMA (Figs. 3.11–3.12) and on the other hand, with those from Sob Tuang camp, marketed by the Sob Tuang Refugee Project (Figs. 3.13–3.15). The Nong Khai designs, under the impact of CAMA policy, are considerably simplified and the number of colors used is reduced to two to suit Western preferences. The designs are sparse and large, and much of the space is taken up by very wide marginal decorations, which could have been made quickly and easily. The Sob Tuang material manifests an opposite tendency: while the project's guidance finds expression in the reduction of the number of colors to two, and in the choice of colors and color combinations deemed to appeal to Westerners, the elaborate complexity of the designs reflects the project's policy of encouraging inventiveness and originality. The products marketed by both agencies, though still within the orthogenetic tradition, represent a greater movement towards hetero-geneity than the Nam Yao products, albeit in opposite directions: towards standardized mass products in the case of CAMA, and towards more individualized products in the case of the Sob Tuang project.

Other Hmong patterns underwent similar metamorphoses as the scroll pattern, but our example is representative of the general trend. I would like, however, to point out an interesting, innovative phenom-enon, found among the Hmong refugees: the emergence of figurative motifs (Plate 4–Fig. 3.16). The point to note is that, although figurative motifs are unknown in traditional Hmong culture in Thailand and Laos, their emergence in Hmong refugee art was a purely spontaneous phenomenon, which has not received encouragement from either the

Figure 3.23 Mien Cushion (Sob Tuang Refugee Project).

Figure 3.24 Mien Cushion (Sob Tuang Refugee Project) (author's collection).

marketing agencies or the private intermediaries. Both figures, which are representative of the trend, record the various traditional costumes, lifeways, and pastimes of the Hmong. This phenomenon is difficult to classify within our scheme of types of dynamics of change; while clearly not orthogenetic, it is not heterogenetic in the sense of absorption and re-integration of some alien cultural influences. Rather, it seems to be a genuine, indigenous development reflecting the desire of people torn out of their traditional habitat to recollect their customs and valued past experiences and to broadcast them, through the market, to the world at large. Paradoxically, though by style they are alien to Hmong culture, they probably possess more cultural meaning for the Hmong refugees than do the fanciful variations of their traditional non-figurative designs on commercialized products (see Ch. 6–7).

2. The Mien: in comparison with the Hmong, the traditional Mien designs are more formalized and less varied. Moreover, the general outlay of different types of designs on traditional objects such as women's trousers, was fixed by tradition (Layton 1968) – though the choice of some specific designs within this outlay, especially of the small squares, was left open to the artisan's choice. The base-line from which the commercialization of Mien arts commenced was thus, despite considerable richness, less 'open,' than that of the Hmong arts. Moreover, owing to their greater internal homogeneity, the crafts of the village and refugee Mien differ less from one another than those of the respective Hmong groups. Consequently there are also fewer differences between the commercialized products of village and refugee Mien than there are in the case of the Hmong.

Spontaneous production is found primarily among those village Mien whose settlements were frequented by tourists, with conse-quences very similar to those found in the touristic Hmong villages: a replication of designs in traditional colors on commercial items – for example, the embroidery of the women's trousers on a piece of black cloth; as in the Hmong case, this was accompanied by a marked decline in quality, for example, the designs were simplified and their density drastically parred down.

In the at least partially sponsored Mien crafts from resettlement villages and refugee camps, several concomitant trends can be observed, each usually associated with, but not exclusive to, a given marketing agent. The process of change in these crafts will be illustrated by two principal examples, which are fairly representative of the process as a whole: the design on the Mien bridal veil and on the women's festive trousers.

Figure 3.25 Mien Commercial Square (Highland Tribal Crafts, Chiang Mai).

The Mien bridal veil (Cambell et al. 1978), originally embroidered in the five traditional Mien colors, is characterized by a square centerpiece, in the middle of which is located a small Mien square (Fig. 3.17). More recently the veil has been embroidered with industrially dyed threads for use by the Mien themselves, and lastly, for commercial purposes. The basic structure of the centerpiece has been borrowed, in a wide range of variations, for different commercial products. At an early stage of commercialization, it was fairly faithfully copied onto decorative squares, for example, by the resettlement Mien whose work was sponsored by 'Hmong Mien Handicrafts' (Fig. 3.18), a religious non-profit organization. Later, the centerpiece design of the original veil underwent further change, and its colors were adapted to Western tastes as, for example, in Fig. 3.19, also produced by the resettlement Mien. The decoration on many of the bigger Mien shoulder bags (Fig. 3.20), at the time of research one of the most

Figure 3.26 Mien Commercial Square (Border Crafts of Thailand, Chiang Mai).

popular touristic items, produced in a great variety of specific designs by both resettlement and refugee Mien (Fig. 3.21), is apparently a further, simplified adaptation of the centerpiece design. This line of development led to simplification and the mass production of cheap items, which were, owing to their popularity, often copied by other groups, especially refugee Hmong, and even ethnic Thais. Though it remained, on the whole, firmly within the boundaries of orthogeneity, this line of development led to standardized 'tourist art.'

There is, however, an opposite line of development, exemplified primarily by the products marketed by the Sob Tuang Refugee Project. Here, as can be seen in Figs. 3.22–3.24, the basic form of the centerpiece was retained, but came to be ever further removed from the original. In Fig. 3.24 the formal outlay of the centerpiece is still recognizable, but the design itself is highly stylized. This, in fact, is as far as Mien commercialized crafts have moved in the direction of heterogeneity; but the designs themselves are, even in these extreme cases, still related to traditional Mien designs.

A similar line of development can be followed when one departs from the traditional design on the Mien women's trousers. At an early stage of commercialization of Mien crafts in the resettlement villages, the general outlay of the pattern on the trousers was copied, in a simplified form, on pieces of cloth to be sold as decorative items (Figs. 3.25 and 3.26). This, however, involved a great amount of labor, which has either increased the price of the product so much that no large market could be found for it, or contrariwise, so much reduced the artisans' income that producing the item would not be worthwhile. Hence, one of the foreign relief workers, in collaboration with some Mien women, evolved a set of several dozen 'samplers' – master patterns on which traditional Mien designs were re-arranged in an innovative manner; the sparseness of the design is compensated by skillful distribution, so that the impression of plentitude is preserved (Fig. 3.27). Later on, the basic designs were further developed into more complicated ones, particularly by a Thai designer for the THCF, as, for example in Fig. 3.28. This is a highly sophisticated design, heavily influenced by Western aesthetic ideas – specifically the coloration of the design changes in tune with the color of the background cloth; the design itself, however, is strictly within the confines of orthogeneity. The very sophistication of this design, however, demanded strict adherence to the master-pattern – hence, the production of these Mien items, similar to the Hmong items made for the UNDPAC program, tended towards standardization; it is, thus, a high quality example of 'pseudo-ethnic' art (Shiloah and Cohen 1983), evolved by a non-Mien designer for replication by Mien artisans.

Conclusions

Our study reinforces the conclusion of several contemporary ethnographers and anthropologists that the commercialization of folk crafts is not identical with their destruction. Rather, under the specific conditions prevailing in northern Thailand, and especially among the Hmong and Mien refugee population, commercialization keeps the folk arts alive; indeed, in its absence, they would wither away.

It is true that commercialization changed the Hmong and Mien folk arts; but the people drew a distinction between production for an external audience and for their own use. Insofar as they continued to produce them for themselves, their crafts changed little, although they

Figure 3.27 Mien Commercial Square (Thai Tribal Crafts, Chiang Mai).

Figure 3.28 Mien Table Runner (Thai Hill Crafts Foundation, Chiang Mai).

have adopted some new materials and colors. The changes, wrought through contact with the crafts market and its mediating agents, in the crafts produced for the external audience, were many and complex. In fact, my principal finding is that, as a consequence of the specific marketing policies adopted by the external agents and the nature of collaboration between them and the producers, several directions of change in Hmong and Mien arts can be distinguished.

Spontaneously produced products in the touristic villages, sold directly to visiting tourists, were usually poor replications of products and designs used by the tribal people themselves. Production sponsored, to varying degrees, by external agents for 'indirect tourism' (Aspelin 1977), namely, sale on the market, was at the outset also mainly replicative. Soon, however, more substantive changes began to appear. The bulk of this production falls into one principal type of dynamics of change, which we termed 'transitional' – the new craft emerges as a collective production of the external sponsoring agents and the spontaneous efforts of the artisans. While innovative, it is firmly anchored within the orthogenetic tradition of the tribe, but also absorbs some heterogenetic elements.

Within this type, however, several strains can be distinguished, according to the manner in which the major dilemmas of the commercialization process have been resolved: the emphasis on quality versus quantity of production, the desire to preserve as against the tendency to alter tribal styles and designs, and the degree of freedom left to the artisan by the marketing agent. While some agents lent support to the artisans' creativity within the orthogenetic tradition, others favored simplification and standardization. Indeed, some kinds of 'transitional' crafts tended to degenerate into cheap 'tourist art.' Though a substantial part of the commercialized Hmong and Mien crafts tended towards this end of the spectrum of the 'transitional' type, it was not the dominant one. Despite the low prices received by the artisans, the crafts of these two tribal groups preserved – at least for a considerable time – a remarkable vitality. Though constantly changing through frequent innovations, however, Hmong and Mien commercialized crafts only rarely became completely heterogenetic; no tendency among the artisans themselves to copy the styles of others has been found except that the Hmong continue their tradition of borrowing Mien designs. Nor did the external agents attempt to induce the Hmong or Mien people to produce styles or patterns completely foreign to their own culture. Paradoxically, the closest the Hmong (but not the Mien) came to heterogeneity was the spontaneous attempt of a few gifted refugee women to render their traditional culture and customs in a figurative style, itself foreign to their very culture.

While in most cases the artisans retained some degree of creative freedom, in some instances concern with quality and adaptation to market demand led to a virtually complete abrogation of that freedom – the artisans being asked to reproduce faithfully a designer's master pattern, thus leading to the emergence of art of the 'pseudo-ethnic' type.

Though not destructive of the traditional crafts, commercialization does have some problematic cultural consequences. Although most tribal production remained within the realm of 'orthogenetic innovation', the proliferation of changes in traditional designs was not, in general, inspired by spontaneous artistic impulses or responses to a changed life situation, nor by a desire to give expression to inner moods of the artisans – but rather by the need to invent designs which would attract the eye and suit the tastes of a new audience whose culture was foreign to the artisans themselves. The innovations, often sponsored by the external agents, were thus not meaningful in terms of the artisans' own culture. And while they were fanciful, they were also alien to the producers. The proliferation of new and imaginative color combinations, designs and products in the commercialized Hmong and Mien arts should hence not be equated with a cultural 'revival'. Paradoxically, the Hmong artisans who did do figurative work, which was foreign to their own culture, represented a more important artistic attempt to respond to the radical changes in the life of the people, than the many purely decorative innovations in the traditional ornamental styles.

Notes

1 I am grateful to the Harry S. Truman Institute, the Hebrew University of Jerusalem and Stiftung Volkswagenwerk for providing grants to support this research in the years 1977–1980. Thanks are due to the National Research Council of Thailand and the Tribal Research Center in Chiang Mai who assisted me in many ways and whose cooperation was vital for the success of the project. I am also obliged to Mrs. Elaine Lewis for her useful comments.

4

FROM TRIBAL COSTUME TO POP FASHION

The 'Boutiquisation' of the Textiles of the Hill Tribes of Northern Thailand[1]

Introduction

Between the 'authentic' ethnic culture and modern popular culture there is a gray intermediate area which has been condemned by culture critics but, up till now, given little attention by serious researchers. This area embraces the various forms in which ethnic products, old and new, entered modern popular culture, often after undergoing considerable transformation. This process is widespread, although scarcely docu mented. In the contemporary world, the ethnic products most frequently undergoing this process are those of 'Fourth World' people – the ethnic and tribal minorities of the Third World (Graburn (ed.) 1976). The consumers of such products were at first modern Western youths, especially those belonging to one or another alternative sub-culture; but as ethnic products became more widely marketed in the contemporary West, other social groups adopted their use. In the process, the style of their adaptation to modern tastes and needs has been changed, as we shall see below.

Several types of ethnic products have entered that process. Ethnic jewelry is probably the most popular and the most easily adaptable to modern usage. Thus, the necklaces and other objects of the Bedouins in Israel, and probably elsewhere in the Middle East, have been torn asunder and reassembled in new designs, by urban Arab merchants or modern Jewish designers, and then sold to tourists and local inhabitants alike. Textiles, particularly ornamented ethnic costumes and other garments have in the last few decades found their way into Western fashions. While original textiles are only rarely used in an unadapted form by Westerners, old ethnic clothing or even new items, specially produced for the market, are frequently adapted to modern uses. This can vary from a mere inclusion of a piece of ethnic embroidery into an otherwise wholly Western piece of garment, to a complete refashioning of an ethnic outfit to correspond to the measures and conventions of modern Western clothing. Examples abound from all over the world. Bedouin and other nomadic textiles have been so used, as have those of Native Americans in the United States and of South American Indians. This case study is meant primarily to open this gray area between ethnic and popular culture to discussion.

Background

As he toured the tourist shops and the night markets of Chiang Mai in the 1980s, the visitor was confronted with a curious and slightly confusing spectacle: He encountered a rich array of dresses, vests, skirts and other garments, which at first looked like pop fashions, but on closer inspection turned out to be made, wholly or partly, from hill tribe textiles, and sometimes actually from old hill tribe clothing. Most of these woven, embroidered, appliqued or batiked tribal materials have been originally produced, or even used, by the tribal people who inhabited the mountainous areas to the north and west of the city and the drab refugee camps along the Thai-Laotian border to the east of it. The visitor was faced with a peculiar kind of hybridization or fusion of the cultural products of the remote, 'primitive' people of the tribal highlands of Southeast Asia, and of the pop fashions of the youth of the contemporary West, with its penchant for the incorporation of 'authentic' ethnic or 'primitive' elements in their outfits, without, however, thereby 'going native.' I shall here refer to this specific process of incorporation of tribal materials into the pop fashions which appeal primarily to contemporary youth as 'boutiquisation,' and examine briefly its origins, development and economic and cultural significance.

The Process of 'Boutiquization'

The commercialization of hill-tribe crafts was initially sponsored by the Thai authorities as part of their efforts to incorporate the tribal people of northern Thailand into the Thai state and national economy (Ch. 2). The process began already in the 1960s, as the authorities and some non-profit organizations (NGOs) endeavored to find new, alternative or supplementary sources of employment and income for resettled tribal people. The commercialization of their products was at the outset oriented primarily to the expatriate market; however, the production of the tribal villagers gradually penetrated the local and the tourist markets (Ch. 3).

A variety of national and foreign religious and humanitarian NGOs undertook to commercialize the hill tribe products, mainly textiles, but also some basketry and jewelry. The process of commercialization was considerably expanded when tens of thousands of tribal refugees, primarily Hmong, entered the country after the 1975 communist takeover in Laos. Highly skilled, often destitute, and with plenty of free time at their disposal, the tribal refugees, especially the women, provided an enormous potential labor force for craft production; however, since they were restricted to the refugee camps, their products could only be sold through NGOs or private middlemen who have gained access to the camps (Cohen 1982c). With increased production, in addition to the expanding local tourist market, a growing export business in tribal textiles developed.

The necessity to provide employment for ever more tribal, local, and refugee producers, faced the promoters of tribal crafts, primarily the NGO's, with the problem of evolving new uses for their textile products in order to attract additional customers. The marketing agencies therefore began to look for ways to adapt the products to the needs, tastes and preferences of a broader Western public, consisting of people who never even heard of the tribes, or knew only a little about them and their predicament, and had no particular 'folkloristic' interest in their products. A wide variety of new, adapted products, such as embroidered, appliqued or batiked decorative 'squares,' hangings, table-cloths and bedspreads, and a variety of souvenir articles, such as shoulder-bags were evolved. These products combined tribal designs and ornaments, often adapted in color and elaborated or embellished to suit Western tastes, with forms and functions which were foreign to the tribal people, but familiar to the new buying public (Ch. 3, Dewhurst and MacDowell (eds.) 1983, Randall (ed) 1984, *Hmong Art* 1986).

The one area in which there was relatively little production for the market remained, paradoxically, that of the original use of tribal textiles: clothing. The 'authentic' tribal costumes and apparel, though exquisitely made and very attractive to tourists' eyes, proved to be marketable, if at all, only in very small quantities. The garments of the Karen, Hmong, Mien and other tribes are rich in colors and boldly ornamented, and hence held little promise of attracting the rather sedate tastes for clothing of the middle-class Western travelling public. In addition to a few collectors, only the rich and extravagant would buy expensive original pieces that might be worn at exclusive parties or at

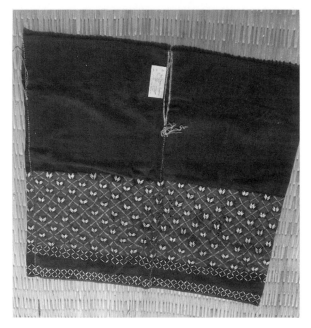

Figure 4.1 Karen Women's Shirt, Thai Tribal Crafts, Chiang Mai (1981).

masquerades. Most Westerners found the color of tribal garments too loud,and their cut too ungainly or uncomfortable to wear in their original form.

Experiments in two directions were made and eventually met with success: The re-designing of tribal apparel for Western usage, which often meant a change in its form, appearance and function; and the preparation of semi-finished small, ornamental 'patches' and similar items which could be incorporated, often by non-tribal seamstresses or designers, into fashionable clothing. Here are found the beginnings of the 'boutiquisation' of the tribal textiles. These products appealed primarily to young tourists, immersed in the contemporary pop-culture and with an interest in pre-industrial, hand-made ethnic products.

The re-designing of tribal apparel initially took the simple form of cutting original and commercialized tribal products into richly ornamented vests and jackets, which resembled in their form the current Western hippie and pop fashions. Thus, the square, woven Karen woman's shirts (Fig. 4.1) were cut into unisex vests (Fig. 4.2); and so were pieces embroidered in the style of Mien women's trousers

Figure 4.2 Vest Cut from Karen Woman's Shirt, Thai Tribal Crafts, Chiang Mai (1981).

(Fig. 4.3; see Lewis and Lewis 1984: 139–141). Commercial appliqued Hmong 'squares' were similarly sometimes cut into colorful jackets (Ch. 3, Fig. 3.12).

However, even after being so redesigned, the garments made wholly of tribal materials sold only in modest quantities. More popular and more marketable were the fashionable clothes, cut from ordinary cloth to fit the tastes of the younger foreign travellers, and subsequently conspicuously decorated with small tribal embroidered or appliqued patches and similar items. Very popular products in that line were long women's dresses, made of simple linen material, with a small Hmong or Mien 'patch' on the chest, which were sold in great quantities on the Chiang Mai night-market and in many tourist shops in the city. The production of such items became increasingly more and more sophisticated, as can be seen, for example, from a woman's vest, decorated with a complexly designed embroidered Hmong 'square' (Plate 5). The incorporation of tribal elements in modern clothing is not

Figure 4.3 Vest Cut from Mien Woman's Embroidered Trousers, Hill Tribe Sales, International School, Bangkok (1979).

limited to relatively cheap pop fashions. Some elite Thai designers also incorporated tribal elements in their *haute couture* creations; these were available in some of the most exclusive Thai shops in Chiang Mai and in Bangkok, patronized by the royal family and the Thai upper-class. Indeed, the Queen herself occasionally dons costumes richly adorned with tribal ornaments (e.g. SUPPORT, 1992: 245). Such garments are of importance not merely as high fashion setters; they are also of political significance in that they symbolize the royal patronage of the tribal people and the Queen's desire, through personal example, to help uplift their social standing and make their cultural products more widely acceptable in Thai society.

FROM TRIBAL COSTUME TO POP FASHION

As the process of 'boutiquisation' of the commercialized tribal products evolved, a parallel process took place, involving old clothing discarded by the tribal people. Original, used tribal clothing is a collector's item, purchased by only a few foreigners and Thais. However, pieces of discarded tribal clothes, such as the varied, complexly ornamented 'sailor's collars' of the Hmong women's jackets (Lewis and Lewis 1984: ills. pp. 112–3; Ch. 5), were already in the 1970s bought up by young travellers, made into shoulder bags, and sold to their peers as fashionable hippie apparel. This was the antecedent of a whole industry of 'secondary elaboration' of discarded tribal garments, which flourished in Chiang Mai later on (cf. Barnard 1984:3).

The widespread production of garments cut from old tribal clothing was also initiated by a Thai *haute couture* designer from Chiang Mai, a woman who studied art in Germany. When she returned to Thailand in the early 1980s she bought old and discarded Hmong clothes – particularly the richly ornamented blue batiked women's skirts – which she employed to great effect in producing strikingly designed dresses, suits, and skirts. These relatively expensive garments were well received by both foreign and Thai customers. However the innovations of this designer soon found many imitators among local Thai seamstresses, and gradually also among some Hmong women who maintained stalls in the Chiang Mai night market. Big quantities of simpler, less sophisticatedly designed, and cheaper clothing, made of discarded Hmong and Mien garments, and catering to the tastes of Western, and increasingly Thai, youth, soon flooded the Chiang Mai tourist market. What started as *haute couture* eventually also became pop fashion.

Squeezed out from the market by the cheaper products of her competitors, the designer who had originally introduced the fashionable garments made from discarded Hmong clothing, gradually abandoned this line of production and turned to the creation of women's costumes from new Karen woven textiles, and to the designing of sophisticated-looking model dresses, which upon closer inspection, turn out to be somewhat refashioned two-color versions of the cumbersome, multi-colored Lisu women's dress (Fig. 4.4; comp. Lewis and Lewis 1984, Ch. 8). The Lisu textiles, which had until then remained largely outside the mainstream of commercialized products, thus also finally found a modest outlet into the market.

Figure 4.4 Fashionable Dress Adapted From Lisu Woman's Dress, Prayer Shop, Bangkok (1983).

Conclusion

What are the consequences of the process of 'boutiquisation' and its *haute couture* counterpart? One could easily dismiss the whole affair as just another example of the exploitation of tribal people and of the banalization of their 'authentic' arts and crafts by outsiders. However, the situation in is fact more complex and its various pros and cons have to be weighed carefully before a judgement can be made.

From a purely economic standpoint, it is true that as commercialized tribal textile products came to be utilized for the production of

96

fashionable Western clothing, the tribal component was reduced in scope in the final product, and may have constituted as little as 10% or even less of the production cost of some garments, such as the long dresses with a tribal patch in the front. However the varied uses to which such small items can be put, significantly increased the market for them and thus encouraged their production. Also, less skillful producers who were not capable of making the complex and refined designs on the big commercialized pieces such as Hmong 'squares' and 'tapestries' (see Chs. 6 and 7), but were able to produce the relatively simple and standardized small patches, gained access to the market.

The use of cheaply-bought discarded tribal garments to produce new, Western costumes may be similarly seen as exploitation, or even worse, as a destruction of the material culture of the hill tribes. It has, however, to be borne in mind that the tribal people would otherwise throw away these garments, and that, in fact, their novel uses recycled them. Moreover, the prices demanded for these items by the tribal people have over time risen considerably, as they discovered that they can be put to new uses. Indeed, some tribal people have themselves penetrated this new line of production.

Another objection which can be raised to the processes here described is that they lead to a misuse of tribal products indeed, that the refashioning of tribal clothing and its utilization in a novel context amounts to the destruction of their distinctive value and cultural meaning. There is certainly much to be said for this argument. But one can look at the 'boutiquized' and other fashionable products here described from a new perspective: not as aberrations of tribal arts and crafts but rather as a new hybrid art-form, fusing the old and the new, the tribal and the modern, in an unexpected and often original way, which has at its best an aesthetic appeal of its own. These products are of a similar order – though not necessarily on the same level – as works which are in the world of modern music known under the label 'fusion,' i.e., musical productions in which elements taken from the music of one culture are utilized to compose works in the style of quite another: for example, elements of Oriental music are incorporated into modern Western musical forms. 'Ethnic rock,' which is presently popular in Thailand itself, is a good example of precisely such a fusion in the field of music. The hybridized textile products, fusing tribal items into modern Western garments fashionable among the younger generation of foreigners and Thais, are a material counterpart to such ethnic rock and should therefore be appreciated by similar aesthetic criteria.

Notes

1 This chapter reports some of the findings of my larger study of the commercialization of the arts and crafts of the hill tribes of northern Thailand, conducted during several field trips between 1977–1985, under a grant from the Harry S. Truman Research Institute for the Advancement of Peace at the Hebrew University of Jerusalem, whose support is herewith gratefully acknowledged.

THE HMONG CROSS

A Cosmic Symbol in
Hmong Textile Designs[1]

The designs on Hmong costume are distinguished by great variety, complexity, and richness. First noted by Bernatzik (1947:124–126) in a study conducted prior to World War II, this has become fully manifest in two later volumes on the crafts of the hill tribes of Thailand (Campbell et al. 1978; Lewis and Lewis 1984, 104 ff.). The very diversity of Hmong designs, however, has apparently hindered attempts at analyzing their cultural meaning. According to some authors, the nonrepresentational Hmong designs are stylized geometric representations of natural objects such as flowers and animals (Bernatzik 1947: 124). This claim seems to find support from the names of some of the ornamental motifs as reported, for example, in a catalogue of Laotian Hmong refugee work in the United States (Dewhurst and MacDowell (eds.) 1983: 70–71; see also Campbell et al. 1978: 128–129). But the simple listing of names is unreliable: names can serve as mere identifiers, perhaps even conferred a *posteriori* simply as playful 'interpretations' or 'brand names' by which certain motifs are widely known, without thereby revealing either their origins or their hidden cultural meaning. Moreover, some motifs may have several different and unrelated names: in the above-mentioned catalogue, for example, one motif is called 'seed,' 'chicken eye,' and 'water vegetable seed,' another 'rooftops,' 'snail,' and 'tiger' (Dewhurst and MacDowell (eds.) 1983: 71). This same multiplicity of names for motifs is found among the Mien (Yao), a tribal group culturally akin to the Hmong with whom the Hmong have many designs in common (Butler-Diaz 1981: 14).

Students of Hmong culture seem to share a common tacit assumption that the rich ornamentation of Hmong costume is merely decorative and devoid of more profound cultural meaning. All seem to deny that Hmong designs have a magical or religious significance. This has been explicitly stated for Mien designs (Lewis and Lewis 1984: 138), despite the fact that these designs have been found to be closely related to Mien mythology (Butler-Diaz 1981: 12–13). As a consequence of such assumptions, no student of Hmong culture has yet attempted to discern any general underlying regularity of form and symbolic meaning in the variety of Hmong motifs and ornamental designs.

In contrast to the prevailing tendency, this chapter aims to demonstrate the existence of a significant relationship between basic Hmong designs and some wider magical and religious themes in Hmong culture. Specifically, I shall show:

Firstly, that underlying the apparently unlimited variety of Hmong textile designs, some common 'ground forms' (de Beauclair 1970: 205) can be discerned. I shall limit my discussion to one ground form that appears to be of particular significance, to be called here the 'Hmong cross' (Figs. 5.1 and 5.2);

Secondly, that this particular ground form has a magical and religious significance in Hmong ritual;

Thirdly, that the ground form of the cross is at root an iconic cosmological representation, possessing a deep-structural symbolic meaning in Hmong culture, of which, however, most or all members of the culture are generally unaware. Special attention will be paid to the designs on a most salient component of the Hmong woman's costume, the 'sailor's collar' of her jacket (Lemoine 1972b: 116–117; Lewis and Lewis 1984: 108 and ills. on pp. 111–113);

And fourth, that this ground form is preserved even in commercialized Hmong textile products, which are intended for an 'external,' mostly Western, public that is unaware of and largely uninterested in Hmong culture.

The Hmong cross

The Hmong have a complex religious system: they believe in and worship a variety of gods and spirits and practice a form of shamanism, whose major purpose is the healing of illnesses (Morechand 1968; Chindarsi 1976; Mottin 1981). It is in the context of magic and religious ritual that the symbol of the Hmong cross is frequently encountered.

In the Hmong house there are usually several altars or 'spirit platforms' devoted to a variety of spirits and other supernatural beings (Bernatzik 1947: 202–205; *Meo Handbook*, 1969: 54; Chindarsi 1976: 60–61; Mottin 1979: 24 ff.; Kasemani B.E. 2527: ills. 40, 42). The central altar in the house is decorated with three elongated paper-cuts

Figure 5.1 Collar of Blue Hmong Man's Burial Cloth; Thai-Finn Handicrafts, Chiang Mai.

Figure 5.2 'Sailor's collar' of Blue Hmong Woman's Jacket (author's collection).

(Mottin 1979: ill. 6, opposite p. 24; *Meo Handbook* 1969: 54, fig. 23, here reproduced in Fig. 5.3). Referring to these papercuts, Lewis and Lewis (1984: 131) report that 'the focus of the main altar in a Blue Hmong house is a piece of white paper about one hand-span square put on the wall opposite the doorway. At this altar, protection is sought for all of the people and animals of the household.' Bernatzik (1947: 129, author's translation) similarly reports that Hmong altars are 'decorated with bamboo-paper, into which simple ornaments are cut [by the Hmong] with their own punches.' His meticulousness notwithstanding, Bernatzik appears to have paid little attention to the precise design on

Diagram 5.1: The ground form of the Hmong cross and its principal
permutations on altar papercuts

a) The basic prototypes of the ground form

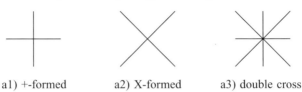

a1) +-formed   a2) X-formed   a3) double cross

b) Permutation of the prototypes on altar papercuts

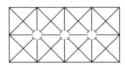   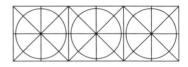

b1) Interlocking double cross   b2) Encircled double crosses
    (Meo Handbood 1969:54;   (Lewis and Lewis 1984:132,
    Fig. 5.3)   lower left Figure)

the paper; in his drawing (Bernatzik 1947: 202, table 41) he renders it
as a kind of stylized flower. This seems to be incorrect. A careful
scrutiny of all available photographs of papercuts on Hmong altars in
later publications indicates that they are invariably based on the ground
form of the Hmong cross. The cross appears in three prototypes: a +-
form, an X-form and a double cross; the latter is obtained when the
former two are superimposed upon one another (diagram 5.1a 1–3).

These prototypes of the Hmong cross do not appear on the altars in
isolation. Rather, they tend to be repeated several times, over the
elongated surface of the papercut; in some cases they form a simple
row of +'s or X's (e.g., Kasemani B.E. 2527, ill. on pp. 8, 40; Lewis and
Lewis 1984: 132, lower right ill.). On some papercuts, however, a more
complex design of double crosses appears (as, for example, on the
shamanic altar in fig. 5.3, also depicted in diagram 5.1 .b1). This design
is obtained when a piece of paper sized 1 x 2 is folded once (creating a
square), then folded diagonally four more times, and the borders are cut
out in a zigzag pattern. The design is of special importance for our
study, since it presents a complicated, multistable image (Ihde 1979:
66–79) that can be seen in at least three different ways: (1) as two rows
of X's separated by horizontal and perpendicular lines; (2) as a series of

Diagram 5.2: Breakdown of multistable image design on diagram 5.1, Fig. b1)

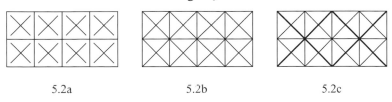

5.2a   5.2b   5.2c

three interlinked double crosses; or (3) as a middle double cross surrounded by a diamond-shaped square flanked by two halves of the same design (diagram 5.2.a–c).

The multistability of that design – which appears to be the most common one on Hmong altars – is of fundamental significance for the following exposition. This design harbors most, if not all, potential permutations of the Hmong cross and their variations in Hmong textile designs. It is therefore important to interpret the meaning of this prototype of the Hmong cross and the possible ways of seeing it.

It should be emphasized that my exposition of the different ways in which the design on diagram 5.1.b1 could be seen is not merely an arbitrary listing of possibilities derived from the visual characteristics of the design. Rather, the Hmong themselves also seem to see it in various ways, and to emphasize these differences in the manner in which they execute its permutations and variations. On the altars, they apparently see it primarily as possibility (2) above: as if to emphasize the way of seeing the design as three interlinked double crosses, each set into a diamond-shaped square, a small rosette sometimes appears in the central points of the crosses (as in fig. 5.3). This way of seeing the design is reinforced in another permutation, in which the diamond-shaped middle square is turned into a circle (for example, in diagram 5.1.b2, taken from the paper-cuts on the altar in Lewis and Lewis 1984: 132, lower left figure; the three encircled double crosses are thereby separated from one another and do not intersect, as they do in 5.1.b1). In other permutations, appearing particularly on the 'sailor's collars,' the other two ways of seeing the design of the multiple double crosses also appear, as we shall point out below.

To the fundamental question 'What is the meaning of the Hmong cross and of its permutations in Hmong religion and worldview?' the voluminous literature on the Hmong offers no clues at all. I therefore propose my own interpretation, based on an analysis of the situations in which the cross is used in Hmong life. I shall first deal with the cross on paper-cuts on the altar and then refer to some of its other uses.

The Hmong probably acquired the custom of hanging paper-cuts on their altars from the Chinese. This is suggested in Graham's description of the altar in the houses of the Chu'an Miao of China. He reports that, while the Miao 'completely reject the Chinese gods and their images' (Graham 1961: 70), nevertheless 'in some homes there is a family god representing the ancestors. It consists of a string of spirit money, hung up . . . in the imitation of, and a substitute for the Chinese house god . . . .' (p. 71). The Chinese origin of the Hmong paper-cuts is further supported by the fact that they are made of bamboo paper (Bernatzik 1947: 129; Campbell et al. 1978: 43), and that paper-cuts are a common Chinese folk art (e.g., Bewig 1978). In Thailand and Laos the paper used is white. Some Hmong in China and Tonkin, however, used red paper (de Beauclair 1970: 101). This is a conspicuous color in Chinese culture; the Chinese usually use red paper for calligraphies to be hung up in houses on festive occasions (Graham 1961: 145). The most important fact to note concerning the Hmong paper-cuts, however, is their location: they are hung in the center of the house altar, which itself is located on the wall precisely opposite the main entrance of the Hmong house (Graham 1961: 71; cf. Lewis and Lewis 1984: 131, and diagram of Hmong house on p. 122). The use of the paper-cuts is thus similar to the use of the magic 'eight Diagrams' (or Trigrams, Chinese *pa kua*) hung over the house door 'as an emblem of felicity' (Williams 1960: 149; Comber 1969: plate no. 8). Magic mirrors too are similarly used in Chinese households: they are hung up on a wall or a roof 'to reflect back evil influences' (Dennys 1968: 45), and thus to protect the inhabitants. We can thus infer that the designs on the paper-cuts on Hmong altars serve essentially as symbols of protective magic. This interpretation is corroborated by other situations registered in which the cross is used ritually among the Hmong. Following are some instances, related to shamanistic practices, which are reported in the literature.

The Hmong shaman, when practicing, wears the sign of the cross, made of white cloth, on his back. Bernatzik (1947: 177, table 40) renders it in the form of a +-formed cross. Schrock et al. (1970: 633), however, report that the 'mark [on the shaman's back] resembles a cross or square x'; and it also appears in the X-form on an illustration in the *Meo Handbook* (1969: 57, fig. 24). The fact that the two forms of the cross, the + -formed and the x -formed, here appear to serve the same function lends support to my contention that they are interchangeable prototypes of this basic Hmong symbol.

Figure 5.3 Hmong House Altar or 'Spirit Platform,' from *Meo Handbook* 1969: 54, Figure 23.

In another instance reported, the cross appears on the back of the jacket of a person who underwent a shamanistic healing ceremony; the symbolism here appears to be more complicated and differentiated. The fullest description and explication of this use of the cross can be found in Mottin's book on Hmong shamanism. His explanation of the drawing of two versions of the cross[2] is worth quoting in full:

> Cross in several colors, about 8 cm in size, which the sick person preserves on his jacket until it falls to rags. It signifies that the route, or the routes, of reincarnation are henceforth cut for the vital spirits of the sick. One of the stripes is black, the other white, and the third red. The black is the color of the invisible world, the white, in opposition, is the visible world; with respect to the red, it frightens the demons and hence serves to cut the first two colors (Mottin, 1981: 289, author's translation).

The black-and-white cross thus, by preventing reincarnation, preserves the sick person's life. The red stripe forms an additional protective device, which shelters the sick person from the demons. It is clear, hence, that the resulting double cross, as illustrated in Lewis and Lewis (1984: 111, lower right ill.), is a doubly protective sign. The single cross on the shaman's back can be interpreted, on the basis of Mottin's explanation, as a sign intended to frighten away the demons.

Other instances of the use of the basic prototypes of the Hmong cross have also been recorded. Thus, what seems to be a black-and-red X-formed cross on a white square background appears on the back of the jacket of a male Hmong, on an illustration in Campbell et al.'s (1978: 57) book; the caption merely reads: 'Jacket with applique cross to lengthen the life of the wearer.' This is obviously another protective use of the symbol, but it is not clear whether it is identical with the preceding one.

It is thus obvious that the Hmong cross, as ritually used, is a protective magic sign, whether it appears on the back of the shaman's jacket as he engages in a perilous business, on the back of a sick or recently healed person, or elsewhere. The fact that in all these instances the cross is located on the back of the person is important, for the back is the most vulnerable part of the body. However, the Hmong cross is not merely an arbitrary magical sign; rather, it is an iconic symbol, whose meaning derives ultimately from Hmong religion and cosmology.

On a most general, 'archetypal' level, the +- formed cross is a generic cosmic symbol, an iconic image of the basic structure of the world – its center and four cardinal directions (Eliade 1971: 6–17); this virtually universal symbol can thus be interpreted to serve in Hmong culture, as it does elsewhere, as a microcosmic sign, whose function is to symbolize the basic homology between the cosmos, the house, and the human body. This interpretation helps explain the location of the cross either in the center of the altar opposite the main entrance to the house or in the center of the back of the shaman's or the healed person's body.

My interpretation, based on the general meaning of the cross in many cultures, would be much reinforced if we found that the specific Hmong cosmological concepts also reflect the image of the cross. The literature on the Hmong, unfortunately, says little about their view of the world. One of the few explicit reports on their cosmology, however – Chindarsi's study of the religion of the Blue Hmong – corroborates the above interpretation:

The Miao [Hmong] believe that the earth is flat, and that four gods hold it up one at each corner . . . . The Hmong name four major directions: sunrise, sunset, upland and downland.

Figure 5.4 Hmong Traditional Coin Bags (author's collection).

Figure 5.5 Sailor's Collars of White Hmong Woman's Jacket (author's collection) a. Upper left. b. Lower left. c. Upper right. d. Lower right.

Upland

Sunset   Sunrise

Downland

These four gods . . . are seen as largely responsible for the form of the
earth as the Miao [Hmong] see it. (Chindarsi 1976: 19)

This description of the Hmong view of the world and Chindarsi's
diagram of it lends specific support to our general interpretation of the
Hmong cross as a microcosmic symbol: the form of the Hmong image
of the cosmos is obviously that of a cross. Moreover, Mottin's (1981:
289) statement quoted above – that the black and white colors of the
stripes of the +-formed cross on the sick person's back represent
respectively the invisible and the visible world – again clearly
reinforces our interpretation: it suggests that the black-and-white cross
is a Hmong variation of the Chinese *yin* and *yang* cosmic symbol.

The Hmong cross on costume: The ornamentation of the 'sailor's collar' of the woman's jacket

The Hmong are adept at a variety of textile arts: they use the techniques
of embroidery, appliqué, and batik with great skill and imagination.

All the literature on Hmong costume reports on the extraordinary
richness and variety of its ornamentation (e.g., Bernatzik 1947: 124 ff.;
de Beauclair 1970: 203–205; Lewis and Lewis 1984: 104 ff.). However,
the very variety of techniques of ornamentation, of motifs and their
variations, and of colors and color combinations on Hmong textiles
seems to have precluded any attempt at their systematic analysis. Only
de Beauclair, dealing with the Pa Miao, a subdivision of the Miao in
China, has attempted a rudimentary stylistic classification. She
distinguished two basic styles: one, which she considers as the original
Pa Miao style, is essentially 'geometrical'; the other consists of
patterns representing flowers and animals in stylized form (de
Beauclair 1970: 205). Such a distinction would be difficult to make
in the work of the Hmong of Thailand and Laos, however, since even
flower and animal motifs, insofar as they exist, are usually
'geometrized' almost out of recognition. In his study in the 1930s,
Bernatzik (1947: 124) established that there were no figurative
representations in the Hmong textile arts in Thailand. More recently,

108

Figure 5.6 Sailor's Collar of White Hmong Woman's Jacket (author's collection).

Figure 5.7 'Sailor's collar' of White Hmong Woman's Jacket (private collection).

realistic figurative representations appeared on the commercialized textiles of Hmong refugees in camps in Thailand; these, however, are recent innovations in Hmong culture (Ch. 6–7).

Within the geometric style, de Beauclair (1970: 205) distinguishes several 'ground forms,' such as triangles, rhombs, crosses, and meandering lines. These ground forms appear in many variations: 'The variations consist of the changing filling of interstices and in the coloration' (205, author's translation). These same 'ground forms' are also found among the Hmong of Thailand and Laos; however, while de Beauclair mentions the cross just as one ground form among others, and interprets neither, at least some of those she mentions can be reduced to the symbol of the cross or to one of its permutations.

The cross, in its various permutations, is not only the most frequently used, but also the most distinguishing of the Hmong designs. The high prominence of the cross in Hmong design is attested to by the fact that the Mien (Yao), who also use it, refer to it as the 'White Meo design' (Butler-Diaz 1981: 37, ill. 58). Butler-Diaz herself calls the design 'Meo Forks,' a designation that is also used by others. This 'Meo Forks' design is also frequently used by the Hmong (fig. 2), and occupies a central position in their own ornamental repertoire. It is significant that two other Mien designs that are named after the White Meo also embody the ground form of the cross (Butler-Diaz, 1981: 37, ills. 55 and 56).

The cross and its permutations appear particularly frequently on one of the most prominent and distinctive components of the Hmong costume: the 'sailor's collar' of the Hmong woman's jacket (Lewis and Lewis 1984: 111). It is also found on many other parts of the Hmong costume, for example, on the coin bags of the Hmong festive attire (fig. 5.4; Lewis and Lewis 1984: 110, lower right figure), on the ornamental bands of the Hmong woman's 'apron,' on the Hmong baby hat (Lewis and Lewis 1984: 125, upper left figure), and, significantly, on the upper part of the Hmong baby carrier (Lewis and Lewis 1984: 107, upper left and middle ills.). On both the sailor's collar and the baby carrier the cross occupies a similar position: it is located on the back of the woman, or of the baby as it is carried on the woman's back. Significantly, this location is similar to that occupied by the cross on the jacket of the shaman or the recently healed person. The cross is not as prominent on any part of the Hmong male's costume. Since women and babies are more vulnerable than adult males, it can again be inferred that the cross on the former's costume plays a protective role.

Authorities agree on the prominence of the 'sailor's collar' on the Hmong woman's costume. Thus, Bernatzik (1947: 320) states that this is the most remarkable component of the woman's attire, and Lemoine (1972b: 116) reports that the most exquisite decorations are found on that collar. This richly embroidered or appliqued rectangular ornament is frequently worn inverted, so that its design cannot be seen without turning it over, a habit that is apparently intended to preserve it (Bernatzik 1947: 320; Lemoine 1972b: 116). The variety of the collars is enormous, as can be seen from the rich sample of collars in the Lewises' book (Lewis and Lewis 1984: 112–113), but most (about two-

Figure 5.8 'Sailor's collars' of White Hmong Woman's Jacket (author's collection). a. Upper left. b. Upper right. c. Lower left. d. Lower right.

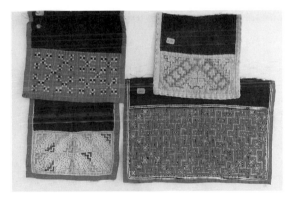

Figure 5.9 'Sailor's collars' of White Hmong Woman's Jacket (author's collection). a. Upper left. b. Upper right. c. Lower left. d.Lower right.

thirds) are based on the Hmong cross in one permutation or another. The great frequency with which the Hmong use the cross in their ornamentation of textiles – especially on the woman's sailor's collar – may have escaped the attention of the students of Hmong art because it appears in a large number of permutations and variations that in turn are frequently multiplied over the face of the cloth several times, creating distinctive patterns. Only careful analysis, therefore, can show that apparently diverse designs are structurally related to the basic prototypes of the Hmong cross.

The permutations and variations of the cross on Hmong costume and especially on the 'sailor's collars' are much greater than those found on the crosses in ritual use. This state of affairs confirms the observation made by Campbell et al. (1978: 43) that 'most of [the] religious articles [made by the hill tribes, including the Hmong] are simple in design and involve none of the skill devoted to secular crafts.' Indeed, Hmong women vie with each other to evolve and execute the most original and complex ornamental designs; their inventiveness is widely appreciated in Hmong society (Bernatzik 1947: 125–126). It is therefore the more remarkable that, despite innovations and outside influences, the basic ground form of the Hmong cross should be so frequently reproduced in their designs.

On the Hmong coin bags a single Hmong cross ordinarily constitutes the center of the design (Fig. 5.4). On the 'sailor's collars', this is generally not the case; rather, in the simplest designs, a series of two, three, or more +-formed, X-formed, or double crosses appears horizontally arranged, sometimes resembling their layout on the paper-cuts on the house altars. Thus, in Fig. 5.5a, a row of three thin, green, embroidered, X-like crosses, separated by small white diamonds, forms the basic design of the collar. The design on figure 5.5b is based on three +-like crosses. The most common design on the collars, however, is based on a pair of X-formed crosses (Figs. 5.2, 5.5c). While on some collars these X-formed crosses are separated and hence clearly recognizable, on others they merge into one another and create a zigzag pattern, in which the individuality of the constituent crosses gets lost (Fig. 5.5d). On some collars the two simple prototypes of the cross (the + and X) merge into a double cross, as in figure 5.6, where the white lines form two +-formed crosses, while the broad dark bands form a pair of X-formed crosses. In the center of that collar, a third +-formed cross can be seen, resembling that in Fig. 5.1; it is surrounded by an octagon of broad red bands that also constitute the inner arms of the two X's flanking it. Here we have an instance of a multistable design on a collar, closely resembling that on the altar paper-cuts.

Some other designs based on a pair of double crosses are also multistable. The multistability is sometimes produced by the combined effect of line and color, and therefore is not wholly discernible in black-and-white reproductions. Thus, the design on Plate 6a can be seen as two double crosses, the arms of which are formed by the alternative red and green coloration of the little triangles of the design, which surround the crosses' centers (represented in black-and-white in diagram 5.3a).

Figure 5.10 Samples of Hmong Commercial 'Squares' (from Camacrafts 1984:13).

Figure 5.11 Hmong Commercialized 'Patch,' Probably from Ban Vinai Refugee Camp (author's collection).

However, if one concentrates merely on the horizontal and vertical lines defining the edges of the more saliently colored red triangles (the dark ones in diagram 5.3a), each cross becomes a swastika (diagram 5.3b).

The swastika and the sauvastika (reverse swastika; see Williams 1960: 377–378) are, of course, widely disseminated Indian and Buddhist symbols, commonly found throughout the area. Williams (1960: 378), in fact, argues that the swastika, the Latin cross (i.e., the +-formed cross) and St. Andrew's cross (i.e., the X– formed cross) are all derived from the same ancient source, the Aryan or Vedic sun and fire worship. The design of the collar in Plate 6a in fact provides an

113

Diagram 5.3: Analysis of multistable design on Plate 6a

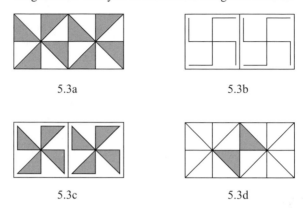

5.3a   5.3b

5.3c   5.3d

unexpected corroboration of this argument, since it conjoins all three of these forms: the swastika emerges from the double cross (i.e., from the combination of a + and an x) and thus in fact becomes one of its permutations.[3] The swastika, or sauvastika, however, appears also independently on other Hmong collars, either simply, as in Plate 6b, or in more complex, meandering permutations,[4] as in Fig. 5.7. The commercialized version of the latter design will be discussed below.

The analysis so far, however, does not exhaust the possible ways in which the design on Plate 6a may be seen. Thus, if one concentrates on the red triangles as a configuration, one gets two red X- formed crosses with triangular arms resembling those of a windmill (the dark triangles in diagram 5.3c); this form of the cross is very common in Hmong textile ornamentation (e.g., Lewis and Lewis 1984: 115, lower right ill. of Hmong man's jacket). Finally, if one concentrates on the center of the design, one gets a zigzag pattern of light lines, with a +-formed cross surrounded by a diamond-shaped square in the middle, flanked by three half-diamonds on each side (diagram 5.3d).

We have seen above that from one perspective, the Hmong altar paper-cuts can be seen as rows of simple X -formed crosses, while from another they appear as double crosses surrounded by diamond-shaped squares (diagrams 5.2a, 5.2b). These possibilities are also inherent in the design on the sailor's collar on Plate 7a, which reproduces most features of the paper-cuts – omitting, however, the +-formed crosses. It can be seen as consisting of two rows of four small X -formed crosses, or as three large interlinking X's, each surrounded by three diamond-shaped squares. This latter design serves, in turn, as a point of departure

Diagram 5.4: The permutations of the X-formed cross surrounded by a diamond-shaped square

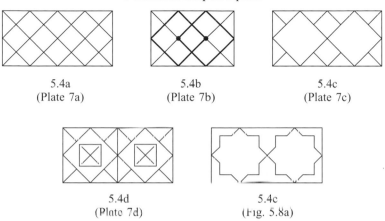

| 5.4a | 5.4b | 5.4c |
| (Plate 7a) | (Plate 7b) | (Plate 7c) |

| 5.4d | 5.4e |
| (Plate 7d) | (Fig. 5.8a) |

for a large number of further permutations, successively ever more remote from the basic prototypes of the Hmong cross, as illustrated in diagram 5.1. al–3. Here only some of these permutations will be shown, by way of example, but the presentation is by no means exhaustive. We begin with the triple X's surrounded by diamond-shaped squares (diagram 5.4a). This design is varied on the collar on Plate 7b in that there appear only two diamond-shaped squares, which intersect in the middle of the collar. The small diamond formed by their intersection is rendered in a different color, as if to stress the intersection, while the center of each of the two X's is emphasized by a rosette (diagram 5.4b).

In a further permutation, the diamond-shaped square is emphasized at the expense of the cross. Thus, on the collar in Plate 7c, the two blue, diamond-shaped squares are flanked by the remnants of the arms of two X-formed crosses (diagram 5.4c). In a more complex permutation (Plate 7d), the diamond-shaped square contains a smaller, regular square from the corners of which protrude the arms of the X's (diagram 5.4d); the X's are also inscribed inside each of the smaller squares. When the square inscribed in each diamond is enlarged and made to intersect with it, as on the collar in Fig. 5.8a, the arms of the X's disappear and the Hmong double cross is indicated only by the corners of the eight-cornered star so created (diagram 5.4e).

While in the above series of permutations the point of departure was the X-formed cross, designs based on the +-formed cross manifest similar permutations. We start with the double cross on the collar in

Figure 5.12 Hmong Commercialized 'Patch,' Probably from Ban Vinai Refugee Camp (author's collection).

Figure 5.13 Hmong Commercialized 'Square,' Ockenden House, Nam Yao Refugee Camp Project (private collection).

Fig. 5.6. As indicated above, the center of the design can be seen as a + surrounded by an octagon, formed of the inner arms of the two broad dark X's (diagram 5.5a). This way of seeing the design may, in turn, serve as a point of departure for the interpretation of permutations. Thus, the design on the collar in Fig. 5.8b can be seen as two white crosses surrounded by two red octagons; a further, thin white cross can be seen in the middle of the collar (diagram 5.5b). The dark components of the octagons are decorated by S-formed 'snails' (Dewhurst and MacDowell (eds.) 1983: 71). Snails or coils in various

Diagram 5.5: The permutations of the X-formed cross surrounded by an octagon

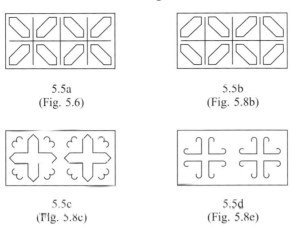

5.5a
(Fig. 5.6)

5.5b
(Fig. 5.8b)

5.5c
(Fig. 5.8c)

5.5d
(Fig. 5.8e)

forms are an extremely common Hmong motif (Campbell et al. 1978: 127). Significantly, however, they appear on many collars around a central I-formed cross, in the same place as the dark bands on the collars in Fig. 5.6 and 5.8b. Thus, in Fig. 5.8c four snails surround a pair of pointed crosses (diagram 5.5c); and in Fig. 5.8d the +-formed crosses are created by four heartlike shapes with coils at their ends (diagram 5.5d). It thus appears that the very common Hmong 'elephant foot' design (Dewhurst and MacDowell (eds.) 1983: 70) is a remote permutation of the Hmong cross, with snails taking the place of the octagon surrounding the central + -formed cross.

Another line of permutations of the Hmong cross can be seen as starting with an arrangement of five small X's or +'s that merge into a big X (or +) with crossed arms (Figs. 5.9a, 5.5a, and diagrams 5.6a-b). The same design is also frequently appliqued on the batiked Hmong baby carriers (Lewis and Lewis 1984: 107, upper left and middle ills.). If the arms of the four smaller crosses on diagram 5.6b are extended until they meet (diagram 5.6c), the emerging design (diagram 5.6d) becomes an X–formed cross surrounded by a diamond-shaped square, identical in form with those found in diagram 5.4a (Plate 7a). This example indicates that there are complex structural affinities between the various lines of permutation of the Hmong cross.

Until now I have argued that many concrete Hmong textile designs on sailor's collars can be interpreted as permutations of the basic

Figure 5.14 Hmong Commercialized 'Square,' Probably from Nam Yao Refugee Camp (author's collection).

Figure 5.15 Hmong Commercialized 'Square,' Probably from Nam Yao Refugee Camp (author's collection).

prototypes of the Hmong cross. The last and most speculative topic to be discussed here is the relationship between the ground form of the Hmong cross and some other ground forms of Hmong textile design. I do not have a complete inventory of such ground forms, but at least two kinds of design in addition to the cross are distinctive enough and frequent enough to merit this designation, particularly an inverted V design commonly found on sailor's collars (Figs. 5.9b,c) (compare to the lower half of the design on the collar in Fig. 5.6), and a mazelike design, which has been variously called 'reverie' *(bouw chua,*

118

Diagram 5.6: The transformation of the design on Fig. 5.9a into the design on Plate 7a

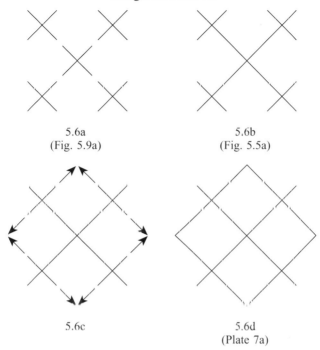

5.6a
(Fig. 5.9a)

5.6b
(Fig. 5.5a)

5.6c

5.6d
(Plate 7a)

Campbell et al. 1978. 128–129), or in another variation 'worm track' (*cua nab*, Dewhurst and MacDowell (eds.) 1983: 70). Both of these ground forms can be in some way related to the Hmong cross.

The inverted V design can be interpreted simply as a bisected X. It should be noted, however, that the V is always inverted, that is, it reproduces the lower, rather than the upper, half of the X. However, I was unable to detect the symbolic significance of this particular ground form.

The ground form of the maze lends itself more easily to interpretation, Symbolically, the maze appears to be a polar opposite of the cross: if the latter is a cosmic symbol, that is, the basic structure of the ordered world, the former symbolizes chaos. Its 'unordered,' unstructured, or 'liminal' (Turner 1977) character is indicated by the above-quoted name 'reverie.' It is interesting, therefore, that the maze pattern is often developed from the cross, or is intertwined with it in a complex ornament. The maze design often starts with a +-formed cross

Figure 5.16 Hmong Commercialized Pillow Cover, Probably from Nam Yao Refugee Camp (author's collection).

Figure 5.17 Hmong Commercialized 'Square', Thai Tribal Crafts, Chiang Mai.

as illustrated by the pattern on the illustration in Campbell et al. (1978: 128–129) and on the collar in Fig. 5.9d. On some collars, the maze pattern appears as a filling between the familiar X -formed crosses. An even more complex intertwining between the two contrasting ground forms obtains on the collar in Plate 7c. Here the dark-colored elements of a maze pattern in fact create the outlines of meandering sauvastikas, but they also form dark, diamond-shaped squares that fill up the larger,

120

light-colored diamonds. These, in turn, with their protruding arms, form a variation of the Hmong cross (diagram 5.4c). In a variety of ways, then, the ground forms of the cross and of the maze intertwine with one another in complex designs, which could well be interpreted as attempts at integrating the opposites of cosmos and chaos, or of structure and flow.

The Hmong cross on commercialized Hmong textile products

Following the Hmong insurgency in northern Thailand in the mid-1960s (Abrams 1970), many Hmong villages were resettled in the lowlands. Among the steps taken to rehabilitate these resettled Hmong (Hearn 1974), various Thai and foreign relief organizations and individual local middlemen initiated the commercialization of Hmong textile products (Ch. 2 and 3). Following the influx of tens of thousands of Hmong refugees from Laos and their internment in refugee camps in Thailand in the mid-1970s, the production of the Hmong commercialized textiles was vastly expanded. This expansion engendered a veritable explosion of forms, variations, colors, and color combination on Hmong products that flourished for a number of years; only in the course of the 1980s did it begin to undergo increasing standardization and routinization. Although remuneration was low, the refugee women – with ample time on their hands and their basic needs supplied by the UN commissioner for refugees – applied themselves to an imaginative development and embellishment of their traditional ornamental designs with new materials, and on new products.

Despite the apparent proliferation of new designs on the commercialized textiles, in virtually all of them the ground form of the cross can be rediscovered, as, for example, on almost all of the twelve designs on Fig. 5.10, taken from the catalogue of one of the relief organizations marketing the refugee crafts, Camacrafts.

In the simplest cases, the design of the cross was reproduced on a commercialized product in one of its traditional permutations. In some such instances, the basic prototype of the Hmong cross appears in high relief without further elaboration, as, for example, the X -formed cross in Fig. 5.11, where it is worked out in broad, parallel appliqued bands of green and white. In other instances, the design of the cross is merely indicated by the coloration of an underlying pattern, as in Fig. 5.12, where the image of an X emerges from the contrasting white and red coloration of the small +-formed crosses of the underlying pattern. Finally, there are instances in which the prototype of the Hmong cross

Figure 5.18 Hmong Commercialized 'Square', Ban Vinai Refugee Camp (author's collection).

is barely recognizable without careful inspection of the design, as, for example, the double cross formed by the leaflike shapes in Fig. 5.13.

Even more complicated are some of the designs on commercialized products derived from the various permutations of the ground form of the Hmong cross that were discussed above. The X-like cross surrounded by a diamond-shaped square ('sailor's collar' on Plates 7a–b and diagrams 5.4a,5.6d) serves as the basis of a wide variety of designs on such products (see, for example, the illustrations in Dewhurst and MacDowell (eds.) 1983: 29). A variation of that design appears on the 'square' in Fig. 5.14, where the X-formed cross is contained *within* the diamond, so that its arms do not protrude from it as in Fig. 5.13. Other permutations of that same design, presented in diagram 5.4, also appear in different variations on some commercialized articles. Thus, on the pillow cover in Fig. 5.15, the permutation of diagram 5.4c appears in a heavily embellished variation: in place of each single line, there appear several alternating appliqued brown and white lines, but the basic form is that of a diamond with the protruding arms of an X-formed cross. The design also appears in Dewhurst and MacDowell (eds.) 1983: 70) under the name 'spider web'; since such a 'web' is found only on commercialized products, this name is probably a mere designation without symbolic significance.

Other permutations of the Hmong cross underwent a similar process of embellishment in their commercialized variations. Thus, the starlike permutation on the collar of Fig. 5.8a and diagram 5.4d is in its commercialized variation developed into a more complex design through the multiplication of parallel appliqued lines.

122

Diagram 5.7: Analysis of multistable design of Fig. 5.18

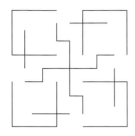
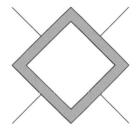

Diagram 5.7a	Diagram 5.7b	Diagram 5.7c
Central sauvastika	Central diamond with	Swastika within
(Fig. 5.18)	protruding x-formed arms	central diamond

While in all these examples the basic 'traditional' designs are easily discerned, in some of the more extreme commercialized variations they are barely recognizable. Thus, the design on the appliqued pillow cover in Fig. 5.16 is a variation of the diamond with protruding arms, the coils forming the diamond, and the small x's the protruding arms of a large X.

The swastika-formed permutation of the Hmong cross has also been used as the basis of interesting commercialized variations: thus, the design on the collar in Fig. 5.7 is quadrupled on the appliqued 'square' in Fig. 5.17. The four identical designs form a weakly emphasized + - formed central cross. Each quarter reproduces the basic design of Fig. 5.7, embellished by alternately colored lines, which fill out the whole surface of the square. The design on the quarters has also been used on other commercialized Hmong products, as, for example, on the 'square' illustrated in Dewhurst and MacDowell (eds.) 1983: 48–49).

A particularly high degree of complexity is achieved on the appliqued 'square' in Fig. 5.18. The multistable design on this square integrates two permutations of the Hmong cross – the swastika and the diamond with protruding arms – all through a sophisticated use of alternating colored lines. At the center of the design is a sauvastika (diagram 5.7a) inside which nestle four crosses, as on the collar in Fig. 5.9d; however, they are surrounded by alternating colored lines, which fill out the whole surface of the square. These lines give rise to a pattern that forms a central diamond with protruding arms (diagram 5.7b); within that central diamond the lines create a swastika (diagram 5.7c), whose arms fill out the whole area of the diamond.

Many other designs on commercialized Hmong textiles could be similarly analyzed as variations of one or another of the traditional permutations of the ground form of the Hmong cross. Catalogues such as that of Camacrafts (1984) or the volume by Dewhurst and MacDowell ((eds.) 1983) show this clearly. Enough has been said, however, to show that the apparent explosion of new and varied ornamental forms characteristic of the recent 'baroque' of commercialized Hmong textiles is deceptive. The Hmong have embellished and elaborated their traditional designs, but on the whole they have preserved their ground forms; their nonrepresentational commercialized designs hence have remained essentially orthogenetic (Redfield and Singer 1969), despite external influences and the pressures of the market;[5] and among the traditional designs on commercialized Hmong products, no ground form is more frequently and consistently encountered than the Hmong cross.

Conclusion

In this chapter, a symbolic interpretation of the wide variety of the apparently merely decorative designs on Hmong costumes has been presented. For that purpose, the most common ground form underlying these designs, that of the Hmong cross, has been singled out for analysis. As in other regions and cultures, the ground form of the cross in Hmong culture is basically a cosmic symbol – it symbolizes the basic structure of the universe, as conceived in Hmong mythology (Chindarsi 1976: 19). However, it appears in several permutations and many variations that are specific to Hmong culture. It seems, indeed, that the Hmong proclivity to innovate and vary the presentations of their symbols helped to conceal the underlying symbols on their ornaments from students of their culture.

I have shown that the cosmic symbol of the cross serves in Hmong ritual a protective magic function; I have argued by extension that it performs the same function when used in the designs on Hmong costumes. This argument is supported by the following facts: firstly, the cross is placed on a similar spot when tacked ritually onto people's clothes and when used as ornament on their costume; secondly, it is oriented in a direction from which a place may be most threatened or a person most vulnerable: opposite the entrance of a house, or on the back of a person; thirdly, it is used by people most in need of protection: the shaman when performing, the sick or recently healed person, and on the clothes of women and babies (but *not* of Hmong men).

No relationship was discovered between the ground form of the Hmong cross, or its permutations and variations, and Hmong social organization; in this respect, the Hmong differ from other, more isolated ethnic groups, whose designs reflect basic structural features of their society (see, for example, Adams 1980). I speculate that the reason for this discrepancy can be found in the exogenous origin of Hmong cosmic symbolism and of the Hmong cross, which may well have been adopted from the Chinese, under whose influence the Hmong lived for hundreds of years (Geddes 1976: 9–12). This explanation is supported by the close resemblance between some Chinese and Hmong ornamental designs, but needs further investigation.

Finally, in this chapter only one – albeit the most widespread – ground form of Hmong designs has been explored. While the existence of several others has been noted, and the links between them and the Hmong cross indicated, no systematic 'vocabulary' of such ground forms and their interconnections has been proposed. The preparation of such a vocabulary may well yeiled deeper insights into the connections between Hmong cosmology, mythology, magic, and design.

Notes

1 This chapter is based on data of a study of the commercialization of the crafts of the hill tribes in northern Thailand, collected during several field trips between 1977 and 1984. The study was part of a larger project supported by grants from the Harry S. Truman Research Institute for the Advancement of Peace at the Hebrew University of Jerusalem and, for 1979, by a grant from Stiftung Volkswagenwerk. Their support is hereby gratefully acknowledged. Thanks are due to U. Almagor for his comments on an earlier draft of this chapter. All diagrams are by Tamar Soffer, Department of Geography, the Hebrew University of Jerusalem.

2 Unfortunately, Mottin's drawings are imprecise. He renders two versions of the Hmong cross, one a + -formed cross with a red vertical stripe crossing a black horizontal one, the other a black and white X -formed cross, over which a single vertical red stripe is drawn. I have never encountered the latter form of the symbol. The illustration in Lewis and Lewis (1984: 111, lower right ill.), appears to render its correct form: a vertical white stripe crossed by a horizontal black one, constituting a + -formed cross, and this in turn is overlaid by a red x -formed cross; both crosses together form a double cross, as in diagram 5.1.a3.

3 This should not be construed to mean that the + or the X in any sense precede the emergence of the swastika; mine is a purely synchronic analysis and has no bearing on the process of development of Hmong symbolism.

4 The design on figure 5.7 strikingly resembles, but is not identical with, the Chinese meander pattern (Williams 1960: 120, pattern no. 11). This similarity is further evidence of the close relationship between Chinese and Hmong designs.

5 The only completely new development in commercialized Hmong textiles is the emergence of figurative representations. This is dealt with in Ch. 6.

6

HMONG COMMERCIALIZED REFUGEE ART

From Ornament to Picture[1]

Introduction

The process of emergence of pictorial art, in a culture which previously had only highly stylized non-representational ornamental art, has rarely, if ever, been documented in detail in anthropological literature. In this chapter I shall describe such a process, as observed over a period of approximately seven years among Hmong refugees from Laos in northern Thailand, and analyze it against the dramatically changed circumstances of their lives and the functions of their art. It is a study of commercialized tribal art products, intended for sale to non-members of the tribe, particularly Westerners, who have little or no knowledge of Hmong culture or of the recent historical experiences of the Hmong people. While commercialized tribal arts have received some attention on the part of anthropologists (for example, Graburn, 1976b; *Cultural Survival Quarterly* 1982, Cohen, 1992c), the problem of their distinctive meaning has, as yet, rarely been touched upon. It is by now commonly recognized that commercialization does not necessarily destroy tribal arts and may even lead to their revival (cf. Boyer 1976). However, most anthropologists would probably consider the proliferation of designs and colors which sometimes occur in the commercialization of folk arts as a meaningless 'baroque', of the kind which, according to Levi-Strauss (1963:265), accompanies the break-down of the traditional tribal social structure. Few students, indeed, have claimed to have discovered any meaning in such processes (but see, Silver 1979).

Such a conclusion, however, is too simple and appears to be based upon too restricted a concept of meaning. It essentially assumes that meaning is deep-structural, and, as such, implicit, diffuse, synchronic and internal to the group. Hence, meaning has to be discovered by the

Figure 6.1: 'Hmong Cross' on Collar of Woman's Jacket (author's collection).

Figure 6.2: Stylized Flower Pattern, Probably Produced in Nam Yao Camp, 1978 (photo by author).

anthropologist, who relates the art to the wider socio-cultural structure of the group[2]. The deep-structural meaning of art has been analyzed in this sense by Levi-Strauss (1963:255–268) and later on by Adams (1980). The contents of a work of art have no place in such a conception of meaning which concentrates exclusively on its formal aspects. A structural analysis of art, like that of myth (Levi-Strauss 1963:206–223), aims to discover the constant formal elements, reflecting basic traits of the group's social or cultural structure, beneath the surface variations of pattern or content (e.g., Hirschfeld 1977; Adams 1980). In the following discussion I shall show that deep structural meanings may well be preserved even under conditions of proliferation of designs in commercialized traditional art – though their relevance may well decline; there occurs instead an ascendance of surface messages in new genres of artistic expression.

The Baseline: Hmong Textile Art in Laos Prior to their Flight

The involvement of the Hmong of Laos in the Vietnam conflict from the 1960s onward on the side of the Americans had a catastrophic consequence for these people: their communal life was completely disrupted, hundreds of thousands perished in the war and by the hands of the victorious communists and about 100,000 fled to Thailand after the communist takeover of Laos in 1975. There they spent years in refugee camps until most were eventually resettled in third countries, principally the United States (Ch. 2; Yang Dao 1982, Hamilton-Merritt 1993, Warner 1996, Parker 1997). As a consequence of their traumatic experiences in the war, the fate of these previously unknown people became a matter of knowledge and concern to organizations and individuals throughout the Western world. Their experiences found expression in their art, and, through contact with the outer world, led to the emergence of a novel, representational art style. In this chapter we shall follow the stages of this process of transformation of their textile designs from geometrical ornaments to representational pictures.

The baseline of our analysis will be the Laotian Hmong traditional arts, namely, those which they practiced prior to their intensive involvement in the political events of the region, their flight and their appearance on the world scene. The Hmong were adept in a wide variety of arts and crafts, but the most distinctive and the richest aspect of their art was the ornamentation of textiles (Bernatzik 1947; Campbell et al. 1978; Lemoine 1972b:114–121; Lewis and Lewis 1984:104–115). In the past, Hmong women wove their own hemp-

Figure 6.3: Hmong Embroidered 'Square' with Cross-like Ornamental Design and Integrated Animal Figures (author's collection).

cloth; in recent times, however, they have preferred to buy ready-made cloth from itinerant traders or in local markets (Lewis and Lewis 1984:104). They used the ready-made cloth to make their traditional clothing, which they ornamented in a rich variety of designs. They employed three basic methods of ornamentation: batik, embroidery and applique. The patterns of their ornamentation were highly varied: many of them have been borrowed from other ethnic groups, most recently from the Mien, but in the more distant past probably also from the Chinese.

Hmong traditional designs are invariably purely non-representational, geometric and ornamental. As Dhuravatsadorn (1923:171) pointed out many years ago. 'The Meo [Hmong] have no knowledge of drawing or painting' (cf. also, Bernatzik 1947:124). There are no recognizable figurative representations in the traditional textile designs of the Hmong either in Thailand or in Laos, except for an occasional, highly stylized flower or plant. Many motifs, however, are given names of natural objects, such as 'snail', 'spider web', 'crab claw' (Dewhurst and MacDowell, 1983:70–71), or firefly' (Schrock et al. 1970:626); or sometimes of abstract notions such as 'reverie' (Campbell et al. 1978:128–129). Many of these names appear to me as rather arbitrary 'brand-names' for customary geometric motifs. In any case, even if current motifs did develop in a process of stylization from representations of natural objects, those objects are presently mostly unrecognizable in the ornamental designs. Similarly, the designs presently have no commonly recognized and accepted cultural meanings (White 1982a:11)[3].

Hmong traditions appreciated originality and innovativeness of design (Bernatzik 1947:125–126; Lemoine 1972b:116), a fact which accounts for the astonishing variety in the ornamentation of Hmong textiles. The great variability of Hmong designs has already been noted by Bernatzik (1947:124–129) and is richly illustrated in the volumes by Campbell et al. (1978) the Lewises (1984:104–115) and Kanomi (1991: 159–192). There are some differences between Blue and White Hmong designs, and there may have existed in Laos some regional differences in the designs within each of these subgroups. Beyond this, however, Hmong designs do not seem to be related to any specific aspect of the social structure: they are devoid of emblematic significance and they are not specific to any particular clan or any other social formation.[4]

The various authors who have studied Hmong arts discovered few regularities. The designs on women's clothing seem to vary with the age of the wearer, being most elaborate on the costume of young Hmong women and less so on that of children or older women (Schrock et al. 1970:626; Lewis and Lewis 1984:108). The patterns, however, are not strictly age or sex specific.

The richness and variety of the Hmong designs undeniably reflect the inventiveness of the individual producers, as well as their readiness and even eagerness to absorb innovations from the manifold external influences which impinged upon their culture throughout history[5]. The pace of this impingement and, consequently, of absorption and adaptation of external influences, was dramatically increased as the Hmong emerged from their relative seclusion into the modern world, following recent historical events (Ch. 2).

The very variability of Hmong design appears to preclude any attempt to discover beneath their manifold contents any basic structural uniformities. Indeed, in the various anthropological studies of the Hmong no attempt has been made to analyze their ornamental designs. However, a brief reference to ground forms is found in an early ethnography of the Southwest Chinese Miao (of whom the Hmong are a subdivision) (de Beauclair 1970:205). My own analysis of traditional Hmong textile ornamentations, however, revealed that a significant proportion manifests one such ground form which I called the 'Hmong cross' (Fig. 5.1; Fig. 6.1; see also Butler-Diaz 1981:37, Ill. 58), and which reflects the fundamental traits of the Hmong image of the cosmos (Ch. 5). Hmong art thus appears, after all, to harbor a 'deep-structural' meaning, of which both the Hmong themselves and the students of Hmong culture have heretofore been oblivious. This

Figure 6.4: Hmong Refugee Woman Batiking Animal Figures; Ban Vinai Refugee Camp, 1984 (photo by author).

ground form is also preserved in the commercialized Hmong ornamental art.

The Commercialization of Hmong Refugee Textiles

Several foreign relief organizations initiated the commercialization of the textile crafts on the Hmong refugees from Laos, who crossed the border into Thailand from the mid-1970s onward (Ch. 2). The main concern of these organizations was to create a source of income for the destitute refugees. The designs on the commercialized objects were derived from Hmong traditional ornamental geometric, non-representational designs; in the camps, however, the ornamentation of these objects was more varied, complex and colorful than on their own clothing (Figs. 2.2, 3.8, 6.2; Ch. 3). The relief organizations encouraged these developments, but sought to direct production toward the preferences of the market.

At the early stages the concern of the relief organizations was primarily with the form, size and color combinations on the products, and not with the designs themselves. Over the years, as their marketing processes became increasingly more routinized and sophisticated, designs also became standardized – so that the producers' scope for free invention and variation of designs was gradually reduced. The introduction of a catalogue by the marketing agency seems to have contributed significantly to such standardization (see, e.g., the *Camacrafts* 1984 catalogue). Indeed, in 1984 Camacrafts designs were listed and numbered so that customers could order the precise design and color combination they desired. Such standardization was necessitated by the expansion of the export market for Hmong textiles, a market which makes much stricter demands on the producer than the Thai market. Commercialized Hmong art was thus a 'collective action' (Becker 1974) in the literal sense of the word, in that the marketing agencies took a direct part in the creation of the artisans' products. Moreover, it was a process of collective action in the course of which the producers' independence and creativity was gradually restrained by the constraints of an expanding market. However, this tendency towards routinization of their principal products was countervailed by some spontaneous developments, to be discussed below.

The Dynamics of Commercialized Hmong Ornamental Textile Designs

During the first years after the Hmong refugees entered Thailand, their non-representational ornamental designs underwent ever further elaboration and sophistication (Figs. 2.3 and Plate 5), although the rate of design innovation and development gradually declined as standardization and routinization set in. Despite their restricted circumstances or, perhaps, because of them, the Hmong women applied their considerable skills and creative gifts to the production of commercialized textiles. A closer look at the commercialized designs, however, reveals the remarkable fact that almost without exception they remained throughout the period of about ten years merely elaborations of the basic themes already contained in their 'baseline' artistic tradition. The free play of fantasy which the new conditions and demands made possible, particularly in the early stages of commercialization, and the direction of their production by outsiders, did not

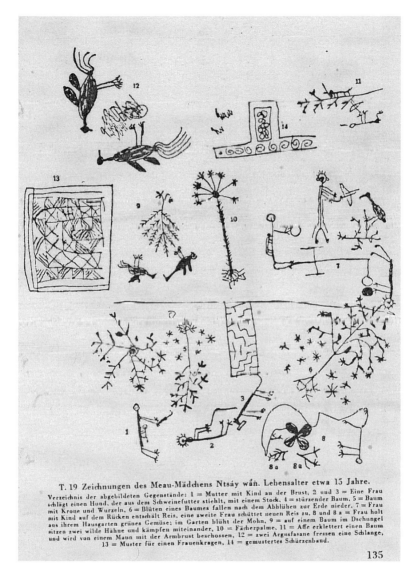

T. 19 Zeichnungen des Meau-Mädchens Ntsáy wáñ. Lebensalter etwa 15 Jahre.
Verzeichnis der abgebildeten Gegenstände: 1 = Mutter mit Kind an der Brust, 2 und 3 = Eine Frau schlägt einen Hund, der aus dem Schweinefutter stiehlt, mit einem Stock, 4 = stürzender Baum, 5 = Baum mit Krone und Wurzeln, 6 = Blüten eines Baumes fallen nach dem Abblühen zur Erde nieder, 7 = Frau mit Kind auf dem Rücken entschält Reis, eine zweite Frau schüttet neuen Reis zu, 8 und 8 a = Frau holt aus ihrem Hausgarten grünes Gemüse; im Garten blüht der Mohn, 9 = auf einem Baum im Dschungel sitzen zwei wilde Hähne und kämpfen miteinander, 10 = Fächerpalme, 11 = Affe erklettert einen Baum und wird von einem Mann mit der Armbrust beschossen, 12 = zwei Argusfasane fressen eine Schlange, 13 = Muster für einen Frauenkragen, 14 = gemustertes Schürzenband.

135

Figure 6.5: A Drawing of a 15-year Old Hmong girl. (Note the similarity between the archer in the upper center of Fig. 3.16 and in the upper right of this drawing) (from Bernatzik, 1947:135).

133

essentially change the fundamental nature of their designs. Hmong commercialized ornamental textile designs, though innovative, remained well within the limits of orthogeneity (Ch. 1; Redfield and Singer 1969; Shiloah and Cohen 1983). A close analysis of the designs revealed that the most frequent ground form, the Hmong cross mentioned above, returns regularly even in elaborate commercialized designs (Ch. 5).

It appears, then, that the Hmong women reacted to the new and drastically changed circumstances, as they did in the past: by selectively adapting elements from the new environment (e.g., new materials and colors), and using them to develop and embellish their traditional basic ornamental designs. The new situation allowed even freer play to their imagination than the old – the limitations now being imposed from the outside, by the market, and not by the available materials and colors and the traditional forms and uses of objects as in the past. But originality and imagination remained well within the canons of their artistic traditions. The baroque of ornamental Hmong art thus continued on the whole to encode the same deep-structural meanings contained in traditional Hmong designs. Commercialization had a liberating effect on the women's imagination, even though market demand soon constrained its free play. But the play of imagination, whatever its scope, did not alter the cultural meaning of Hmong art.

The Emergence and Development of Representational Commercialized Hmong Refugee Art

While ornamental, non-representational Hmong refugee art underwent the baroque flourishing described above, in the late 1970s a completely new, spontaneous and unexpected development took place – the emergence of figurative representations on Hmong commercial textiles.

As pointed out above, the Hmong had no tradition of drawing or painting. However, in a unique experiment conducted in the 1930s in northern Thailand, Bernatzik (1947:130–135) demonstrated that the Hmong, and particularly the Hmong women, were capable of drawing figuratively, even if they tended to 'ornamentalize' their figurative representations (Bernatzik 1947:131). Bernatzik, however, noted that there was a complete absence of composition in their drawings. The Hmong depicted only single objects – animals or plants, or scenes from daily life – and distributed these randomly over the page, so that

Figure 6.6: Corner of Hmong Embroidered Bedspread with Figurative Representation of Hmong Customs and Costume. (Note integration of figures with overall design); produced in refugee camp, 1979. This item is also illustrated in Plate 4 (photo by author).

6.7: Hmong Embroideries with Rows of Figurative Representations on Stall in Ban Vinai Refugee Camp, 1984 (photo by author).

the picture lacked any integration or even direction; it was impossible to tell which was the upper or lower end of the painting, nor was there any proportion between the figures depicted (figs. 16–19 in Bernatzik, 1947:132–135). The Hmong would fill out the sheet of paper randomly and spontaneously, often turning it around so that they could more comfortably fill out any empty space left on it (Bernatzik, 1947:130–131).

135

Bernatzik's description indicates that no concept of a unified 'picture' then existed in Hmong tradition. A fascinating finding of the present study is that, forty years later, Hmong representational textile designs initially very much resembled the drawings which Bernatzik collected. Gradually, however, they evolved into veritable pictures. We shall follow this process of evolution through its principal stages.

In the wake of their displacement in Laos, flight and eventual internment in refugee camps in Thailand, the Hmong came increasingly into contact with selected elements of lowland Lao and modern Western culture. Among other things they came in touch with printed materials, which included various illustrated textbooks used for instruction in the English language – which they were taught in the camps as part of their preparation for eventual resettlement in a third country. In all probability, the idea of figurative representation penetrated Hmong culture from the simple illustrations found in these textbooks and in Chinese pattern-books. In any case, in the camps they began to produce embroideries with figurative designs (Dewhurst et al. 1983:20), possibly with the help of foreigners (cf. Dewhurst and Macdowell, 1983:57). The earliest figurative designs included a variety of animals, some of which were obviously copied from foreign sources, since they were not encountered in the Hmong's natural environment. Other such designs, particularly mythical ones, probably came from Chinese pattern-books. The animals were depicted individually and sometimes integrated with an ornamental design (Fig. 6.3). Animal representations continued to be popular on embroidered commercialized products and later also appeared on batiked cloth (Fig. 6.4).

However, figurative representations among the Hmong soon extended beyond the mere reproduction of purely decorative textbook illustrations. The important development, which took place in the late 1970s, is the emergence of embroidered illustrations (e.g., Plate 4, Fig. 3.18) of a variety of activities and customs of traditional Hmong life (figs. 19–20 in Dewhurst 1983:20); these show Hmong men and women at work and at leisure – carrying loads, hunting, smoking the water pipe, or playing. The figures were embroidered directly on the cloth by the women, and were not first drawn in pencil or ink. There was a complete absence of composition. The figures were dispersed randomly over the face of the cloth: there was no obvious connection between the different figures, which were out of proportion, and the embroidery was lacking in direction, some figures being embroidered sideways to others (see Fig. 6.6, where the direction of the figures on the right changes). Some early figurative embroideries strikingly resemble some of the

6.8: Hmong Embroidery with Figurative Representations of Hmong Customs (detail). (Note ball game in the upper middle section and detailed imitation of design on women's costumes); Ban Vinai Refugee Camp, 1984 (photo by author).

6.9: Hmong Embroidery with Figurative Representations of Hmong Customs (detail). (Note feast on the lower right, particularly person throwing up; Ban Vinai Refugee Camp, 1984) (photo by author).

drawings collected by Bernatzik (compare Fig. 6.6, and Plate 4 with fig. 12 in Bernatzik 1947:135, reproduced here as Fig. 6.5). Occasionally, the figures were part of the overall ornamental design of the embroidery (Fig. 6.6); significantly, however, they did not make an integrated picture.

137

The representation of Hmong traditional life and customs had more than a purely decorative purpose: it was obviously intended to convey to the world outside the camps, namely the external public which saw and bought the embroideries, both the past glory and the present plight of the Hmong people. This message was occasionally reinforced by short inscriptions, recording the place and date of the production of the embroidery: these were at first written in the Hmong language and alphabet (Plate 4), but soon English inscriptions also appeared such as, 'I'm Hmong lady I made on June 3rd 80 at Refugee Camp' (Fig. 2.10). These inscriptions constitute a personal testimony of the artisan, a message about her fate as a Hmong refugee; there were not 'signatures' identifying the artist and authenticating the work, such as appear on Western art products.

The Hmong may well have been assisted in the composition of the English texts by foreigners working in the camps as aid personnel or by missionaries. It should be emphasized, however, that the Hmong refugees were not asked, advised, or encouraged by the relief organizations marketing their crafts to produce figurative designs. Indeed, these organizations concentrated on purely ornamental designs, and marketed the figurative ones only rarely and in negligible quantities. Figurative designs were thus an essentially spontaneous, though heterogenetic, development in Hmong art.

At first, figurative designs appeared relatively rarely in Hmong embroidery, and showed little change. However, the execution of the figures, at first simple, became increasingly more sophisticated and all the figures came to be positioned in the same direction (fig. 3.17). Still, there was no overall compositional order among the individual figures or concern for proportionality in their relative sizes; thus a butterfly could be almost as large as a human being (Fig. 3.17).

With time, a significant expansion took place in figurative products, accompanied by a proliferation of new motifs and a far-going evolution in the structure of their designs. These changes were observed in the Ban Vinai camp in the summer of 1984 and later on in products reaching the Chiang Mai craft market, which originated from that camp.

While embroideries with figurative representations were not particularly prominent in the markets outside the camp, the numerous craft stalls within the camp displayed a large number of products featuring a wide variety of figurative designs (Fig. 6.7). This disproportionate concentration of the market for figurative work in the camp itself can be partly explained by the marketing relief

6.10: Hmong Man Drawing Animal Figures on Cloth; Doi Pui village, 1984 (photo by author).

organizations' and the middlemen's relative lack of interest in this line of products. Partly, however, it can be accounted for by the appropriateness of the location and the theme of the figurative embroideries: they probably appealed most to people who visited the refugee camp and hence had some interest in, or knowledge of, the Hmong and their plight.

As indicated above, at first the figurative designs were directly embroidered on the cloth. The figures were simple and, in comparison with ornamental designs, inexpertly executed, attesting to the women's lack of familiarity with this line of work. By 1984, however, the execution of the figures had become much more sophisticated. The Hmong women learned to render Hmong costume and customs in much greater detail and more vividly than before (Plate 1, Figs. 6.8–6.9). The individual scenes from traditional Hmong life and customs became more complex and varied than at the earlier stage. However, the figures and motifs were no longer spontaneously embroidered by the women. Rather, the figures were first expertly drawn on the cloth, often from models cut in paper (Fig. 6.10), and were subsequently executed in embroidery (Fig. 6.11). Hmong men, some of whom acquired their expertise in illustrating textbooks for the camp school, were often hired to draw the more complex figurative designs.

The overall structure of the figurative embroidery also underwent far-reaching changes. Even in the simplest products, the figures were no longer randomly distributed over the cloth, but were lined up in orderly but artless rows (Fig. 6.7). There was no logical or chronological relationship between the scenes, and the selection and the order of presentation seem to be completely random. The ordered scenes, hence, do not render an integrated picture. Individual scenes, however, may have been used to decorate smaller squares.

A new, more integrated, form of figurative embroidery, however, has been observed in 1984: the sequential representation of Hmong folktales, where individual scenes with their appropriate text are put in chronological order (Plate 8). Like the idea of figurative representation itself, the idea of sequential representation did not come to the Hmong spontaneously. Rather, it was derived, possibly with some help from foreigners, from a series of booklets of Hmong folktales which were, curiously enough, originally prepared in Minnesota as an aid for teaching English to Hmong immigrants from familiar materials.[6] They were illustrated by a Hmong. Some of the most picturesque scenes from the tales were selected and copied, with some adaptations, and then embroidered on the cloth (compare Fig. 6.12 and the scene in the upper left corner of Plate 8), accompanied by the appropriate text in English (Fig. 6.13). I have seen two such embroidered folktales, 'The Woman and the Tiger' (Johnson (ed.) 1981a), and 'The Orphan and Ngao Zhua Pa' (Johnson (ed.) 1981b), but there may well be others of which I am unaware.

The most interesting recent development in Hmong figurative design, however, is the emergence of wholly integrated embroidered pictures, or, more rarely, pictures in batik. The scenes depicted on these products are predominantly dramatic events from the Hmong's recent historical experience, though some depict Hmong traditional life, such

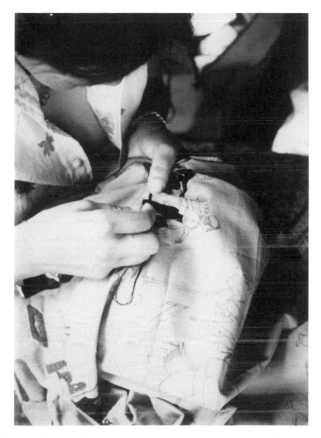

6.11: Hmong Woman Embroidering Figures Drawn on the Cloth; Ban Vinai Refugee Camp, 1984 (photo by author).

as hunting scenes (Fig. 6.14). It is the depiction of recent historical experiences, however, the like of which was not observed before 1984, which is of principal interest here: a good example of such work is 'Warlao' (Fig. 2.7), in which a battle between planes and anti-aircraft gunners from the war in Laos is depicted in vivid detail, complete with tracer-bullets, planes exploding in mid-air and their pilots parachuting to earth. Despite the vivid detail, however, the picture nevertheless incorporates some ornamental elements, creating a curious mixture of abstract pattern and concrete event – for example, the incongruous distribution of trees over the cloth, rhythmically mingled with planes

6.12: A Man Shooting a Monkey; Scene from 'The Woman and the Tiger' a Hmong Folk Tale (from Johnson (ed.) 1981:4).

6.13: Man Killing the Tiger; Scene from 'The Woman and the Tiger' an Embroidered Hmong Folk Tale; Ban Vinai Refugee Camp, 1984 (photo by author).

and parachuters. There is also an element of vertical symmetry in the distribution of the gunners at the bottom of the cloth; such symmetry, reminiscent of Hmong ornamental work, can be found in many figurative representations (Figs. 6.13–6.14). This tendency of the

Hmong towards the ornamental in their representational drawings was already noticed by Bernatzik (1947:131), and is probably a consequence of the long tradition of non-representational ornamental design in their culture.

Other historical representations manifest a sequential character similar to, but less detailed than, that of the embroidered folktales. Thus, one embroidery depicts a fight between Hmong insurgents and a Laotian or Vietnamese communist soldier and below it the capture of the latter (Fig. 6.15). There exist, however, fully-fledged pictures, which began to appear about 1984, depicting salient scenes from the recent Hmong past in a realistic, though simple, manner; the crossing of the Mekong river, which is the last and most traumatic stage on the long escape route of the Hmong refugees into Thailand, is a popular theme (Fig. 2.8; Ch. 7). The essential elements of the flight are depicted in this simple embroidery: some Hmong are walking on their way to the river (upper right), others are crossing it on a raft or swimming with the assistance of a tube (central diagonal), while on the other side (lower left) the bleak huts of the refugee camps already await them.[7] It is thus in the realistic scenes depicting traumatic experiences that the fully integrated pictorial representation finally evolved and became part of the emergent Hmong artistic expression and self-representation to the world.

However, a vague and ambiguous sequential element is still implicitly preserved in many of these pictorial representations. This is occasionally made explicit, as in another depiction of the crossing of the Mekong (Sherman 1988:589), where captions are inserted (similar to those in Plate 8) which describe a sequence of events, from the Hmong's flight from the Vietnamese attack and up to their crossing of the river into Thailand. However, other pictures, like the one depicting a refugee camp in Thailand (*Hmong Art* 1986:109) appear to be synchronic and devoid of any sequential element (cf. Ch. 7).

Conclusions

It remains to bring together the various stages in the process of change in Hmong commercialized art and, particularly, of the process of emergence of pictorial representation. Five major stages can be identified.

1. *Non-representational (ornamental):* this is the baseline situation, in which the Hmong produced, both for their own use and for the market, only purely non-representational, geometric designs on

6.14: Hmong Embroidered 'Square', Representing a Hunting Scene; Ban Vinai Refugee Camp, 1984 (photo by author).

6.15: Hmong Embroidered 'Square' Representing a Fight Between Hmong Insurgents and a Laotian or Vietnamese Communist Soldier, and the Latter's Capture; Ban Vinai Refugee Camp, 1984 (photo by author).

their textiles. As Bernatzik (1947:13–135) has shown, the Hmong had an ability to draw, but this was not realized in their cultural products.

2. *Representational – isolative:* representational designs are introduced into Hmong textiles, but each figure is treated individually,

and in isolation from all others, without proportion, order or direction; occasionally, figures are integrated into the overall ornamental design of the product.
3. *Representational – directional:* the figurative representations on the products are all oriented in the same direction, eventually in simple rows, but still without any thematic or chronological connection between the individual scenes represented.
4. *Representational – sequential:* the scenes on the product are lined up in a chronological order, through which the sequence of an event or a folktale is presented.
5. *Representational – pictorial:* finally, the figurative representations on the product are integrated into a fully-fledged picture, even though some sequential or ornamental elements may still be present.

It should be noted that some of the components of this process have been identified in other cultures. Thus, a transition in modern times from non-representational ornamental to figurative art has been observed elsewhere, particularly in the realm of traditional Islam. Beier (1968:29), for example, points out that, although 'Islam does not allow figuration representation' and that '. . . consequently Islamic art has always been restricted to geometric ornament and calligraphy . . . Khartoum has become one of the most important centers of art in Africa.' He vividly describes the process of transition of one Sudanese artist, Ibrahim El-Salahi, from calligraphy to representational painting (Beier:29–33). The process of his transition, however, differs substantially from that which took place in Hmong textile arts. Again, each of these stages can be found in isolation in tribal and non-Western arts elsewhere. A random distribution of scenes can be found, for example, in some early Greenland Eskimo drawings (Kaalund 1979:104). Sequential presentation of scenes can also be found in contemporary non-Western folk-art: one of the best-known examples is probably the Queen of Sheba legend, which has customarily been painted in Ethiopia in a sequence of scenes from the end of the nineteenth century onward (Perczel 1978:10; cf. also Kaalund 1979:105). In none of these cases, however, has a gradual process of emergence of a fully-fledged picture been identified. Indeed, it appears that the problem of the emergence of the picture as a distinct art form has rarely, if ever, been posed by students of cultures in transition. The importance of our analysis, therefore, lies not only in the uniqueness of the empirical details of the process as described above; perhaps of more general importance is the very thematization of the process of emergence of pictorial representation in cultural change.

This formal process, however, is not unrelated to the specific content of the products. The most important point to be noted in this context is that the fully-fledged picture emerges in close association with the representation of traumatic events from recent Hmong history. While such presentations are quite common in the contemporary art of many Third World people, particularly in Africa (e.g., Szombati-Fabian and Fabian 1976:7ff, *Moderne Kunst* 1979), the connection between the specific content represented and its form of presentation is by no means obvious; its comprehension necessitates a brief recapitulation of the main features of the setting in which pictorial representations emerged in Hmong refugee art.

As has been pointed out above, the gradual emergence of pictorial representation was by no means a wholly indigenous process in Hmong culture; neither, however, was it expressly sponsored or directed by outside agents, as was the process of change in Hmong ornamental designs. All in all, the extent of outside intervention seems to have been smaller than it was in the production of objects with ornamental designs. This is a remarkable fact, considering that the ornamental designs on commercialized products remained, on the whole, within the canons of traditional, orthogenetic Hmong art, whereas the representational designs were a completely new hetero-genetic development, unrelated to anything previously produced in Hmong art. Sure enough, these new products, like those with ornamental designs, were intended for the market. Still, their production was not motivated purely, or even primarily, by economic considerations, as was that of ornamental designs. Many of the representational designs were genuine, and possibly wholly sponta-neous, expressions of sentiments, experiences and aspirations which the Hmong refugees, interned as they were in the camps, desired to transmit to the world outside – be they nostalgic reminiscences of their traditional life and customs in the highlands of Laos, or dramatic renderings of their recent historic and personal experiences and present plight. At first, they were simple self-advertisements to a world unaware of and unconcerned with their predicament. However, as the world increasingly took notice of these heretofore little known people, and relief organizations, volunteers, anthropologists and casual visitors swarmed into the camps, the nature and function of the message began imperceptibly to change: the representational work became ever more varied and accomplished, and manifested more topical themes, at least

Plate 1 Commercial Hmong Embroidered 'Tapestry,' with Motifs from Traditional Hmong Life (author's collection).

Plate 2 Commercial Hmong Embroidered 'Tapestry' with Serial Representation of Shamanistic Ritual (author's collection).

Plate 3 White Hmong Silver Coin Bags (author's collection).

Plate 4 Hmong Bedspread with Representational Design (detail) CAMA (International School Sale, Bangkok).

Plate 5 Fashionable Woman's Vest Decorated with Hmong 'Square,' Hill Tribe Products Foundation, Chiang Mai (1984).

Plate 6 Sailor's collars of White Hmong Woman's Jacket (author's collection). a. Above. b. Below.

Plate 7 Sailor's collars of White Hmong woman's jacket (author's collection). a. Upper left. b. Upper right. c. Lower left. d. Lower right.

Plate 8 'The Woman and the Tiger', an Embroidered Hmong Folk Tale; Ban Vinai Refugee Camp (1984).

Plate 9 The Hmong's Fight, Flight, Escape and Resettlement; Embroidered Cloth (about 1991); (author's collection; photo by L. Gutmanovitch).

Plate 10 Owl.

Plate 11 Earthenware Fountain in Dan Kwien Market (1998).

Plate 12 Painted Figurines of Traditional Thai Musicians (1996).

Plate 13 Partly Painted and Partly Varnished Carvings (1995).

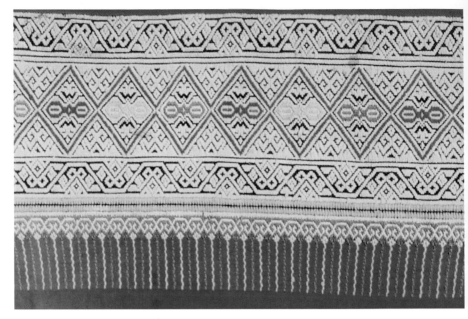

Plate 14 Old *tin jok* in Brilliant Colors (Collection of Wat Saleng, Long district) (detail).

Plate 15 *Krabung*, A Traditional Rice Basket.

partly as an attempt of the Hmong to establish their identity and image in the eyes of the world.

The most important conclusion arising from our analysis is that the nature of the communication transmitted changed significantly as the new form of representational self-expression replaced the older ornamental designs. As I have made clear above, even the latter, despite their variety, are not mere decorations. Rather, many of them manifest a common ground-form (de Beauclair 1970:209), bearing a unified deep-structural meaning, though the artisan and his internal public may be unconscious of it (Ch.5).

It is important for the present purpose to note that the ground-form and its deep-structural meaning is encoded in the ornamental pattern and repetitively expressed in its many variations. For the member of the culture it resonates, as it were, through the concrete ornamental content of any particular piece of work. The ground-form remained enclosed in the orthogenetic designs of the commercialized products, although it is questionable whether its deep-structural meaning found any resonance in its new, external public, for whom the attraction of the products lies primarily in their aesthetically pleasing decorativeness.

The figurative representations, however, of current and historical experiences, do not possess a common ground-form and do not express a deep-structural meaning; rather, they emit concrete and explicit surface messages which the Hmong consciously aim to transmit to their new external public. Hence, the stronger the emphasis on content, the more remote the work is from the traditional concern with pattern. Animals, and even individual human forms, can still be fitted into an overall geometric design. Depictions of war and flight experiences, the more concrete and personal they are, cannot. They are individual expressions, rather than variations of collective representations. However, though occasionally inscribed with a personal message, they remained unsigned; while still in the camps, the Hmong have not yet developed the concept of an individualized work of art[8].

The development of the fully-fledged picture can be seen as a direct consequence of the change in content of Hmong art: the emphasis on the surface message necessitated a novel form for its expression. The Hmong might well have adopted the idea of the picture from the new, outside influences which impinged upon them in the camps. But they would hardly have found use for it, were it not a convenient medium for the expression of the memories and experiences of their recent past and of their present plight, which they strove to broadcast to the world outside the camps.

147

Notes

1 This chapter is based on data on the commercialization of the crafts of the hill tribes in northern Thailand, collected during several field trips between 1977 and 1984. The study was part of a larger project supported by a grant of the Harry S. Truman Research Institute for the Advancement of Peace at the Hebrew University of Jerusalem, and, for 1979, by a grant of Stiftung Volkswagen; their support is here gratefully acknowledged.

2 For an excellent analysis of what could be termed a tribal protoaesthetics in an African tribal society and its relationship to the tribal culture, see: Almagor 1983.

3 My claim that contemporary names of designs are arbitrary is supported by the fact that Dewhurst and MacDowell (1983:70–71) several times report completely unrelated names for the same designs. The same holds true for some designs of the Mien (Yao), a group culturally akin to the Hmong, for which also multiple, unrelated names were reported (Butler-Diaz 1981:18, 20–21).

4 Thus, Lemoine (1972b:114) points out that within each Hmong sub-group there is no uniformity in costume; there maybe some at the village level, but variety is introduced by brides brought in from other villages.

5 Cf. de Beauclair (1970:64) who pointed out that Hmong are '. . . a people of great adaptability . . . readily assimilating heterogenous elements.' This is true of their textile arts as it is for other realms of their culture.

6 A series of about a dozen Hmong folktakes were published, bilingually or separately in Hmong or English, by the linguistics department of Macalester College in St. Paul, Minn., under the editorship of Ch. Johnson, as an auxiliary for teaching English to Hmong immigrants in the U.S., see: Johnson 1982.

7 See also Ch. 7 and *Camacrafts* (1984:2) for a highly elaborate representation of the crossing, inscribed: 'he walked for month (sic!) and crossed Mekong River to Thailand.'

8 Such a concept, however, appears to be developing among the Hmong resettled in the U.S., under the influence of the artistic environment there. Thus, in catalogues of Hmong art in the U.S., products are related by name to their producers and some are expressly signed by them (Ch. 2; Dewhurst and MacDowell 1983).

7

TEMPORAL AMBIGUITY IN HMONG REPRESENTATIONAL TEXTILE ART[1]

Introduction

Hmong 'traditional' textile designs in Thailand and Laos were geometrical and abstract (Lewis and Lewis 1984: 100–133; Kanomi 1991: 159–192). From the late 1970s onward, Hmong refugees from Laos in camps in Thailand started to produce embroidered cloths in an innovative, representational style (Peterson 1988; MacDowell 1989; Ch. 6). The Hmong themselves distinguished between the two styles by calling the earlier one *paj ntaub* (lit. 'flower cloth,') meaning 'flowery' or 'decorative' cloth, and the latter one *paj ntaub dab neej* (lit. 'flower cloth of people and customs') (MacDowell 1989: 1–3), translated as 'story cloth.' The sense in which these cloths constitute a 'story,' however, has remained unexplicated, despite the considerable attention which this style attracted in the literature. Implicit in the term 'story' is the assumption that it reports or narrates something. The so-called Hmong 'story cloths,' however, differ considerably in the degree of their 'narrativeness': while some are static pictures or single scenes (Peterson 1988: 8), others represent loosely demarcated scenes from recent Hmong history or explicit sequences of scenes from Hmong folktales (Ch. 6). The students of recent Hmong representational art have attached little attention to the sense in which these cloths are 'stories,' and especially to the nature of their temporality.

The aim of this chapter is to problematize the temporal dimension in Hmong representational art and point out the complex interplay of stability and sequence, synchronicity and diachronicity inherent in them.

149

Time in the visual arts

The problem of temporality in the visual arts has received relatively little attention in the literature (Gombrich 1964: 293). The more general treatises on the problem depart from Lessing's early (1979 [1766]) distinction between succession and simultaneity, as two fundamental categories of esthetic expression, the first characteristic of literature, the second of the visual arts (McClain 1985, Mitchell 1986). The basic conclusion of these analyses is that Lessing's distinction is untenable and that 'works of art . . . are structures in space-time'; hence 'the interesting problem is to comprehend a particular spatial-temporal construction, not to label it as temporal or spatial' (Mitchell 1986: 103). McClain, indeed, on the basis of his analysis of Western art objects, sketched out a typology of such constructions; he concluded that 'time in art ranges from a passive coexistence with space in the expression of timelessness, to active instantaneousness, prolonged duration, and a dramatic intraspatial tension' (McClain 1985:41).

These typological distinctions are important and relevant for our purposes. But equally relevant are several issues which have not been given sufficient attention in the extant literature on temporality in the visual arts, namely the differences between the presentation of various temporal scales, like movement and biographical or historical time; the degree of implicitness of the representation of temporality; and the underlying conceptions or images of time.

Much of the discussion of temporality in visual arts relates to the problem of movement in static representations (Gombrich 1964, Ward 1979). I would submit, however, that the analysis could profit from a clearer distinction between the representation of micro-temporal processes, such as movement, and of those on a more macro-temporal scale, such as the depiction of the life of a saint (Pächt 1962), or of a period in the history of a people. Movement, morever, is often only implicitly represented, and can be only inferred by the observer; analyses like those of Gombrich and Ward, therefore, focus primarily on the perception of the observer, rather than the explicitness of representation on the part of the artist. However, the very perceptibility of movement depends on the explicitness of its representation: it is much more difficult to infer movement from, for instance, the instability of a figure in a picture (Gombrich 1964: 304), than from a sequential representation of a figure, as in Marcel Duchamp's *Descending Nudes* (Clair 1977, Plates 11 and 12).

The same applies to the representation of biographical or historical temporality: thus the biographical dimension in the 'simultaneous narrative' of Munch's paintings (Loshak 1989) becomes accessible only after a detailed analysis, whereas the lives of saints in medieval Christian paintings have often been depicted in 'pictorial narratives' (Pächt 1962), namely in a sequential series of two or more scenes; moreover, even if the life was depicted in a single painting, the biographical dimension – the saint's progression towards salvation – was rendered in multiple representations of the saint according to conventional, vertically or spirally ascending schemata (Hahn 1990:3). In such cases, the temporality of the representation is more explicit, and hence more directly perceptible by the viewer, than that inherent in Munch's paintings.

This leads to the last issue mentioned above, namely that of the underlying concept or image of time. I submit that there is a fundamental difference between the concept of time underlying its visual representation in different periods and cultures. Western secular time, informing, for example, Munch's paintings, is linear: biographical events are unique and unrepeatable. Medieval Christian illustrations of saints' lives combine the duality of uniqueness and repetition; according to Hahn (1990: 3), '. . . each saint is a unique historical entity yet . . . each saint is . . . also ontologically one with all the other saints in an affirmation of the eternal. The saint, in a seeming paradox, represents both stasis and progress.' Although Christian theologians may have 'resisted both linear and circular [temporal] schemata' (Hahn 1990: 3), the temporal mode of representation of saints' lives appears to come quite close to the combination of the two.

Finally, a mythical circular concept of time informs the visual representations of 'primitive' societies. Thus Layton (1991: 138), basing his analysis of the bark paintings of Australian aborigines of northeast Arnhem land on Morphy's (1977) ethnographic studies, claims that 'A simple painting can . . . simultaneously depict landscape, ancestral and present events,' presumably because events are assumed to repeat a prototypical primeval circular pattern (cf. Eliade 1971).

The Hmong 'story cloths'

Throughout the late 1970s and most of the 1980s between 40,000 and 60,000 Hmong resided in various refugee camps in Thailand (Srisongmuang 1987, Long 1993: 58). Destitute, jobless and with an uncertain future, most of the refugees wasted their time in the camps. Various NGOs sought to assist the refugees economically and morally by helping them, and especially the refugee women, to develop their crafts for the tourist and the export crafts market (Ch. 3). Under their tutelage, non-representational, ornamental Hmong designs were adapted to the demands of the market and produced in great quantities. However, according to MacDowell (1989: 3), 'From the late 1970s, [the Hmong] began to deviate from the use of the more traditional geometric and abstract designs and began to incorporate in their work embroidered figures, animals, and scenery. This genre became later known as 'story cloths'.'

The origins of this radically innovative representational genre in Hmong commercialized textile production are not entirely clear. One source claims that it first emerged spontaneously, in the Ban Nam Yao refugee camp about 1977 (MacDowell 1989: 3). According to another source, '. . . the idea to depict scenes from their old life, their escape, and especially to illustrate myths and stories came from relatives of Hmong in the refugee camps who had moved to the United States and were homesick for Southeast Asia' (Bessac 1988: 27, cited in MacDowell 1989: 3–5). However, it is also possible that some refugee camp workers encouraged the Hmong to depict their culture and recent war experiences on cloth (Dewhurst and MacDowell 1983: 57, MacDowell 1989: 3). According to my own information from fieldwork in the late 1970s, foreign workers helped the Hmong refugee women in their tentative attempts to introduce figurative representations into their textile work.

Whatever the precise origins of this new style, it is fairly certain that it represents an instance of 'contact arts,' a consequence of the interaction of the Hmong with representatives of other (especially Western) cultures. The new style quickly became popular in Thailand and in the United States; the designation of products in this style as 'story cloths' appears to have originated in the latter. The question which emerges is, in what sense do 'story cloths' tell a story?

The Hmong 'story cloths' have been described and analyzed in numerous publications (*Hmong Art* 1986: 107–112, Ills. 185–190, Fournier 1987, *Embroidered History* 1987, Bessac 1988, Peterson 1988, Bellion 1991, Zeitlin 1992); however, the term 'story' in this designation remains strangely unexplicated. The authors appear to assume that the connotation as well as the denotation of the term are unproblematic and that everybody knows what a story is. A glance into the literature on the concept of 'story' or 'narrative' quickly dispels this notion. In fact, as Leitch (1986: 4) has noted, *'Story* is a difficult concept to define . . . it is almost impossible to establish a definition which includes all stories but excludes everything else.' If this is the case with respect to the genre of stories in literature, the difficulty is compounded in the visual arts, in which 'temporality must be *inferred* in a painting [or any other visual representation]'(Mitchell 1986: 100). This is not the place to discuss at length the problem of the definition of 'story.' For the present purpose it suffices to adopt a minimal definition, which, though not strict, would be acceptable to most students of Hmong art. Following Chatman (1983: 45), I propose that a story narrates, at the very least, an interrelated, especially causative, sequence of events. I shall adopt this as a working definition and ask whether and to what extent it is applicable to the various kinds of Hmong textile products which are generally referred to as 'story cloths.'

In Chapter 6 I have attempted to outline schematically the principal stages of the transition from 'ornament to picture' in Hmong refugee textile art. My point of departure were the 'traditional' non-representational, ornamental designs on the textiles of the Hmong of Thailand and Laos. These designs may have been in the past abstracted from natural objects, such as flowers, but such links have over time become completely lost, and there is presently no agreement among the Hmong as to what most of them represent. In Chapter 5 I have attempted to show that underlying the apparent great variety of Hmong designs, there is the form of the cross. I argued that the cross symbolizes the conception of the cosmos in Hmong mythology. If we accept this analysis, then Hmong ornamental designs reflect a fundamental spatial characteristic of the world, and are therefore essentially static, because they represent an eternal, atemporal reality.

Before the emergence of the so-called 'story-cloths', the Hmong of Thailand and Laos did not embellish their textiles with representational motifs, nor did they show much drawing ability. Bernatzik, who conducted drawing experiments with the Hmong in Thailand in the 1930s, found that they completely lacked a 'sense of composition.' The Hmong depicted isolated objects, like animals or plants, randomly over the page; the picture lacked any integration or even direction – so that one could not tell which was the upper or lower end of the painting; nor was any proportion maintained between the depicted figures (Bernatzik 1947: 130–135, ills. 16–19).

The Hmong representational textiles went through several stages of development (Ch. 6): At the outset they reflected a similar lack of composition; gradually, the figures began to be uniformly matched, but remained mutually isolated and dispersed over the cloth without attention to scale. Over time, the figures came to be organized in neat lines, and were drawn to scale.[2]

Such linear representations became increasingly more complex; thus scenes from Hmong traditional life were depicted, but not in any, even implicit, chronological order (Fig. 7.1; Ch. 6, Fig. 6.7–6.9; *Hmong Art* 1986: 111, ill. 189). All these are not yet 'story cloths,' even in the minimal sense of depicting a sequence of scenes or events.

Lineally depicted individual scenes were eventually integrated into explicit sequences, 'story cloths' in the full sense of the term. The most prominent in this body of work are Hmong folk stories embroidered onto cloth, in distinctly separated, sequential scenes with accompanying captions (Ch. 6, Fig. 6.13). The texts of the captions were usually taken from a series of illustrated translations of Hmong folk stories published by Macalester College in the U.S. from 1981 onwards (Johnson and Johnson 1981, Johnson (ed.) 1985; cf. *Hmong Art* 1986: 110, Figure 188; MacDowell 1989: 10).[3] These were originally prepared to assist Hmong immigrants to the United States to learn English with familiar materials; they found their way back to the refugee camps in Thailand, where they were put onto cloth. The most popular amongst those 'story cloths' is that of 'The Tiger and the Hunter' (MacDowell 1989: 17 – 22; Ch. 6, Plate 8) but several others have also been depicted on the embroideries, both in the camps and in the United States. Other fully sequential 'story cloths' depicting, for example, Hmong customs such as a shamanistic healing session (Ch. 2, Plate 2) show a fairly clear series of events, even without accompanying captions.

Another representational form in Hmong embroidered cloths is a fully integrated 'picture' (Ch. 6). The most popular such picture is that of the Hmong in flight crossing the Mekong river into Thailand (Ch. 2, Fig. 2.8; MacDowell 1989: 40, Peterson 1988: 12, ill. 1); but a variety of other themes was also depicted in such an integrated 'pictorial' form (like, for example, the Ban Vinai refugee camp: *Hmong Art* 1986: 109, ill. 187). In contrast to the explicitly sequential 'story cloth,' such integrated 'pictures' appear to be static, depicting, as it were, an instant in the flow of an event, or a given situation. Close examination of such works, however, indicates that, although not explicitly sequential, such 'pictures' are often also not unambiguously static. The temporal ambiguity characteristic of such embroidered cloths therefore merits further investigation.

Figure 7.1 Scenes from Hmong Traditional Life; Embroidered Cloth (early 1990's); (author's collection; photo by L. Gutmanovitch).

A case study of temporality in a Hmong embroidered 'picture'

In 1991 I acquired at the night market in Chiang Mai a large (151x169 cm.) embroidered Hmong representational cloth (Plate 9), almost certainly produced in the principal Hmong refugee camp of Ban Vinai in Loei province, northeastern Thailand. This cloth is the most complex representation of the fight, flight, escape and resettlement of the Hmong that I have seen in Thailand in close to twenty years of observation and collection of Hmong textiles; it at least matches in complexity and richness of detail any 'story cloth' depicted in books and catalogues of Hmong art published in the United States. The cloth lends itself perfectly for the purpose of the present analysis, although simpler examples also contain many of the themes embodied in this particular cloth.

In order to be able to analyze fully the temporal ambiguity of the cloth, I shall first present a detailed account of its structure and contents. For the sake of clarity, I found it useful to analyse separately its two dimensions, the vertical and the horizontal.

The vertical dimension of the cloth has the form of a rough map, embracing synoptically a huge territory, stretching from Laos and Thailand, over the Pacific Ocean, to the United States. It is not, however, a topographically correct or geographically properly scaled map. Rather like the 'maps' on the bush-paintings of Australian aborigines, it is 'modified in order to represent conceptual relationships between . . . events' (Layton 1991: 138). The Hmong cloth refers to recent events in Hmong history, and the map is similarly modified to emphasize those areas, features, localities and relationships among them which played a significant role, in the Hmong perception, in these events. Even the scale of the map varies accordingly: disproportionately large space is devoted to the area in which the Hmong suffered the most traumatic experience of the period, the flight through Laos after their defeat by the communists, while the Pacific Ocean is reduced to a small quadrangle.

The map can be divided geographically into four main sections, each of which also represents a principal theme in the Hmong recent history. These are, from top to bottom, the fight (Section I), the flight (Section II), the escape (Section III), and the process of resettlement (Section IV).

Section I comprises a narrow band along the top of the cloth: it represents a stretch of mountainous territory and bears the label 'Laos.' These are the highlands in which the Hmong fought the communists. The principal sites marked in this section are 'Ban Long Chieng' and 'Phou Bia,' both in reality located in the highlands to the south of the Plain of Jars (not indicated on the cloth). Ban Long Chieng served during the war as the headquarters of General Vang Pao, the commander of the Hmong 'secret army,' and was also one of the principal CIA bases in Laos (Hamilton-Merritt 1993: 130 – 143; Warner 1996, *passim*); it was also a major refuge for Hmong who were forced to leave their traditional habitat. Phou Bia, the highest mountain in Laos, was the site of the last resistance of the Hmong against the new communist regime; it had been finally subdued only in 1978, three years after the establishment of the Lao People's Democratic Republic (Hamilton-Merritt 1993: 400–403).

Section II comprises the territory between the highlands and the Mekong river. It is not clearly marked off from Section I, but can be analytically separated. This section is distinguished by a different perspective: in Section I mountains and clouds are depicted almost horizontally; Section II is devoid of distinctive topographic features and, like the following sections, is depicted from a diagonal perspective. At the bottom of this section, on the bank of the river, are marked two cities: the capital 'Vieng Chan' (Vientiane) with its distinct *chedi* (pagoda) and the city of 'Paksan' (Paksane).

Section III, marked the 'Mekhong River' (Mekong river), represents a section of the Mekong across which Hmong escaped into Thailand.

Section IV comprises primarily the southwestern, Thai bank of the Mekong, on which unnamed refugee camps are represented. Beyond these, geographical accuracy is overridden by exigencies of space; concomitantly, the scale of the map is ever more radically reduced. To the left of the refugee camps is marked the transit camp of 'Phantnikhom' (Phanat Nikhom) (Benyasut 1990), beneath it, 'Bang-kok' (actually, the Don Muang airport), the 'Pacific Ocean', and eventually the 'U.S.A.' Phanat Nikhom is in reality located to the south of Bangkok; and Bangkok is not quite located on the shore of the Pacific. However, these departures from geographic fact are not random errors: rather, they are necessary simplifications, serving to emphasize those localities and relationships between them which are significant in the recent Hmong experience.

Within each of these geographical sections, a sequence of events is horizontally represented. However, contrary to a first impression, a close scrutiny of the cloth shows that there is no continuity between the sequences represented in each section. Each section is, as it were, a separate 'chapter.' The dominant orientation of all the sections is, from the Hmong standpoint, from right-to-left: most Hmong face in that direction and insofar as movement is represented it invariably proceeds from right to left.

The narrow top section (Section I) depicts the war between the Hmong and the communists in the Laotian highlands: in the top right corner, a plane emits white flakes – probably an allusion to the 'yellow rain' (Chagnon and Rumpf 1983a, 1983b, Westing and Williams 1983, Hamilton-Merritt 1993: 390), a poison allegedly used by the communists to exterminate the Hmong resistance after the communist takeover. Hmong on Phou Bia defend themselves against an attack by the Laotian and Vietnamese communist soldiers, while further to the left Ban Long Chieng has already fallen.

The following section, Section II, depicts the Hmong in the period between the communist victory and their flight from Laos. It combines a presentation of Hmong agricultural pursuits with that of their persecution by communist soldiers and of their overland flight.

The Hmong are surrounded, with a few communists attacking them along the right margin of the cloth, while the principal persecution takes place further to the left; here sits 'Kaisone,' the leader of the Pathet Lao, secretary-general of the Lao People's Revolutionary Party, first prime minister, and later president, of the LPDR (Brunnstrom 1991; *Bangkok Post* 1992), on a throne-like chair; a Hmong man is forced at gun point to kneel in front of him. Some Hmong are in the process of surrendering, while others are driven into a prisoners' camp or being shot by communist soldiers, after they have dug their own graves. Communist soldiers are confiscating Hmong cattle and otherwise interfering with Hmong life.

Those Hmong in this section who are not disturbed by the intrusion of the communists, are shown engaging in planting or pounding of rice, harvesting corn, growing opium poppies, and feeding pigs. However, partly mingled with these peaceful pursuits, other Hmong, some armed, flee in single file towards the river. They descend diagonally from right-to-left passing through the jungle (which is metonymically symbolized by wild animals, such as tigers, elephants, and monkeys on a tree) and are arriving on the left bank of the Mekong between the cities of Vientiane and Paksane, with communist soldiers pursuing them up to the riverside (on the lower right of this section).

Section III shows the Hmong escaping across the Mekong river into Thailand. The crossing, after an arduous and often prolonged journey, was the critical last stage of the flight, during which many Hmong were caught or killed by Laotian soldiers, or returned by the Thai authorities into the hands of the communists (Hamilton-Merritt 1993: 11–14). Various modes of crossing are depicted: some Hmong cross by boat or by raft, whilst others use banana stems or inflated inner tubes to support themselves. They are pursued by a Laotian motorboat.

This section, too, is spatially unrelated to the preceding one: the Hmong are escaping along the whole length of the river, and not just from the points between the two Laotian cities, to which they are shown arriving in Section II. We do not see them embarking on the Laotian side, or disembarking on the Thai side. As in their flight in the preceding section, the Hmong cross the river from right-to-left – even though in actual fact they would probably be crossing from left-to-right, since the river, flowing from west to east, would carry them in that direction.

Section IV is again unrelated to the preceding one. It represents in a highly condensed manner the process of resettlement of the Hmong refugees, in a clear geographical and temporal right-to-left sequence: the Hmong are shown on the extreme bottom right of the cloth as queueing in front of a barrier, behind which sits a uniformed man, probably a Thai official, processing their admittance to the refugee camp. The tense situation is stressed by two more uniformed men in a bunker, located behind the seated official. In front of the Hmong are the barracks of an unnamed refugee camp; these constitute the background to the further processing of the refugees: some are shown approaching a desk behind which sit two white civilians, probably NGO officials or representatives of a 'third country' into which the Hmong refugees are to be resettled. Both are writing on some papers in front of them. A group of Hmong, with suitcases in their hands, approach two buses at the bottom of the cloth, while a Hmong woman, with a suitcase, apparently takes her leave from another woman, without a suitcase, who is left behind. We see the Hmong next in Phanat Nikhom, the transient camp (Benyasut 1990), where refugees destined for resettlement underwent language training: on the cloth, a very tall white teacher introduces a group of Hmong to the Latin alphabet. From here the scale of representation becomes radically reduced: beneath the transit camp the city of Bangkok is marked, but the city itself is not depicted; rather, there is only the airport terminal of Don Muang, on the outskirts of Bangkok, from which the Hmong departed for resettlement countries. A huge airplane, presumably carrying the refugees, crosses a narrow stretch of gray water, marked 'Pacific Ocean.' Beneath the ocean, in the lower left corner, there is the 'U.S.A.,' the principal resettlement country. A big American accompanies a suitcase-bearing Hmong into a room, where a Hmong family sits around a dining table, while another couple views television; next to them are two private cars. These three symbols of Americanization indicate the apparently successful (material) assimilation of the Hmong in their country of resettlement.

Discussion and conclusions

Throughout the description of our example, care was taken not to prejudge the issue of the nature of its temporality. It is, however, obvious from our discussion that this is an ambiguous issue; the cloth contains both static and dynamic elements: dynamic events are depicted on the background of a static map. Unlike 'story cloths' consisting of a series of distinct scenes, the cloth is, in one sense, an integrated picture, without internal divisions; however, it can be divided into several sections, even if those are not sharply delineated. Moreover, the sections, as our analysis has shown, appear to be discontinuous: each can be seen as self-contained, and not explicitly linked to the one preceding or following it. Finally, the problem of individual continuity between the various sections is ambiguous: while all Hmong, belonging to the same gender, look alike, the groups depicted in the various sections differ in terms of number and gender composition. The question of whether the same or different persons are depicted on the cloth thus remains unresolved.

This summary indicates that the cloth under consideration is ambiguous in two different respects: it is unclear whether it is a static or a dynamic representation; and, whatever the case may be in that respect, it is also unclear whether it depicts the general fate of the Hmong in recent times, or whether it depicts the fate of particular individuals. The crossing of these pairs of alternatives renders four possible readings of the cloth (Table 7.1):

(1) *Personal (biographical) narrative:* The cloth can be read as a story of a period in the life of some individual Hmong, beginning with their fight against the communists in the Laotian highlands, continuing with their flight and escape to Thailand, and ending with their resettlement in the U. S. This reading is closest to that of a 'story,' as a sequence of causally related events: the story would thus resemble the biographical stories of individual Hmong, as represented, for instance, in Chan's collection (Chan (ed.) 1994). Such a reading, however, is weakened by the standardized, impersonal depiction of the individuals involved, and the absence of a readily recognizable continuity of identities of individuals or groups in the various sections.

(2) *Snapshot:* The cloth can be read as a synchronic representation, an instantaneous depiction, of different Hmong in various but simultaneous stages of fight, flight, escape, and resettlement: while some Hmong still fight in the highlands, others flee and escape, while still others are already entering refugee camps or being resettled. This reading – which denies that the cloth is a story at all – is resisted by the extraordinary range of events depicted – from fight in the highlands of Laos, to the eventual resettlement in the U. S. However, simpler cloths, depicting only the flight, the escape over the Mekong and the entrance into Thai refugee camps (Fig. 2.8; MacDowell 1989: 40), can plausibly be seen as snapshots of the process, with different individuals caught in its various stages.

(3) *Historical narrative:* The cloth can be read as a generalized representation of the main stages of the recent history of the Hmong

	Generality	
	Individual	General
Dynamic	(1) Personal (biographical) narrative	(3) Historical narrative
Temporality ————		
Static	(2) Snap-shot	(4) 'Mythical' emblem

Table 7.1 Four Possible Readings of the 'Story Cloth'

people – not as an individual story of certain Hmong, but of the Hmong people as a collective. Hence it is set in historical not in individual time. The sequence does not seek to depict the same people in different stages of the historical process but merely to illustrate the sequence of these stages in a general manner. However, this reading encounters the difficulty that the various stages are not historically discrete. Thus, while some Hmong were still fighting the communists on Phou Bia, others had already fled or reached the refugee camps in Thailand, and may have even resettled in the United States.

(4) *'Mythical' emblem*: Finally, the cloth can be also read as an emblematic representation, outlining a modern Hmong myth – a myth of loss, exodus and salvation, consisting of defeat in the old homeland, Laos, the sufferings on the flight from Laos and during the sojourn in the refugee camps in Thailand, and the ultimate attainment of a new home in the United States. As a historical myth it is set in time, but it is also 'out of time': in a sense a generalized, stable background to the innumerable biographical experiences of individual Hmong, who went through the stages charted by it. Their repetition of the mythical cycle, in turn, endows their sufferings with meaning. The temporal dimension of the cloth, according to this interpretation, is dualistic: it is both atemporal on a general level and temporal on the individual level. As such its temporal nature is similar to that of the mythical drawings of Australian aborigines or of the lives of medieval saints. The underlying myth, however, unlike for instance the myths of Australian aborigines and other 'primitive' peoples, is not set in some primeval time, in *'illo*

161

tempore' in Eliade's (1971) terminology, but in historical time – the cloth represents, as it were, a mythologized history.

We do not know how the producers of the so-called 'story cloths' here discussed or other Hmong would interpret them. But I would suggest that they would hardly be able to form a clear or consensual opinion. In contrast to the example of Australian aboriginal drawings or illustrations of Christian saints' lives, the genre of representational designs on Hmong cloth is new to Hmong culture and heavily influenced by outside forces. Therefore it is doubtful that any conventions regarding a preferred common reading of such cloths have already emerged, as they have in other cultures. For the time being, at least, the temporal dimension of the Hmong 'story cloths' appears to remain irreducibly ambiguous and indeterminate. I would suggest, however, that, as time passes and the variety of individual experiences lose their sharpness, the 'mythical' reading of the cloths will become predominant. Hmong 'story cloths', of the kind described here, will thus become one of the means of integrating the turbulent events of the war in Laos into the Hmong collective mytho-historical memory.

Notes

1 Thanks are due to Zali Gurevitch, Danny Rabinowitz and Shelly Shenhav-Keller for their comments on an earlier draft of this chapter.
2 Similar linear representations of individual scenes can be found on the walls of temples in Laos (e.g. *Lao* 1985: 85). I have no information regarding the influence of such representations in lowland Lao culture on the work of Laotian Hmong in the refugee camps in Thailand.
3 The stories were originally published separately in little illustrated booklets and some were later collected in the cited publications.

Part II

Lowland Village Crafts

8

TOURISTIC CRAFT RIBBON
DEVELOPMENT IN THAILAND[1]

Introduction

Shopping is one of the principal touristic activities, but has received insufficient attention in the sociological literature. Two main topics of research in this area can be distinguished: (1) studies of tourist shopping behavior, including its spatial aspects (Kent et al. 1983, Jansen-Verbeke 1991) – this is the more frequently studied topic, particularly by researchers in the field of business administration; (2) the location, distribution and structure of tourist (and leisure) shopping facilities; this is the less frequently and less systematically studied topic. Most of the work on this topic has been done by geographers and planners (Butler 1991, Getz 1992, 1993b) rather than sociologists and anthropologists. This work refers primarily to rather massive clusters of shopping facilities in highly developed countries; there are no systematic studies on the subject in a Third World country.

Several locational configurations of touristic shopping facilities have been conceptualized or described in the literature: the most general is the concept of the 'tourist precinct', which includes, among other things, 'shopping centers' (Leiper 1990): somewhat narrower and morphologically more concretely definable is the concept of the 'tourist business district' (Getz 1993a) which tends to be part of the inner-city shopping area, (Jansen 1989), and the concept of 'tourist shopping villages' (Getz, 1993b). While these concepts refer to two-dimensionally distributed clusters or areas, some authors also mention linear arrangements of touristic shopping facilities, such as strips, arteries, malls, or even toll roads (Ben-Amos 1977, Butler 1991, Getz 1992, McIntosh et al 1990). I shall refer in this chapter to such linear spatial patterns of location of tourist shopping facilities as 'ribbons'. The chapter deals specifically with one subset of such ribbons: ribbons of shops selling exclusively or primarily tourist crafts.

The purpose of this chapter is twofold – on the one hand, to present, through a series of systematically selected case-studies, a phenomenon of growing importance, not only in Thailand but in many Third World countries: the dynamics of a locational process, emerging in a spontaneous and unplanned manner in response to the opening up, through road construction and increased motorization, of hitherto remote and not easily accessible craft-producing regions to domestic and international tourism; and, on the other hand, to resuscitate and refine the concept of 'ribbon development', which has been largely neglected since the 1970s, as the attention of urban geographers and ecologists turned to novel, large-scale shopping complexes. I shall show its usefulness for the study of new, tourist-orientated commercial developments in less developed situations.

I became aware of tourist craft ribbons in Thailand in the course of my anthropological study of the commercialization of Thai crafts for the tourist market conducted in the years 1991 – 93. The following presentation is based on a survey of such ribbons, in several locations in northern and north-eastern Thailand.

Types of Ribbon Development

Ribbon development is an urban retail shopping pattern, identified by Berry (1963) as a subsystem of retailing activity catering for casual or passing trade. 'Ribbons' have been defined as 'beaded clusters of activities strung out alongside major roads . . . that may contain a large number of shops but also contain a high incidence of services and sometimes a mixture of small wholesale and manufacturing establishments' (Davis 1984: 31). There is a difference between ribbon developments in the UK and the USA, which is of analytical significance for our purposes: In British cities such developments:

> . . . constitute the oldest and most blighted retail configurations [reflecting] mainly a former, uncontrolled marketing response to public transport staging points with only relatively little recent adaptation to the needs of consumers using private vehicles (Davis 1974:94).

Such developments in the UK are primarily inner-city affairs. In the USA, in contrast, the ribbon pattern developed in response to motorization and, though older ribbons are located in the inner cities (and as in the UK, tend to degenerate into 'skid roads'), the newer ones are suburb and highway orientated, catering to passing private motorized traffic (Scott 1970). As we shall see, these particular, historically determined forms of ribbon development in the two countries can be employed as elements in the construction of a more sophisticated typology of ribbon developments, to be applied in the analysis of our case studies. But prior to this, we need some background information.

Tourism and Commercialized Crafts in Thailand

Tourism arrivals have multiplied rapidly in Thailand in the last three decades, and especially in the 1990s. This rapid growth followed vigorous efforts to promote Thailand as a major international destination as, for example, by such projects as the 'Visit Thailand Year' in 1987 (*Business Review* 1986, *Saen Sanuk* 1988b). In 1960 only about 80,000 foreigners visited Thailand; their number grew to more than 600,000 in 1970; from then on, throughout the 1970s and 1980s, there was a growing expansion. The one million mark was passed in 1973, the two million mark by 1982; in 1987, the 'Visit Thailand Year', tourism grew by 23% and reached 3.4 million; by 1996 7.2 million foreign visitors were recorded.

The rapid development of international tourism was accompanied by a significant, although less spectacular and less easily perceptible expansion of domestic tourism. Thais traditionally embark on pilgrimages (Cohen 1992a, Pruess 1992); however, such visits to popular sacred places are usually accompanied by recreational activities of a touristic character. Middle-class Thais also engage in secular forms of tourism. Organized weekend group tours, usually by bus, to historical, natural, ethnic or cultural sites are highly popular. With growing affluence and the improvement of the road system, motorization has accelerated; consequently, growing numbers of Thais engage in tourism by private cars to an expanding number of destinations throughout the country.

Foreign tourism tends to concentrate in a small number of locations: Bangkok, Pattaya, Chiang Mai and the southern islands of Phuket and Koh Samui are the principal destinations. The Thai government, however, makes efforts to disperse tourism, developing and promoting additional destinations, particularly in the north and the northeast of the country. These efforts at dispersion go hand in hand with an effort to promote the country's arts and crafts. This endeavour has a dual goal: to preserve and revive traditional culture and to create a new source of income for the producers of often declining folk crafts. The principal expression of such efforts was the organization of the 'Arts and Crafts Year 1988–89' (*Holiday Time in Thailand* 1988, *The Nation* 1988) intended as a conspicuous undertaking to bring the considerable variety and attractiveness of Thai folk crafts (*Thai Life* 1988) to the attention of the tourist public. Interest in crafts has grown considerably in recent years not only among foreign, but also among domestic tourists. Some locals take regular antique- and craft-hunting trips through the countryside.

Many of the craft-producing localities are located well away from the major cities and tourist destinations, especially in relatively remote rural areas of northern, northeastern and southern Thailand. In the past they were not easily accessible, and sold their products either to a local clientele or, through intermediaries, to the tourist market, thus becoming part of the process of indirect tourism (Aspelin 1977). With improved roads, the growth of motorized domestic tourism and the expansion of craft production in response to growing interest, outlets for tourist crafts began to relocate to the roadsides; thus touristic craft ribbon patterns emerged.

Types of tourist craft ribbon developments in Thailand

Contemporary craft production in Thailand is primarily orientated to an 'external audience'(Graburn 1976b:8). The principal target audience are tourists, both foreign and domestic; but the craft market is not so specialized or segregated as to exclude other audiences. These include local villagers and townspeople, who have traditionally purchased functional craft objects for domestic use directly from the local producers, other non-touristic domestic users throughout the country, reached through hawkers, stall keepers and shop-keepers in markets and fairs, and a foreign non- touristic audience, reached through export – import enterprises (Ch. 9). A degree of continuity has often been preserved in Thailand in the transition from production for an internal, local audience to production for external touristic and other audiences; some craft-producing localities are even at present still at the early stages of that transition and have not yet tapped the foreign tourist market (Ch. 11); while production in other craft-producing localities has already undergone considerable heterogeneization in an effort to reach a variety of new markets (Ch. 9–10).

In the different segments of the market a variety of marketing chains have emerged, differing in length and composition. Most craft producers sell only a fraction of their production directly to ultimate consumers, whether local or external; most of the business is mediated through a network of middlemen, traders, wholesalers and exporters. While some of these may be located in the craft-producing locality itself, others come from outside – whether from a regional urban center or from major cities such as Bangkok and Chiang Mai.

In the past, tourists did not ordinarily reach most of the craft-producing villages, whereas transactions with intermediaries were mostly conducted at the producer's workshops, dispersed throughout villages or small towns. However, with the expansion and improvement of the network of roads throughout the country, the rapidly growing motorization and the growth in tourism, a change in the geographical pattern of marketing craft products has taken place: roadside location gave sellers – whether the producers themselves or shopkeepers – direct access to the passing touristic and non-touristic traffic. Mostly locally owned workshops, stalls, shops and trading establishments began to locate along the roads within the craft-producing villages and beyond them, primarily in the direction of major urban tourist centers. Thus small ribbons eventually emerged, composed of craft-producing and marketing establishments catering primarily, though not exclusively, to the tourist market. Other, bigger ribbons developed along major artery roads, leading out of major urban tourist centers, towards crafts-producing settlements, as big craft stores, craft trading establishments and craft factories relocated from the city onto the roadside.

Two kinds of dynamics of tourist ribbon developments can thus be distinguished: from a craft-producing locality towards a major tourist center, and from that center towards the periphery. As a consequence, two polar types of ribbons can be conceptualized: the *localized* ribbon and the *ramified* ribbon.

The *localized ribbon* corresponds to the street ribbons within cities, as described in the literature on British cities. It is located on a single kind of road, and is, initially, relatively short – not longer than a few hundred meters – and homogeneous in terms of products offered and the kind and size of establishments. The latter are relatively simple affairs, and are at the outset composed mostly of locally owned stalls, shops and workshops.

Localized ribbons undergo a process of evolution as they mature: they tend to extend beyond the limits of the craft-producing settlement, and become more heterogeneous in terms of products offered, and kinds, size and ownership of establishments. Not only is local production growing more varied, but products originating from outside

169

and unrelated to local craft specialization are increasingly marketed by the shops on the ribbon. An upgrading of some establishments takes place, while others remain unchanged; new establishments, some small and locally owned, others even from the outset large and outsider owned, further increase heterogeneity. In so far as the craft-producing locality is close to a major tourist center, a mature localized ribbon may eventually link up with a ribbon expanding from that center and merge into a ramified ribbon pattern.

The *ramified ribbon* is longer and more complex than the localized one; it resembles to a degree the highway ribbons in the United States. It is composed of several sections of roads, of different grades: from village street in the craft-producing locality to the highway leading into a major urban center.

Such ribbons extend for several kilometers and are heterogeneous in terms of products offered and the kind and type of establishments located on them. The latter range from simple shops and workshops to large stores and trading enterprises, as well as various types of transport and catering services. Ownership of establishments in *ramified ribbons* is mixed: smaller establishments, particularly those within or in the immediate vicinity of craft-producing villages, tend to be locally owned; bigger ones, especially those on the major artery roads, tend to be owned by outsiders. The evolution of ramified ribbons is bi-directional, rather than uni-directional (like that of localized ribbons): on the one hand, they expand out of the craft-producing locality in the direction of the highway leading into the city; on the other hand, they expand out of the city, along the highway, towards craft-producing localities. Once the two directions of expansion meet, the ramified ribbon pattern emerges.

The emergence and evolution of the two types of craft ribbon patterns will be illustrated by several examples taken from my survey.

Localized tourist craft ribbon developments

This type will be illustrated by three examples; though all of them are localized, they represent different evolutionary stages.

(1) Ban Hua Dong. This example illustrates the initial stage of the emergence of a ribbon pattern. The village is located a few kilometers from the remote northern provincial center of Phrae, and is in a forested area, rich in valuable kinds of wood, which are threatened by illegal exploitation (Suksamrarn 1988). The village is a traditional center of furniture production for the local market. Until about the mid-1980s,

both the production and the sale of furniture were conducted in the many small workshops dispersed throughout the village. With the improvement of the road, a considerable expansion of production took place. The improvement also induced local producers to move to the roadside: by 1993, 41 shops had located along both sides of the road; some had small workshops attached behind them, in which the finishing stages of production were performed. The raw furniture was still made in workshops within the village. The shops are owned by local Thais and Chinese.

The shops offered a variety of plain or carved furniture in sets or as individual pieces: tables, chairs, cupboards, bedsteads and a variety of smaller objects. Some of these are ornamented by elaborate carvings in Thai or Chinese style. The products are destined for the domestic market; they are purchased by domestic visitors for their own use, or by middlemen and shopkeepers for resale in urban centers around the country.

The province of Phrae, long marginal to the principal tourism itineraries of northern Thailand, has been targeted for tourism development (Yee 1988, Theptong 1991) as a stop-over between the cities of Nan and Chiang Rai. The village of Hua Dong, located on that route, has thus begun to experience regular visits from tourist groups. The local response to this novel audience for craft products and souvenirs has as yet been slight. One or two shops sell carved figurines, copied or brought in from the carving village of Ban Thawai (see below). Basketry and textile products, originating outside the village or even outside the province, are sold in a few shops on the in-bound lane of the road from Nan to the city of Phrae. The local furniture makers have not yet turned to the production of souvenirs or other products specifically oriented to the foreign tourist market. But one important innovation has been introduced: wall clocks in ornately carved, coloured wooden cases. While these products, priced at about US $70–100 each, and weighing several kilograms, will certainly not become a popular purchase for foreign tourists, they seem to be attractive to domestic tourists: for those who pass through the village in private vehicles the bulk and weight of the clocks do not pose a significant constraint on their purchase.

(2) Ban Tung Hom. This village represents a more advanced example of a localized ribbon development. Located about 6 km from the city of Phrae, this village is a well-known center of production of *mohom* cloth, a blue or ultramarine hand-dyed cotton fabric, from which are cut shirts, jackets, trousers, skirts and other items (Yee

1988:52, *Chiang Mai Travel Holiday* 1991). *Mohom* clothing for the peasant market was a traditional product of this village for many years prior to its opening to tourism. The raw cloth is presently mostly industrially produced outside the village. It is dyed in the households dispersed throughout the village, and sewn by local seamstresses. However, in the last decade, *mohom* clothing shops, catering to locals as well as tourists, some of them with attached sewing workshops, began to locate along the road passing through the village to the city of Phrae. The shops usually farm out work to local seamstresses, providing them with the materials. In 1993, 31 *mohom* clothing shops, most of which engaged in both retailing and wholesaling, were counted on the road.

The *mohom* products of Ban Tung Hom, unlike those of Ban Hua Dong, have been, from the mid-1980s on, largely adapted to the mostly domestic tourist market: there is a proliferation of fashionable cuts, and many embellishments were added to the plain blue surface of the cloth. The variety is also greater than in Ban Hua Dong: in addition to *mohom* products, other kinds of clothing as well as souvenirs, brought in from the Chiang Mai area, are sold in some of the shops along the road. Moreover, the *mohom* shops do not constitute an isolated ribbon, as do the furniture shops in Ban Hua Dong, but are interspersed between a variety of non-touristic shops and services, serving the local population. Since international tourism to the Phrae area is still in an incipient stage, the *mohom* shops in Ban Tung Hom have not yet become a significant tourist attraction on the itinerary of foreign visitors; they serve primarily domestic tourists.

(3) Dan Kwien market. This is the most developed of the three examples of localized ribbons. The market is located within the pottery-producing *tambon* (sub-district) of Dan Kwien (Ch. 9), at a distance of 14 km east of the city of Nakhon Ratchasima, the largest urban center of north-east Thailand (a region also called Isan). The market stretches for a few hundred meters along both sides of the road leading from the city to the provincial center of Buriram and the ancient Khmer temple of Phanom Rung, which was recently restored and opened for tourist visits. This project was part of a wider effort to open up the region of Isan to tourism (*Manager* 1991).

The villagers of the *tambon* of Dan Kwien have been producing pottery utensils for the local market for at least 200 years. From the 1950s onwards several art teachers and artists, attracted by the distinct metallic lustre of the local pottery, moved into the *tambon* and began to expand production in new directions. These outsiders established their workshops on rice fields along the road; later on, they opened shops facing towards the road. These establishments eventually became the nucleus of the Dan Kwien market; gradually other establishments, owned by outsiders as well as by locals, sprang up along the road. The number of new establishments has increased rapidly in the 1990s, since the road has been improved and broadened and tourist visits, both domestic and foreign, have become more regular. Much of the tourist traffic consists of Thai tourists on buses, who pass through the market on the return leg of a tour to Phanom Rung. Since the buses stop on the southern lane of the road, the shops there have a significantly greater number of visitors than those on the opposite, northern side. The shops on the south side are hence more numerous and larger. In the summer of 1992 there were 44 stalls and shops in the Dan Kwien market, 30 of them on the southern, and only 14 on the northern side of the road. Four of these were big enterprises, producing and selling large quantities of pottery products. All save one, and many of the other shops, are owned by outsiders to the *tambon*. Local villagers, although producing pottery in the villages, were late-comers to the market. Though they are gradually penetrating it, they mostly own only stalls and smaller shops.

Most of the establishments on both sides of the road are simple open wooden structures. But in 1991, a row of 10 new shops, built of hard materials, was constructed on the southern, more active, side of the road. (On later developments see Ch. 9).

The bulk of the products offered at the Dan Kwien market are locally produced pottery objects; these have undergone a growing heterogenization in terms of style, design and form; a huge variety of products, including earthenware jewelry, is offered for sale. In addition to this variety of locally produced objects, the market shopowners are also rapidly introducing diverse kinds of craft products originating in other localities.

The Dan Kwien market caters to foreign and domestic tourists, but the latter are its principal direct customers; foreigners purchase mainly small items, such as earthenware jewelry; most pottery objects are not very suitable for direct sale to foreign tourists, owing to their weight and bulk.

The Dan Kwien market is frequently visited by middlemen, shopowners and exporters; indeed, most of the business, especially of the big enterprises, is conducted through these intermediaries; and the proportion of business through various marketing channels, rather than by direct sales to ultimate consumers, is expanding rapidly. One indicator of this expansion is that two big enterprises recently began to ship their wares abroad directly (Ch. 9).

Ramified tourist craft ribbon developments

This type will be illustrated by two examples, which represent different stages of development.

(I) The Ban Thawai – Hang Dong – Chiang Mai Ribbon. Ban Thawai (Ch. 10) is a wood-carving village, located about 5 km from Hang Dong, a district town, 11 km south-west of the major urban tourist center of northern Thailand, Chiang Mai. Hang Dong is situated on a principal artery road leading to the main urban centers of western North Thailand, Mae Sarieng and Mae Hong Son, an area of rapid tourist expansion. The ribbon of craft-producing and selling enterprises stretches, in four fairly distinct sections, from the village of Ban Thawai all the way to the city of Chiang Mai. Although it is not wholly continuous throughout this long route, the enterprises dotting the sides of the roads are dense and conspicuous enough to endow it with a distinct character. The four sections are:

- the main street of Ban Thawai (about 1 km);
- the track from the entrance to the village to the secondary road leading to the town of Hang Dong (about 1 km);
- along the secondary road to Hang Dong (about 3 km);
- along the artery road from Hang Dong to Chiang Mai (about 11 km).

I turn now to a brief description of the four sections. Ban Thawai, is probably the best known wood-carving village in Thailand (Yee 1992). Although commercial carving began in the village only about 25 years ago, it developed rapidly and became the principal source of employment and income of the villagers. The village is the hub of a complex system of production, encompassing several other wood-carving villages in northern Thailand. Most raw products are carved in those villages and then sent to Ban Thawai, where they are finished and from where they are marketed. In the village itself there are several workshops in which wood is carved but most workshops are engaged in the processes of gilding, ornamenting and otherwise finishing the rough carvings made elsewhere. Although production is conducted in many households throughout the village, its main street was in 1991 lined on both sides with an almost uninterrupted ribbon of workshops and shops stretching from the end of the main street of the village to its entrance, a distance of about 1 km. There were altogether 41 establishments on the main street of the village, all selling, producing or finishing a wide variety of wood carvings. Except for a few small eating places, there were no other shops on the street; nor were other kinds of crafts sold in the village. In a few shops, paints and other production materials were carried for sale to local craftsmen. Most of the establishments on the street began as workshops attached to the craftsmen's households; afterwards simple shops were added in front of some of the workshops. These consisted mostly of a few open shelves on which finished products were displayed. In some shops, the products were simply placed on the floor. A few shops put up modern, urban-type premises, with plate-glass windows and partitions between the shop and the workshop.

Although carving and finishing was going on in many other households in the village, no shops have been established beyond the main street. These other households sought to find suitable alternative locations as outlets for their products; some of them have found such outlets in the prolongation of the ribbon from the main street onto the track leading to the village.

The track from the entrance to Ban Thawai to the secondary road from Hang Dong, about 1 km long, formerly passed through the rice fields of the village. However, the rice fields adjoining the track were filled in and turned into solid land; on that land, dotting most of the track, 28 new establishments, selling wood carvings, have sprung up by 1991. Most of these were recently established small shops, owned by villagers, but there were also three or four big enterprises displaying huge quantities of mass-produced carvings in larger compounds, each comprising several workshops as well as big storage rooms, which also serve as showrooms. This section of the ribbon pattern was an extension of the ribbon within the village. However, since it was established on previously uninhabited land, the shops on this section were mostly dissociated from the households of the owners; there were also relatively fewer work-shops in this section, although in the back of most shops some finishing work has been performed.

The secondary road, from the point where the track to Ban Thawai branches off to the town of Hang Dong, constituted a further extension of the ribbon pattern which started in the village; however, it was more heterogeneous in terms of kinds of establishments and their ownership than the preceding two sections of the ribbon. The dynamics of this section was also more complex. At its far end, at the point where the route to Ban Thawai branches off, was found one of the oldest and biggest locally owned carving establishments. At the opposite, near end of the section, at the point where the secondary road reaches the town of Hang Dong, several older wood-carving shops were located. Between these end-points of the section, a distance of about 3 km, a series of newer establishments have opened up shop. In 1991 this section embraced altogether 48 establishments, all save four selling wood carvings. There were also three major packing and transporting companies located along the road, all of which are engaged in the shipping of carvings to major centers in Thailand or abroad. Their presence bears witness to the scope of the wood-carving business conducted in the area of Ban Thawai. (On later developments see Ch. 10).

This section of the ribbon pattern was more sparsely occupied by business establishments than were the preceding two sections. Although a few of the establishments were small shops, in which only some finishing was done, most were substantial enterprises, occupying large areas of land and combining production with retailing and wholesaling. One of the largest enterprises was a huge, modern compound, built by a limited liability company – the first of its kind in the area; here a big showroom displayed high-quality carvings, while a series of buildings in the compound served as workshops in which products were finished, stored or prepared for dispatch.

Although in one sense an extension of the ribbon starting in Ban Thawai, this section was also marked by a growing external penetration of enterprises owned by outsiders. Most of the bigger enterprises were owned by outsiders, who have been attracted to this section by the proximity of Ban Thawai, as the source of the products in which they were dealing. This section was thus of an intermediate character, featuring characteristics of both of the two preceding sections, as well as the last one.

Before turning to the last section of the ribbon pattern, some of the common characteristics of the first three sections should be noted. In contrast to the Dan Kwien market, the village of Ban Thawai and its immediate surroundings was not a popular tourist destination. Most visitors were shopkeepers or intermediaries, who bought products to be sold in more than a thousand tourist gift and souvenir shops in the provinces of Chiang Mai and Lamphun (Charasdamrong 1991b) or in markets, tourist shops and galleries in major urban centers throughout Thailand; a good many were also sent abroad.

Again in comparison with Dan Kwien, the sections of the ribbon pattern within Ban Thawai and on the track to it were rather homogeneous in terms of products carried by the establishments located on them. Some heterogeneity existed in the third section, the secondary road to Hang Dong, but even here it was not very remarkable; all three sections were heavily dominated by wood-carving products. However, in the third section there was a markedly greater heterogeneity in the size of enterprises and in their ownership.

The section of the main artery linking the town of Hang Dong with the city of Chiang Mai is approximately 11 km long. This section was not studied in depth, and will hence be presented in less detail. Fig. 8.1, taken from a tourist publication, lists the principal enterprises on this section (and on a small stretch of the secondary road from Hang Dong to Ban Thawai). These enterprises are all externally owned. It is evident from the map that this section is much more heterogeneous in terms of products and services offered than any of the preceding ones. Though wood-carving enterprises are still the principal businesses on this section (marked on the map as 'antiques' or 'art' shops), several other kinds of craft and non-craft tourist enterprises are also located on it.

This section of the ribbon pattern differs from the other sections in its dynamics and the nature of the businesses located there. It grew out of the city of Chiang Mai towards Hang Dong (rather than the other way round), and is dotted with enterprises catering to the tourist traffic along this major artery road to the west of North Thailand. There are few small shops on that road, but only relatively large enterprises, including a big ceramics factory, all of which are conspicuous enough to catch the eye of passing motorists, and spacious enough to accommodate tourist buses and private vehicles on their parking lots. Huge billboards were put up by some establishments to attract visitors, while others employed such gimmicks as building a wood-carving shop in the style of a Shan Buddhist temple, so that it would stand out conspicuously from its surroundings.

(2) The Sankamphaeng – Bo Sang – Chiang Mai Ribbon. Bo Sang is the well known 'umbrella village' ('Amethist' 1991, Chunpraseri 1988) located about 8 km east of Chiang Mai, a little more than halfway between that city and the town of Sankamphaeng, another well-known tourist craft center of northern Thailand. Along the main artery road between Chiang Mai and Sankamphaeng has emerged the longest and most heterogeneous tourist-oriented ribbon pattern in Thailand (Tettoni 1992).

In the course of the 'Visit Thailand Year' of 1987, the 'Chiang Mai – Sankamphaeng Road [was declared] the Handicraft Route of Chiang Mai' ('Amethist' 1991:51). Along that route are located mostly big, relatively high-quality craft factories and shops. This pattern is particularly dense on the section of the artery road between Chiang Mai and the junction of the secondary road leading into the village of

177

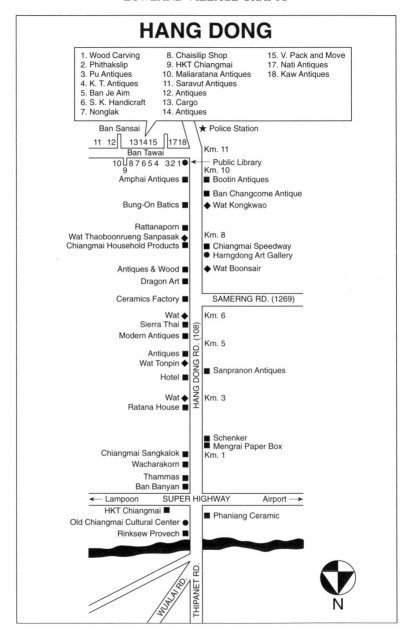

Figure 8.1 The Hang Dong-Chiang Mai ribbon section
Source: Chiang Mai Travel Holiday 1992 (Dec.).

Bo Sang. The major enterprises on that part of the artery road can be seen in Fig. 8.2, which is taken from a tourist publication.

As in the preceding example, here too the ramified ribbon pattern developed from two opposite polar points: on the one hand from the village of Bo Sang, which was originally located about 500 m from the junction, on the secondary road to the town of Doi Saket (Hudson 1973:95), but now reaches the junction itself; and on the other hand, from the city of Chiang Mai to the junction of the secondary road to Bo Sang and, from that junction, along the main artery onwards to Sankamphaeng. I shall describe separately each of these two sections of the ribbon.

The village of Bo Sang was for the last 200 – 300 years a center for the production of umbrellas, made of *saa* (mulberry tree bark) paper. However, commercial production for the tourist market was initiated only in the early 1970s (Linklater 1988:33). In the late 1970s, owing to declining demand for umbrellas, wood carving was introduced into the village as an additional line of craft production (Suvapiromchote 1988). Umbrella production later recovered and diversified: in addition to *saa* paper, cotton and silk were used in the manufacture of umbrellas, fans (Chunpraseri 1988:56–57), butterflies and paintings. Over the years, umbrellas and fans came to be decorated with ever richer and more diversified designs of flowers, birds, Chinese dragons and many other motifs. An Umbrella Festival was instituted during the 'Visit Thailand Year' of 1987, and is now celebrated every year.

Many of the local producers have over the years opened workshops and shops along the main street of the village, creating a ribbon, which extends all the way to the junction with the main artery road coming from Chiang Mai. In 1991 105 establishments were located on this stretch of the ribbon pattern. However, though the development of the ribbon in Bo Sang resembles that of Ban Thawai, the former is much more heterogeneous. Only 57 establishments (54%) produced or sold *saa* and associated products; among these, only 14 (13%) produced or sold umbrellas – although umbrellas are the 'traditional' product of the locality, which gave it its nickname and reputation. In 1991, the most ubiquitous product were fans, produced or sold in 48 establishments (46%). Forty-eight establishments (46%) sold a wide variety of other crafts. The principal category among the latter was furniture shops, 20 in number, whose products were apparently mostly locally made. The others sold products which originated outside the village of Bo Sang, such as basketware, textiles or a mixture of diverse crafts.

Two traditional markets are located on the ribbon, as well as two major factories, one of them employing up to 200 workers

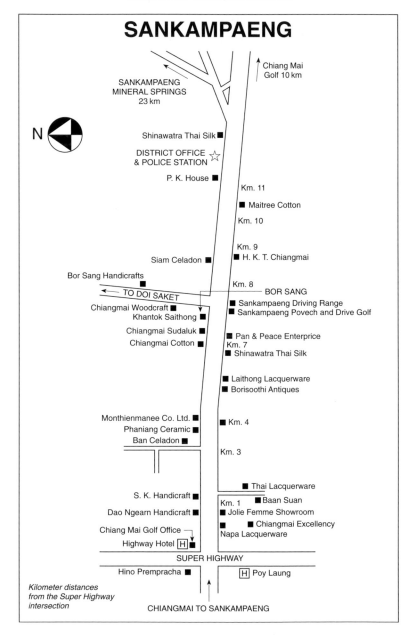

Figure 8.2 The Chiang Mai-Bo Sang ribbon section
Source: Chiang Mai Travel Holiday 1992 (Dec.).

180

(Suvapiromchote 1988). The latter produce umbrellas and fans in great quantities, and offer a very wide selection of other craft products in their spacious shops. Busloads of foreign and domestic tourists regularly stop at these two establishments; a stream of individual tourists passes daily through the village, their number reaching into thousands during the Umbrella Festival. However, as of 1988, only about 40 percent of the umbrellas and kindred products were sold locally to visiting domestic and foreign tourists; about 60 percent were exported (Suvapiromchote 1988).

The Chiang Mai – Sankamphaeng Handicrafts Route has not been surveyed in detail: however, as can be seen from Fig. 2, which lists the most prominent establishments, the route is dotted with a variety of factories and large workshops in which diverse craft products are manufactured. ceramics, celadon, silk, cotton, lacquerware and many other kinds of crafts are represented along the road. Restaurants cater to the tourist traffic. In contrast to the Chiang Mai – Hang Dong road, no craft is dominant on this route. Many of the establishments have built impressive modern structures, maintain large showrooms and permit visitors to observe production in their workshops as part of their promotion efforts. Many have printed flashy brochures or advertised in tourist periodicals. Most establishments have spacious parking lots for buses and private cars which regularly ply the road. In contrast with Bo Sang, where most establishments are small, locally owned, private businesses, the establishments on the artery road are predominantly owned by companies, many of which are based in Chiang Mai or even in Bangkok. This section of the ribbon pattern is thus the most developed, and in most respects represents the very opposite of the incipient localized ribbon, as exemplified by Ban Hua Dong.

Conclusions

Much of the recent literature on tourist shopping facilities has been concerned with developments in the contemporary western world, particularly with large-scale concentrations of such facilities. While some of the concentrations have emerged spontaneously over time, such as the 'tourism business district'(Getz 1993a), others, such as the large shopping complexes, have been planned and constructed by big companies, which implanted them into central city areas, often in the process of urban renewal.

Such tourist facilities are also emerging at an accelerated rate in the bigger urban centers of those developing countries in which tourism is an important branch of the economy. Thus, Bangkok possesses the equivalent of a 'tourist business district' in the centrally located 'Siam Square' area, as well as dozens of large shopping complexes, combining a big department store with a large number of individual stores, eating and entertainment facilities; some of these complexes, such as the 'World Trade Center', are major tourist shopping attractions.

However, in this chapter attention has been drawn to tourist shopping patterns which developed in Thailand as a consequence of road improvements, growing motorization and craft promotion, and which are probably also found in less central and less developed tourist regions of other countries – namely spontaneously emerging ribbons in which locally produced as well as imported craft products are sold to passing tourist traffic. This pattern harks back to a phenomenon in western urban development, which occupied urban geographers a generation ago, but was overcome by more massive recent developments of the kind mentioned earlier. However, this chapter has advanced beyond the conceptualizations of the ribbon pattern in the earlier literature. That literature did not deal with differences in the dynamics of ribbon patterns, and with the different types of ribbons engendered by those differences. On the basis of the case material from Thailand, two kinds of dynamic processes of emergence and expansion of ribbons have been identified: on the one hand, the relocation of craft establishments from within villages to local thoroughfares; on the other hand, the location of urban businesses along major artery roads leading to craft-producing localities. Two types of ribbon developments have been distinguished and their evolution empirically demonstrated: the simple *localized* ribbon and the complex *ramified* ribbon. It remains to spell out some of the broader implications of these developments.

Getz (1993b) has recently proposed the concept of 'tourist shopping villages', which offer various visitor-oriented retailing and other services in tourist destinations or near-urban settings. In the process of their evolution some craft villages in the present studies, especially those of the ramified ribbons, tend to approximate the 'tourist shopping villages', mainly in two respects:

- With the heterogeneization of the products offered, fewer products are made locally, while more are imported from other localities; the village therefore increasingly specializes in retailing, i.e. shopping facilities, rather than production;

182

- As a craft-shop ribbon attracts growing numbers of visitors, new shopping facilities tend to be established in areas in the hinterland of the ribbon; thus, in Bo Sang, several rows of shop-houses have been recently built in an area close to the crossing leading from the main road into the village. This may presage a future development of side-streets, branching off from the main ribbon; such a process has indeed taken place in popular tourist resorts, such as Pattaya and Patong (on Phuket island), where a growing number of side-streets offering a variety of tourist facilities have branched off from the principal road along the beach.

The emergence of the ribbons has contributed significantly to the expansion of the total volume of sales of crafts by the establishments located on the ribbons, and thus to overall local and even national craft production. Location on the ribbons enhances access to tourists, domestic as well as foreign, to craft-producing and marketing establishments. The ease with which tourists can directly observe craft production, and the considerable choice of products offered by many closely adjoining establishments, has made some ribbons into a tourist attraction in their own right; such an attraction was formally institutionalized in the official proclamation of the Chiang Mai – Sankamphaeng road as the 'Handicrafts Road'. It should be noted, too, that the ribbons not only helped to augment direct purchases by visiting tourists, but also contributed to the growing world-wide reputation of Thai crafts, and thereby to their sale in other localities in Thailand as well as abroad. Indeed, purchases by intermediaries, shopkeepers and exporters constitute a more significant component of the total sales of the establishments on the ribbons than direct purchases by tourists.

The impact of the emergence of ribbons on the benefit to local craft producers is more complex; on the one hand, it has helped increase their total production and, in so far as they have established an outlet on the ribbon, their direct sales to tourists, which – although perhaps small in volume – are more profitable than sales to intermediaries. However, most local producers are usually not able to take full advantage of the opportunities offered by the expansion of the ribbon patterns. They usually lack the means, initiative and know-how to establish big and ostentatious trading enterprises with show-rooms and trained sales personnel. The local producers are hence relegated to the smaller shops in the local and more peripheral sections of the ribbons. Outsiders tend to own the larger shops on the localized ribbons and to dominate the sections of ramified ribbons outside the craft villages, and especially on the artery roads, with their large enterprises. Since profits in the craft business accrue predominantly to the sellers, rather than the producers, these outsider owners often reap the principal benefit from the crafts trade on the ribbons: they are able to place large orders with many small producers in the villages, concentrate products in their stores, and sell them in great quantities and at a considerable mark-up to tourists, intermediaries and exporters. It appears therefore, that in the future the ribbons, and particularly the ramified ones, will continue to expand, but as they come to attract growing numbers of both domestic and foreign tourists, the larger, outsider-owned enterprises will gain a growing advantage over the smaller, locally owned ones. It is this takeover by outsiders – a common phenomenon in other types of tourist developments (Greenwood 1972) which may eventually force the smaller, local entrepreneurs out of the market, and thereby seriously diminish the benefits derived by the locals from the ribbon developments, which they have spontaneously initiated.

Notes

1 The study on which this chapter is based was supported by the K-Mart Center for International Retailing and Marketing at the School of Business Administration, The Hebrew University of Jerusalem. Thanks are due to the Institute and Philip Dearden and Ilan Solomon was their useful comments on an earlier draft of this chapter.

9

DAN KWIEN POTTERY

The Heterogeneization of a Tourist Art[1]

Introduction

You can't miss it, the highway is long and straight, and devoid of any apparent human habitation, then suddenly you are confronted by rows and rows of pottery shops. This renowned ceramic work is simply beautiful in its style, and the process dates back around 250 years *(The Nation* 1992:14).

This somewhat exorbitant advertisement invites the visitor to Dan Kwien, the renowned northeastern Thai 'pottery village'(Katz 1991). In fact, Dan Kwien is not a single village, but a subdistrict *(tambon),* consisting of eight villages *(muban),* six of which actually produce pottery, and a crafts market in their midst. It is located at a distance of 14 kilometers from the city of Nakhon Ratchasima (Korat), the 'Gateway to the Northeast' (Chuenprapanusorn 1988), the biggest but also the most impoverished and least developed of the four main regions of Thailand (also called *Isan).*

Dan Kwien is the best known of several localities in Thailand where pottery products for both local and tourist consumption are made, and the only one that is a tourist attraction in itself. Dan Kwien is mentioned in most tourism brochures and guidebooks as one of the attractions of Isan; and a number of articles in tourist-oriented periodicals were devoted to its pottery. Its location on the route to major Cambodian archeological sites, especially the recently restored Phanom Rung Temple in the adjoining province of Buriram, facilitates its exposure to a flow of tourists. Several busloads of locals and foreigners visit daily the crafts market, mostly as a stopover on the return leg of a tour of Cambodian archeological sites in the region. But the crafts market is neither the only nor the most important outlet for local pottery production. Rather, the sales occur in souvenir and antique shops and on the weekend market in Bangkok, as well as in some other tourism localities. The pottery is also exported in great quantities to Europe, Australia and the United States.

The study of the transformation of Dan Kwien pottery from a simple rural craft to a tourist art was undertaken as part of a comparative study of several rural localities in Thailand in which various types of tourist art are produced, conducted between 1991–1998. The dynamics of the emergence and development of tourist arts proved to be a much more complex and involved process than was originally supposed, not only by those who simplistically dubbed them 'airport arts,' and saw in them a denigration of primitive or traditional folk arts and crafts, but also by those who took their cue from modernization theory, and conceived of them as 'transitional arts' – located, as it were, on a one-dimensional continuum between traditional folk crafts and modern fine arts (Cohen 1992c).

To overcome this limitation, several multidimensional schemes for the classification of tourist arts were proposed (Chs.1,3; Graburn 1976b; Shiloah and Cohen 1983:236–243). Even these more complex typologies, however, are based on the assumption that the arts of a given group at a certain point in time are homogeneous enough to be classifiable into one of the categories in the scheme. However, this assumption also appears to be too simplistic, at least for instances in which contemporary crafts are oriented to a variety of markets, without serious cultural constraints upon their diversification. In such instances, there exists the frequently noted duality between products for internal and external publics (Graburn 1976b:8), and there may also exist considerable variety between the products intended for the different external publics. Such instances are thus typologically not clearly definable. However, the significant problem concerns not mere typological systematization, but rather the processes that engender the heterogeneization of products and their consequences.

Four particular problems pose themselves in this context. One, what is the role of entrepreneurs and innovators in the process of heterogeneization and where do they originate? Two, how do market forces influence the process of production, innovation and diversification and what are its consequences for income growth and distribution between producers and various kinds of intermediaries. Three, which are the principal directions of technological and stylistic change engendered in this process of heterogeneization? Four, how far and in what sense can the heterogeneous products be considered 'authentic,' or capable of encoding some hidden symbolic meaning or message (Jules-Rosette 1984; Silver 1979) regarding the producers' culture or identity – a meaning or message oriented to their new, external audience?

These four problems will be investigated on the example of a study of the highly diversified Dan Kwien pottery production. The study is based on anthropological fieldwork methods, and includes a survey of the local crafts market; open-ended interviews with producers, workshop owners, shop owners, and exporters of pottery; an examination of specimens and printed materials; and photographic documentation.

Background

In the shop of one of the oldest and biggest pottery workshops on the market of Dan Kwien hangs an oil painting picturing buffalo-drawn wooden carts *(kwien)* entering the village of Dan Kwien. In front of a local stall, there are several pieces of dark pottery that in form and appearance resemble the pots with a metallic sheen, available on the market, by which Dan Kwien pottery became known. The painting implies that the products offered in the local shops are the same as have been sold here in olden times, when the village still served as a resting-point for cart caravans plying the main road between the city of Korat and the Cambodian border. Indeed, the name of the locality reflects this ancient role. 'Dan Kwien' means literally 'Wagon [i.e., cart] Boundary' (Chuenprapanusorn 1988.49). The painting, however, is anachronistic. While the production of pottery is indeed an old preoccupation of the villagers, nothing of the kind produced nowadays for the 'external public' (namely, the Thai and foreign tourists and the urban and international markets) was available in the village when it was still a viable cart station. All of the products attracting the eye of the visitor are of recent origin. But the painting is the most express iconic attempt to endow these recently introduced products with the patina of tradition. This is complemented by the rather simplistic endeavor of local producers to 'antique' some of their wares, by smearing them with kaolin or some other grayish mixture.

In fact, during the period when buffalo-carts were still the principal means of transportation in the region, the pottery wares of Dan Kwien were adapted to the needs and demands of the local and regional markets. The principal products then were earthenware mortars *(krok)*, rice steaming vessels *(mo hun khao)*, marinated fish containers *(hái,*

Fig. 9.1), and water vessels *(ang nam)* of varying sizes ('Amaranth' 1990:32). These products were laden on buffalo-carts and bartered in the surrounding provinces for 'salt, rice and other daily necessities' (Tuntirattanakul 1987:58). Then, in the years preceding the Second World War, as conditions of transportation in the countryside improved, the villagers 'began to mass produce [earthenware] lamps and crude crockery for sale to different parts of the country' (Tuntirattanakul 1987:58). Dan Kwien products were also 'in use in most of the households in [the city of] Korat' ('Amaranth' 1990:32). However, these products remained throughout the period simple and cheap utilitarian objects, intended for daily use. Their appearance was plain, and their finish rough. They were decorated, if at all, only at the top with a simple pattern of tiny, parallel incised lines (Fig. 9.1).

With the introduction of industrially produced goods to Thailand, traditional crafts experienced a general decline (Resnick 1970:60). The construction of a new road through the region in the 1950s facilitated the penetration of industrially manufactured metal and plastic household goods into the area of Dan Kwien. As a consequence, local pottery production shrank significantly, but it was never completely discontinued (Tuntirattanakul 1987:58). Most of the simple products of the past, and particularly the mortars *(krok),* are even nowadays produced in considerable quantities, despite the recent proliferation of a variety of new pottery products. Indeed, local vehicles can be frequently observed stopping at the market, as peasants from remote villages, as well as modern urbanites, get off for a few minutes to purchase locally produced *krok* – a utensil still commonly used in contemporary households for the crushing of chili *(prik),* the principal condiment in the Thai cuisine.

However, the production of these traditional wares was gradually over-shadowed by the flourishing, large-scale production of a wide variety of new wares for the tourist and the export markets. It is important to comprehend the factors behind this turn of Dan Kwien pottery producers to the new products and markets.

Dan Kwien is not the only locality in Thailand where traditional skills and techniques of pottery production have been preserved. Pottery making has also been continuous in some other localities, notably in Muang Koong near the northern city of Chiang Mai (Sukphisit 1990a; Suvapiromchote 1987; Suwanachat 1990), and on Koh Kred, an island in the province of Nonthaburi, in the immediate vicinity of Bangkok (Pollard 1987; Windsor 1991). Both localities are closer to major touristic outlets than Dan Kwien, but have not achieved

Figure 9.1 A Traditional Marinated Fish Container (*hái*), Decorated by Parallel Incised Lines (photo by author).

the latter's prominence on the tourist market. Moreover, Dan Kwien clay is harsh and not very pliable, and hence lends itself less to fine shaping than that of some other localities. True enough, Dan Kwien pottery products, when fired at high temperatures 'reveal a dark brown hue with a lustral texture as if they were glazed' (Tuntirattanakul 1987:58). Indeed, the older style of Dan Kwien pottery features a metallic sheen, unique in Thai earthenware production. However, the attractive appearance of Dan Kwien products, though important, is in itself not a sufficient explanation for their prominence and popularity. There is no information to confirm that the lustral texture of Dan Kwien products has a greater intrinsic attraction for modern tastes than the fine decorations on 'traditional' Koh Kred pottery. Moreover, Dan Kwien clay appears not to be as unique as it is sometimes represented, and clays of other localities could be endowed with a similar lustre if

189

appropriately treated. Finally, as discussed below, only part of contemporary Dan Kwien pottery is produced in that distinctive style. It is therefore important to look for specific factors that have facilitated the transition of Dan Kwien pottery from a local craft with touristic potential, to a flourishing tourist art of considerable prominence on the Thai tourism market. As in the case of the commercialization of hill tribe textiles (Ch.2), the realization of that potential was also facilitated by some wider regional and historical circumstances. Significantly, the initiative for the revival did not come from among the pottery producing villagers themselves, but from outsiders. According to Tuntirattanakul,

> The year 1956 marks the beginning of a new era of Dan Kwien potteries when Mr. Vatanyoo Na Thalang, then president of the province's technical college, began to pay great attention to the unique quality of Ban Dan Kwien's soil and the potential of creating diversions [i.e., diverse products] from it. On his initiative, other teachers of the institution came to see what creative work they could produce out of the iron oxide-rich soil. Attempts to make floor tiles and stools from Ban Dan Kwien soil for the newly established institution succeeded, bringing Dan Kwien potteries once more in the lime-light (1987:58),

Vatanyoo's early efforts were still directed to find ways to apply local pottery production to new utilitarian purposes. A further development took place in the early 1970s when

> . . . a son of Dan Kwien Village, Viroj Srisuro, graduated from the Faculty of Architecture, Chulalongkorn University [the major university in Bangkok] . . . . He went back to Dan Kwien and started the process of reviving the age-old tradition of earthenware making . . . while designing and supervising the construction of the temple hall of Wat Sala Loy [in the city of Korat] . . . . The temple hall emerged as a singular symbol of the locality. Clay tiles were used extensively, decorating the walls, the corridors, the paths and the roof ('Amaranth' 1990:30–32).

Viroj Srisuro, who in due course became a teacher *(acharn)* of ceramics at the Technical College in Korat, eventually opened his own pottery workshop in what is presently the Dan Kwien crafts market. He also established a cart museum adjoining his shop, where buffalo carts from different parts of the country are displayed, thus commemorating and symbolizing the historical role of the locality.

During the early 1970s, at the time of the return of Acharn Viroj to Dan Kwien, some important political and cultural developments took place on the national scene. In 1973, a popular revolution toppled the dictatorship of the 'Three Tyrants' and a period of 'open politics,' which lasted until the military putsch of 1976, was ushered in (Morell and Samudavanija 1981). Preceding, and especially following, the 1973 revolution, there was a marked turn to the left among Thai students and among some intellectuals (Wedel and Wedel 1987); this was accompanied by an awakening of interest and concern with rural life and Thai folk culture. While the center of these developments was in Bangkok, they had repercussions on the periphery, including the city of Korat. These repercussions, in turn, had some unexpected consequences for pottery production in Dan Kwien. In 1974, three of Acharn Vatanyoo's left-leaning students moved into the area of Dan Kwien; they were attracted by village life and by the local pottery lore. Together with Acharn Viroj and another teacher from the Technical College, Acharn Pit, this group formed the nucleus of the local crafts market, which grew and developed during the subsequent years. Other teachers and students of the College also showed interest in the Dan Kwien pottery production, although they did not move into the area.

The right-wing military putsch of 1976 was succeeded by a period of suppression and persecution of left-wing students, artists, and intellectuals. While many of them fled to the mountains to join communist insurgents (Morell and Samudavanija 1981:292ff), others escaped into remote areas, until they could safely return to their usual place of residence. Owing to the left-wing leanings of some local leaders, persecuted students from the region, as well as members of two popular musical bands, found temporary refuge in the area of Dan Kwien. Mutual awareness and ties between villagers and young urbanites were further strengthened. Afterwards, young artists from the city would periodically open shop on the crafts market, while others were employed by owners of workshops in special projects, such as the preparation of earthenware relief pictures. In the early 1990s, several young artists worked in the crafts market on such projects.

The outsiders who came to live and work in Dan Kwien initiated a gradual transformation in the style and type of Dan Kwien products, but not in the production techniques, which remained virtually unchanged. It is significant, however, that the newcomers did not seek to switch local production immediately to the tourist market. At the outset, attempts were made merely to produce new utilitarian wares, such as floor tiles and stools (*Saen Sanuk* 1988a: 22). These products were oriented to a regional and national non-touristic public, though wider than the one to which the products of earlier times had been oriented. Soon, however, the range was further extended to include a variety of novel products, which were increasingly oriented to the touristic public, both Thai and foreign, and to the export market. The scope of production expanded and so did the number of workshops in the villages of the *tambon* of Dan Kwien. The area on both banks of the road in which the teachers from Korat and their students have originally established their workshops was turned into a crafts market – with the owners of the workshops opening shops facing the road, in which their wares were displayed (cf.Ch.8). The market expanded significantly once the road passing through it was improved and broadened, enabling tourist buses and other vehicles to park in front of the shops.

Production and marketing

Two structural levels have to be distinguished in the study of the production and marketing of pottery in the *tambon* (sub-district) of Dan Kwien: the villages and the crafts market. While this study has focused primarily on the market, some general information on the villages was also collected.

The Villages: in the early 1990s *tambon* of Dan Kwien consists of eight villages and encompassed about 1,200 households. In comparison to the region of Isan as a whole, the *tambon* was relatively prosperous. In addition to agricultural pursuits, primarily rice-growing, the inhabitants derived a significant part of their income from employment in industry and construction outside the villages, and from pottery production.

Pottery was produced in six of the eight villages in the *tambon,* as well as on the crafts market itself. There were about 100 workshops and about the same number of kilns in the *tambon.* A few hundred inhabitants were engaged, full-time or seasonally, in the various stages of production and sale of pottery in the villages and on the market.

Village workshops were generally small production units, based on the members of a household and a few employees, often relatives. These engaged primarily in the early stages of the pottery production process: clay preparation, potting and firing of the objects (Fig. 9.2). However, they did not usually complete the finishing stages, such as the painting, glazing, gilding, or 'antiquing' of the products.

The Market: The Dan Kwien crafts market flanks the main road linking the city of Korat with the urban centers of southern Isan and the

Figure 9.2 A Village Potter Making a Roped Jar (photo by author).

Cambodian border. It is located between the areas of two of the villages in the *tambon,* but constitutes a geographically and ecologically separate unit.

The market consists of two rows of mostly wooden buildings, shacks, and stalls facing the road on both banks (Fig. 9.3). Some newer shops were constructed of hard materials. The composition of the market in 1991 and 1992 is represented in Table 9.1.

In contrast to the villages, there were only four workshops in the market, each related to a shop. However, these were major enterprises each employing up to 100 employees who engaged in a variety of production, finishing, and packing tasks. The employees came mostly from the surrounding Dan Kwien villages. Some of the smaller shop and stall owners on the market owned their own workshops in the villages, or belonged to families of village producers. Others merely sold products purchased from village producers, often after adding some finishing, such as painting or 'antiquing,' in the shop itself. Owners of the big workshops on the market usually ordered additional wares from village producers as well. Shops generally carried large potteries of a wide variety of types, as well as diverse wares brought from outside the Dan Kwien area. Stalls mostly carried earthenware jewelry, a specialty of Dan Kwien (Chuenprapanusorn 1988:46–47, 49; 'Amaranth' 1990:30).

In the summer of 1991, there were about 35 establishments of various types, ranging from small stalls to large shops, on the crafts market; their number grew to 44 early in the following year. The growth of about 25% in the number of establishments within about

	Location		
Type of Establishment	*South Bank*	*North Bank*	*Total*
1991			
Workshop	–	*1	1
Shop and Workshop	2	1	3
Shop	14	10	24
Stall	7	–	7
Total	23	12	35
1992			
Workshop	–	*1	1
Shop and Workshop	2	1	3
Shop	**18	11	29
Stall	10	1	11
Total	30	14	44

Table 9.1 Composition of the Dan Kwien Crafts Market (1991–1992)

*Shop on the south bank.
**In addition, nine newly constructed shops were as yet unoccupied at time of fieldwork in early 1992

half a year indicates that the market was rapidly expanding. A new shop-house with ten shops, built from hard materials, was constructed – the first of the kind on the market. The market continued to expand rapidly in the following years. Owing to this rapid expansion, land prices on the market and nearby areas facing the road have sky-rocketed. This, in turn, has helped the expansion of some of the bigger businesses on the market, enabling them to use the land as collateral for bank loans.

The expansion of the market was also accompanied by a further diversification of wares offered in its shops. While the great majority were locally produced potteries, some products were imported from other craft-producing localities in Thailand and even from abroad. In 1991, some such products were already found in a few shops on the market. By 1992, the quantity and variety of products originating outside the locality increased considerably. Ceramics from Vietnam brought into Thailand via the nearby Cambodian border, competed well with local pottery products, owing to their low price and relatively good craftsmanship.

Various Thai crafts, primarily from the region around the northern city of Chiang Mai, added variety to the market. Earthenware and

Figure 9.3 General View of the Dan Kwien Crafts Market (photo by author).

ceramic products, differing in function and styles from the local ones, were brought in from several places, and especially from the village of Muang Koong and the city of Lampang. Some of the popular rice-paper umbrellas from Bo Sang (Herring 1985; *Kinnaree* 1991; Ressler 1981) and wooden figures from Ban Thawai (Ch.10, *Exports from Thailand* 1990), were also available on the crafts market. Some of these products have been acquired by direct barter for Dan Kwien pottery wares. There was also some cheap basketware from Cambodia and small quantities of various other crafts, stemming from diverse Thai localities. The rapid multiplication of wares deriving from other places is a further indication of the robust development of the Dan Kwien crafts market during this relatively brief period of research.

The technology of pottery production was essentially the same in both the small workshops in the villages and in the larger enterprises on the market. The most important trait of the production process is its relative technical simplicity.[2] It is a work-intensive process, based on traditional skills, usually transmitted from the older to the younger generation within the family. In the early 1990s, however, pottery lessons were introduced in the village school. Children were taught the basics of the craft one day a week by craftsmen from the village workshops.

The claim that the Dan Kwien wares were handmade and produced according to 'age-old traditions of earthenware making' ('Amaranth' 1990:32) is, thus, not without foundation. In fact, there was very little machinery employed in the production process. The raw clay, brought by pickup trucks from the banks of the nearby river Moon, was mostly trodden by foot to make it pliable. Only three or four of the bigger producers used pug-mills for the preparation of the clay. All the other production stages were purely manual. In contrast to some other, more factory-like enterprises for pottery production located in the central plains, such as those on Koh Kred near Bangkok, which 'use[d] . . . wheels driven by a drive shaft from a gasoline engine' (Cannon 1982:33), in Dan Kwien, the potters' wheels were manually operated even in the biggest workshops (Fig. 9.2). Even tiles, which were in some establishments made in the hundreds of thousands, were handmade in molds, in some cases by tens of workers. Indeed, the fact that they were handmade was their trademark; it made them attractive to prospective buyers, even though their appearance, except for some variation in coloration, is completely standardized. Only one big producer in the market used a press for tiles, and even this was manually operated. The kilns, too, were simple brick and adobe structures, without any modern control or regulating devices. According to one foreign expert, the low quality of the kilns and the absence of adequate heat-monitoring devices caused a high rate of cracks and imperfections that often reached up to 70 percent of the output. For that reason, it was also extremely difficult to achieve the standardized color and quality demanded of export wares.

The labor-intensive production of local pottery has been facilitated by the low labor costs. Ordinary workers earned between 70–100 baht (approximately US$3.00–4.00 at the 1991 rate of exchange) a day, irrespective of whether they were paid by piece-work or received a fixed monthly salary. Master potters, being paid by the level of their skills, earned up to three times more than ordinary workers. However, upward pressure on wages was exercised by increasing alternative employment opportunities in the region, particularly in a new, nearby industrial estate.

Whereas local entrepreneurs in the early 1990s invested little in the mechanization of the production process, which remained highly labor-intensive, some made an effort to modernize their distribution and marketing procedures. Profits have been invested in the acquisition of delivery vehicles, such as pickups; the most enterprising local workshop owner used a fax machine to communicate with his clients. Indeed, it appears that local entrepreneurs were primarily concerned with expanding the market for products, rather than with the improvement of the techniques of production. Production, especially for export, was inhibited by their inability to efficiently produce large quantities of high-quality standardized wares. This limitation stands out when Dan Kwien is compared with another of the craft-villages in my study, Ban Thawai, near Chiang Mai in northern Thailand (Ch.10). That village became the hub of an extensive network of production of wooden carvings, such as Buddhist images, human and animal figures, picture frames, and a variety of other ornamental products, embracing several villages in the Chiang Mai area. Despite serious limitations on the availability of the basic raw material, wood (Charasdamrong 1991a), production of objects for export took on huge proportions in Ban Thawai. Three packing and transporting companies operated in the vicinity of the village in the early 1990s, sending its products directly abroad. Such enterprises failed to develop in Dan Kwien, whose limited exports were heavily dependent upon brokers in Bangkok. Only two of the local producers dealt directly with foreign importers, and only one of them packed and dispatched his products in containers directly from his workshop on the market.

The constraints on export expansion from Dan Kwien, due to the technical limitations of local pottery production, are well illustrated by the failure of an attempt by a foreigner, married to a Thai woman, to establish an export firm in Dan Kwien. Although he succeeded in getting several big orders from abroad, he was unable to fill them, owing to the inability of local producers to supply the wares according to specifications in the required quantities.

There was thus a paradox involved in the production of Dan Kwien pottery: Its distinguishing marks are its handmade character and its production by traditional methods. But these very marks inhibit a significant expansion into exports, since local products are not amenable to standardization and do not correspond to the quality specifications of foreign importers.

The Market and the Villages

Dan Kwien was generally perceived as an entity comprising the villages of the *tambon* and the craft market in their midst. However, there existed significant structural differences and covert tensions between the owners of the establishments on the market and the pottery producers in the villages.

The market was founded by outsiders to the Dan Kwien area and is dominated by them. All the major enterprises on the market, except that owned by Viroj, have been established and are presently owned by outsiders. Even Acharn Viroj, who stems from the area, was absent for

197

a considerable period of time before he returned to the area to start his pottery workshop. Several other shopowners were also outsiders. Some were Chinese who have established general merchandise stores in the market and later added some crafts, others were artists interested in pottery production, and still others married into one of the villages and later established a shop on the market. The locals themselves were latecomers to the market; they primarily own the stalls and smaller shops. Several of them sell the products of their families' potteries, located in the villages.

The pottery producers in the villages were dominated by the market entrepreneurs, particularly by the bigger, outsider-owned enterprises. The outsiders were those who have introduced new styles and types of objects into the village production. The local potters have successfully made the new products by copying them from samples, drawings, or photographs, but have themselves rarely initiated innovations. Most of the local potters were also limited to the first stages of the production process (the making and firing of the products). These are then sold, mostly to the market entrepreneurs, who paint, gild or 'antique' some of them. These finishing stages in the production of Dan Kwien wares add considerable value to them, the profits of which accrue to the entrepreneurs on the market rather than to the villagers.

The market was the principal outlet for the products of the village pottery makers. Shopowners at the market resold village products at considerable profit, usually about 100 percent or more on wares that have not undergone any finishing, and several times more if some finishing had been done in the workshop or shop at the market. The market owners were, therefore, keen to preserve the finishing and marketing stages in their own hands, and to prevent customers from acquiring products directly in the villages. They generally talked deprecatingly of the village potters, claiming that they can only copy but not innovate designs and products, and that they were unable to paint or otherwise finish their wares.

Such attitudes obviously reflect the interests of the shopowners. However, some village potters eventually became aware of the profitability inherent in the finishing and marketing of their products. A few began to paint their wares by themselves. Some customers, particularly shopowners from Bangkok, who purchased pottery wares in small quantities, also discovered the price differentials between the market and the villages, and started to purchase their wares directly from the village producers. However, such shortcuts in the marketing process were as yet of limited proportions. Big customers still found it more convenient to deal with the entrepreneurs on the market, who offer a wider selection of products than the village potters.

In an apparent effort to enable village producers to sell their wares directly – and not through the market – the authorities embarked on the construction of an 'Art Center' (*sun silpakorn*) in an area adjoining the principal cluster of Dan Kwien villages: the project was carried out within the wider 'Green Isan' (*Isan kiao*) program of the Royal Thai Army (Johnson 1988, Manibhandu 1988), supported by a 20 million baht (US$800,000 at the time) grant from the Thai government. Opened in 1993 it was intended to house, among others, local artisans who would be able to offer their products directly to visiting tourists. However, the project failed to attract either artisans nor tourists, and remained inactive, like most other such centers in crafts village (cf.Ch.10). It is presently under reconstruction with an even heftier budget.

The Products

The visitor at his/her first arrival at the Dan Kwien crafts market is impressed by the wide variety of products in manifold styles, which initially seem to defy classification. There is a huge selection of different types and sizes of decorative jars, vessels, vases and lamps, human and animal figures, garden equipment and ornaments, earthenware jewelry, as well as pots, tiles and other utilitarian objects. In addition to these locally produced wares, there is also a choice of products from other places, the variety and quantity of which grew rapidly in the 1990s.

This superficial impression of great variety, however, tells only part of the story. The eye of the visitor captures only the choice of wares actually offered at the moment of his or her visit. The variety of products that are, or could be, produced in Dan Kwien is in fact much greater. One of the major producers on the market, for instance, kept a file of about 1,000 pottery designs that he could produce on request either in his workshop, or order from village potters. Other entrepreneurs on the market, as well as village producers, also possessed many designs that could be produced on request. Moreover, the potential variety of Dan Kwien products is virtually unlimited. Local potters would produce anything within the constraints of their skills and the pliability of the clay they use, insofar as they have a customer for it. They can reproduce designs from any photo, catalog illustration, or postcard, as ordered by a shopowner or a customer. A woman who only recently learned to produce earthenware jewelry in her small shop on the market, picked some of her designs from the *Ceramics Monthly*. A potter made rough copies of Greek amphoras from a photo taken from a catalogue of an American museum. Young artists sculpted a huge relief of a Buddhist religious scene, ordered by a temple, by enlarging a postcard picture. Neither the theme, nor the style or cultural origins of the model constituted an obstacle to the copying skills of Dan Kwien potters.

The manifoldness of Dan Kwien pottery products presents serious difficulties to any attempt at their systematic classification. Rather than present a formal typology of the products on the lines proposed by Graburn (1976b) or Shiloah and Cohen (1983:236–243), this study proposes several classifications, each of which illuminates the development and the variety of the local products from a different angle.

The growing popularity of Dan Kwien products on the broader national, as well as the tourism markets, has engendered a process of differentiation between two broad classes of local products: pottery wares and earthenware jewelry. These classes differ significantly in terms of their origins, production processes, symbolic qualities, and market appeal. Pottery wares, based on the traditional local potting techniques, are mostly voluminous and relatively heavy products, fired in big wood-burning kilns, which reach temperatures of well over 1000 C. They are produced almost exclusively by males. Earthenware jewelry is a new line of local production, which was introduced only a few years prior to my study. It is based on tiny components, which are then assembled into necklaces, earrings, bracelets, keyholders, and similar products. Most components are handrolled, sometimes from a different type of clay than the pottery wares. They are fired in small kilns, some of which are run on electricity, at temperatures of about only 500–600 C. Most of the work is done by women.

Although a novel line of products, it is the jewelry, sold on stalls in front of the shops, rather than the more voluminous pottery wares, that primarily attracts the occasional visitor's eye on the Dan Kwien crafts market. Jewelry products also feature the most expressly tourist-oriented symbols. Thus, in the early 1990s, the centerpieces on earthenware necklaces were often richly colored spoked wheels (symbolic of buffalo-carts) or images of traditional Dan Kwien pots, while small buffalo heads served as appendages of keyholders. Such obvious symbols appeared only rarely on the more substantial pottery products. The reason for this difference is probably the more narrowly 'touristic' character of the jewelry, which is relatively cheap, light, and easy to carry, and, as such, an ideal souvenir or gift to bring back from a visit to the Dan Kwien crafts market. It has, therefore, to be more eye-catching and symbolically more expressly 'marked' as a local product than the more multi-purpose pottery wares. Most of the latter, being big and heavy, are less suitable as souvenirs or gifts. They are sold on several other markets, on some of which (especially the export market) they do not have to be 'marked' specifically as Dan Kwien products, or linked to local history.

Turning now to the pottery wares proper, two developmental typologies can be formulated from contrasting perspectives: an 'emic' and an 'etic' one, the former reflecting the perceptions of the locals, the latter the theoretical categories of the analyst. From an 'emic' perspective, Dan Kwien potteries in the early 1990s fell into three concrete stylistic types, distinguished by color and texture.

The first type was 'Dan Kwien glaze' also known as 'metallic glaze' (Amaranth, 1990) or 'salt glaze' (Quain 1983). This style has made Dan Kwien pottery popular and is considered to be the distinctive mark of the local production. It served as the basis for the tourism image of Dan Kwien as promoted in the media. Products in this style are characterized by a deep-brown or blackish metallic sheen, derived from burning clay rich in iron oxide at high temperatures, and spraying it with salt. The products were usually not further elaborated. They were more expensive than the plain ones, owing to the greater complexity and cost of their production.

The texture of the 'Dan Kwien glaze' style was most closely related to that of the local products in the past. However, the degree of refinement of the texture depended upon the kind of wood used for firing the clay. Since wood for stoking the kilns has become ever scarcer and expensive, and the kinds of wood used in the past to obtain particular textures were no longer easily obtainable (Quain 1983), producers used whatever wood was available, including discarded planks from building sites. Some even burned old rubber tires together with the wood, in order to endow the products with a darker hue. Consequently, the texture of most contemporary products in this style was considered inferior to that of the past.

'Plain' was the second style. It was the simplest and least distinctive of the three stylistic types. The products are characterized by their natural terracotta coloration, derived from firing them, without additives, at relatively low temperatures. The products were usually cheap, often utilitarian wares, such as flower pots and other garden equipment. Some producers, however, further painted, gilded, or otherwise decorated these plain products, turning them into more ornamental and showy, rather than mere utilitarian, objects.

While it is not utterly clear when production in the plain style began in Dan Kwien, it is fairly certain that the style was introduced by the outsiders. It is an undistinctive and 'unmarked' style, ubiquitous not only in Thailand, but around the world. Indeed, the production and appearance of plain pottery wares resemble those of industrial products. Moreover, even when painted in different colors or otherwise finished, these products were not marked as distinctive of Dan Kwien, a fact that is also reflected in their simple designation as 'plain' (and not 'Dan Kwien plain'). It is significant that this type constituted the bulk of local products destined for export.

The third style was 'Dan Kwien antique.' It was a relatively recently developed style, whose emergence was motivated by the desire to endow contemporary products with a superficially antique appearance. This is achieved by the simple method, in Thailand unique to Dan Kwien, of covering the finished objects with kaolin and then rubbing most of it off, while leaving some traces behind. This process gives the objects the appearance of being recently excavated. However, the ruse was easily detectable even by the most superficial examination of the objects; nor did local producers or shopkeepers seek to deceive their customers into believing that these were real antiques. However, it may well be that some of the exported 'antiqued' products were sold abroad as genuine. At least one exporter to a Mediterranean country asserted that locally produced jars in Roman style (Fig. 9.2) are sold in that country as 'real' antiques.

From an 'etic' and more analytic perspective, Dan Kwien pottery products could be classified according to the relationship of their style to the local stylistic traditions, i.e., whether it was based on the style prevailing prior to the expansion of the market for Dan Kwien pottery (ortho-genesis) or whether it introduced new, extraneous elements (hetero-genesis). This is the theoretically most significant classification. It is closely related to the preceding analysis of the dynamics of penetration of the local products into new, external markets. Three principal etically defined stylistic types have been distinguished on the ortho-genesis-hetero-genesis dimension (Ch.3; Shiloah and Cohen 1983: 237).

The first, purely orthogenetic style, represents the continuous production of Dan Kwien wares, in the traditional style, whether in their customary forms or in slightly adapted ones. In contrast to many other craft producing centers in the world where the external markets

Figure 9.4 Variously Ornamented and Glaze-colored Jars, Adapted from Traditional Local Styles for External Markets (photo by author).

came to dominate production, several traditional Dan Kwien products were still made there, selling well to the local public. Therefore, the traditional line of production was not completely displaced by the production for the new, external public. However, some of these products were also adapted to the tourist market: miniaturized Dan Kwien mortars *(krok)* were available to tourists who may like their form, but had no use for the heavy normally-sized object.

The second style, ortho-heterogenetic, was a modification of traditional Dan Kwien products, either by change in form or by ornamentation or coloration, in order to adapt them to the needs and preferences of the new, external markets. This type of products is best illustrated by a variety of jars and vessels whose 'traditional' form has been modified to some extent to adapt them to new functional or decorative uses. They have also often been ornamented by a variety of novel designs or colors to make them more attractive to the external public (Fig. 9.4).

The third style, heterogenetic, represents the introduction of utterly innovative forms and designs, unrelated to local traditions, into local pottery production. In Dan Kwien the source of such heterogenetic products was varied in the extreme. There were copies of classic Cambodian reliefs, Greek and Egyptian vases, Roman jars, European figurines, human and animal forms, and a variety of figures from Thai, Buddhist, and Hindu mythology. There were also some original creations, mostly developed by the workshop owners on the market or

Figure 9.5 Spouting Fish (photo by author).

by artists visiting or living in the area. Some of the most popular objects, like spouting fishes (Fig. 9.5) and owls (Plate 10), have been locally developed on the basis of foreign models. In the course of adaptation, local symbolic elements were sometimes subtly introduced into such foreign designs. Thus, some of the owl designs incorporate a pair of spoked wheels, a metonym for the buffalo-cart *(kwien)*.

One of the most important lines of innovation in the transition from the orthogenetic to the heterogenetic stylistic type, was the introduction of representational motifs. The initial orthogenetic products were decorated, if at all, only with a minimal non-representational geometrical design (Fig. 9.1). While such designs later proliferated, and became much more complex, new, representational decorations were also introduced into pottery products. The designs, mainly flowers, leaves, and similar vegetal patterns, are incised into jars, vases, and vessels (Fig. 9.3). One of the most important heterogenetic innovations, however, was the introduction of figurative representations, at first of fishes and owls (Fig. 9.5 and Plate 10), and later of a variety of other animal, human, and mythological images (cf. Popelka and Littrell 1991). It should be noted that the latter are not merely new motifs or a new genre of pottery production. They are indicative of a new kind of production technique – a transition from potting to sculpting. Indeed, some of these objects, particularly of human images, are unique creations, and come closest, among Dan Kwien products, to what could be defined as artistic sculptures.

A similar process of transition from ornamental to figurative motifs has been observed in the case of Hmong refugee textile art (Ch 6 and 7). However, there is a crucial difference between the two developments. Hmong representational embroideries, which encoded a clear message, were a means of the tribal refugees, closed up in their camps, to communicate the world they lost and their present dire predicament to a global audience. Dan Kwien representational potteries and sculptures, varied as they are, do not encode any such message.

A general trend away from orthogenetic and towards heterogenetic forms, designs, and motifs has been observed in Dan Kwien. This trend was largely a consequence of the competition between producers desirous to attract new customers, combined with the prevalent tendency to copy the products of one another. In order to capture part of the market, producers sought to develop attractive new products. However, their 'monopolistic' power was limited in time, since others would soon copy any successful innovations. Enterprising producers hence had to invent additional novel products in order to renew their market advantage – until these products have again been copied by others. This cycle of innovation and copying, unbridled as it was by any cultural stylistic considerations or customary or legal norms, appears to account, at least in part, for the astounding variety of products on the Dan Kwien crafts market.

It may now be asked, what impact a possible expansion of the export market for Dan Kwien products could have on this variety, and on the prevailing rate of innovation. Export of craft products generally leads to standardization of quality, sizes and designs. One of the principal concomitants of such standardization is the emergence of brochures and catalogues in which the products are illustrated and their specifications detailed. The exporting enterprise consequently becomes known for a relatively permanent mix of standardized products as happened, for example, in the case of some of the bigger marketing agencies for hill-tribe products. In the early 1990s, however, Dan Kwien pottery had not yet taken such a turn to standardization, since it had not yet been dominated by export considerations.

Conclusions

Tourist arts, as commercialized folk arts, never remain identical for long with the baseline products from which their development had taken off. Owing to the imperatives of the market, representing the tastes, preferences, and demands of the novel, external publics to which the producers have to respond, at least partially, if their business is to remain viable, changes are introduced into the materials, sizes, forms, coloration, functions, and production techniques of tourist art products. There is hardly any tourist art anywhere that after commercialization remained viable as well as unchanged. However, tourist arts differ considerably with respect to the degree and kind of change that they have undergone in comparison with the baseline. Some are only slightly changed in one direction while others change considerably in many directions. As this chapter has demonstrated, the latter was indeed the case with Dan Kwien pottery. But Dan Kwien is not an isolated example, even in Thailand. Considerable heterogeneization has been observed in another of my ongoing case studies, that of the woodcarvings of Ban Thawai in the region of Chiang Mai (Ch.10). In two other case studies, that of the weavings of Ban Namon in the northern province of Phrae (Ch.11) and the basketry weaving village of the Pha Bong in Chiang Mai province (Ch.12), the degree of variety and variability was much less pronounced. The same is true for most hill tribe products for the tourist market, even though some tribes, especially the Hmong, developed completely new styles, while retaining older ones (Chs. 5 and 6).

Several questions can now be raised. For example, which are the wider economic, cultural, and social factors accounting for the differential degrees and rates of change and heterogeneization of the tourist arts of a given group of producers? Or, more specifically, since we are here dealing with a single case study, which factors can help to understand the remarkable heterogeneization that Dan Kwien pottery experienced?

The pottery production of Dan Kwien went through a process of 'complementary commercialization' (Cohen 1989:162). Production for a local audience, though diminishing, was still viable when the production for an external market was first initiated. This, however, was not a wholly internal, spontaneous process. Rather, it was mostly initiated by outsiders to the subdistrict *(tambon),* although not to the region. Indeed, the initiators themselves have settled in the area of the *tambon.* Here a crucial consideration comes into play. The alleged uniqueness and distinctiveness of Dan Kwien products was from the outset attributed principally to the materials (clay) and the production techniques of the local potters. In contradistinction (for example, to Ban Namon weavings (Ch.11), or most hill tribe products), the style of the baseline Dan Kwien pottery was not given much salience, whereas the dexterity of the potters was much emphasized. The materials and the processes of production, rather than some reputedly distinctive local style, were emphasized in the promotion of Dan Kwien pottery. Indeed, Dan Kwien pottery was, at the baseline and probably also in earlier times, a simple craft, without marked aesthetic pretensions. It was not a 'folk art' of the kind presently celebrated in art books featuring, for example, traditional northern Thai or hill tribe work.

The innovators who came from the outside to revitalize Dan Kwien pottery also did not initially think of it in terms of 'art,' in the sense of having its own stylistic values and aesthetic canons. Rather, they considered it a valuable local craft, that could be put to new uses. Hence, they were at first looking for a way to apply the skills of the local craftsmen to the production of novel, useful, and pleasing products. As the range of such products expanded beyond utilitarian pots and tiles into ornamental garden equipment and further on into tourist arts proper, appealing to an ever wider heterogenic audience, the products produced earlier did not simply disappear. This helps to explain the enormous range of products offered on the market: from those earliest ones originally intended for a rural public, through those destined for the Thai urban market, to those intended for local and foreign tourists, and eventually, for exports.

The enlargement of the range of products, however, was not merely a function of an expanding market, due to better communications and the growth of tourism. It was also a consequence of internal factors, chiefly the competition between local entrepreneurs. In an effort to achieve at least some monopolistic advantage over other local producers, entrepreneurs invented new products, styles, or finishing techniques. However, as these proved successful in the market, they were quickly copied by other producers, thus diminishing their originator's initial advantage. Such waves of innovation and dissemination were a mark of Dan Kwien for virtually the whole period since the local pottery production was revitalized.

The process of heterogeneization on the Dan Kwien's craft market did not stop with the proliferation of new locally produced potteries. It was further intensified by the growing proclivity of shopowners to carry crafts, including pottery and ceramics, originating in other localities in Thailand and even abroad (Cambodia and Vietnam). While in Dan Kwien this additional heterogeneization of the market was still secondary to that of the local products, it points to a processual pattern that was discerned in the development in other, more mature tourism markets in Thailand. Thus, the rapidly growing tourist shopping area of Bo Sang, the well-known northern Thai 'umbrella village,' features a wide variety of northern Thai craft products, besides the locally made *saa*-paper umbrellas, fans, butterflies, and paintings. Indeed, as new craft factories of various kinds located on the main Chiang Mai-Sankamphaeng Road on which Bo Sang is found (Ch.8), the share of *saa*-paper wares in the total tourist-oriented production of the Bo Sang area seems to have gradually declined. In Sankamphaeng itself, a town whose touristic reputation was originally based on the local silk weaving industry, the development of the tourist crafts market has reached an even more advanced stage. The local shops offer a great variety of diverse craft and industrial products, but the locally produced wares are becoming subsidiary to the products brought in from outside the town.

The crafts market of Dan Kwien is thus still at an early stage of the process of heterogeneization, which is much more advanced in some bigger and more popular craft markets. Heterogeneization itself appears in turn to increase the attractiveness of the market for tourists, and to help thereby in popularizing the local pottery products.

It is, nevertheless, doubtful whether the Dan Kwien market will ever reach such an advanced stage of heterogeneization by outside products as Bo Sang and Sankamphaeng. For one thing, Dan Kwien is not located within a major tourist area, whereas the other two markets are close to Chiang Mai, the center of the tourism industry of northern Thailand.

The new products and styles in Dan Kwien pottery have been almost exclusively introduced and developed by outsiders who came to the *tambon* from the surrounding region – mostly from the nearby regional city of Korat, and specifically, the technical college there. Only very few outside entrepreneurs or innovators came from localities outside the region of northeastern Thailand (Isan). For example, in contrast to the development of hill tribe crafts (Ch.3) for the tourist and export

DAN KWIEN POTTERY

market, foreigners or foreign organizations did not take any part in the development or innovation of local products for tourism or for exports.

On the basis of this discussion, it is now possible to answer the question regarding the considerable heterogeneization of Dan Kwien pottery. Four principal factors facilitating or encouraging this process can be distinguished. First is the absence of culturally sanctioned stylistic canons. In this context, Dan Kwien craftsmanship was appreciated, but more for its potential than its actual production at the baseline. Hence, it has been easy to introduce new products, forms, and styles. Second is the external initiative. The revitalization of Dan Kwien pottery was mostly initiated by outsiders who, though stemming from the region, were knowledgeable of styles of other cultures and periods, and who introduced the local potters to them. These outsiders were, in a sense, 'reverse culture brokers.' Third is the multiplication of markets. The fact that production for the local and regional Thai market continued, even as new touristic and export markets were opened up, led to the emergence of differentiated products directed to different market segments. Fourth is the quest for a greater share of the market. The fact that individual entrepreneurs sought to expand their share of the market, led to frequent innovations, which were rapidly copied by competitors. The most important of these four factors of heterogenization is probably that of external initiative and brokerage.

Owing to the fact that outsiders to the *tambon* of Dan Kwien introduced most of the new designs and styles of pottery production in the recent period, and that these designs and styles were taken from many cultures, unrelated to that of the locality, there arises the problem of the evaluation of the 'authenticity' of local production. In accordance with a general approach to the problem of authenticity (Cohen 1988a), 'authenticity' is not a theoretical concept by which the status of any craft object can be unequivocally or 'objectively' evaluated. Rather, the evaluation of the extent of 'authenticity' of an object, site or event, will depend upon the criteria by which authenticity is conceived. These may vary between different individuals depending on their knowledge, perspective, and depth of concern with, and desire for, 'authentic' experiences and products. No empirical study has as yet been made of visitors' and other purchasers' opinions of the 'authenticity' of Dan Kwien products. It is, nevertheless, possible, to differentiate two basically different approaches to the problem, a more 'conservative' and a more 'liberal' one. The 'conservative' would focus upon the degree of similarity between the baseline products and those produced at present, and thus judge the products less authentic, the more heterogenetic they became. The 'liberal' approach would not focus upon the product, but rather upon the process of its manufacture, and judge its authenticity primarily in terms of the extent to which the traditional skills and dexterity of local potters are expressed in the variety of their products, whether traditional or innovative. A middle position between these contrary approaches would be one that considers 'authenticity' as an 'emergent property' and concedes that some innovative products and styles may over time become 'authentic,' as they come to be part of the local tradition of craft production and an identity mark of the locality.

Since most of the novel products of Dan Kwien potters have been introduced from the outside, there is little point to ask whether any of them, individually, encode some 'hidden message' that would be the analyst's task to decipher. However, the question can be approached from a different angle. It is possible to argue that if Dan Kwien pottery does contain a 'hidden message,' it does not consist of some symbolic meaning, encoded in this or that product. Rather, the message appears to be encoded in the corpus of local production as a whole: namely, that even simple craftsmanship can be creatively applied in an astonishing variety of ways. It is indeed the skill to produce a great variety of products by basically the same simple techniques that endow the potters of Dan Kwien with their reputation and external identity in the wider society and on the tourist market.

Having thus achieved a wider renown, the question can be raised as to the craft's significance for the income and economic well-being of the Dan Kwien potters. Here it should be noted that it is not so much the potters, but the local shopkeepers and entrepreneurs who have reaped the principal benefits of the remarkable development of pottery production in Dan Kwien.

In the literature on tourist arts, there are many examples of a steep rise in the price of products as they move through the marketing channels from original producer to final consumer (Cohen 1992c). Most studies emphasize that the various middlemen and intermediaries who move the products along the marketing channels from the producers to the consumers make the bulk of the profits. In the present study, it was found that the price of the pottery products rose steeply even before they entered the marketing channels proper – namely within the *tambon* of Dan Kwien itself, as they moved from the village producer to the mostly outsider-owned shops in the local crafts market. A price increase of 100 percent or more was common even in products that did not undergo any finishing in the shops. If some finishing was done, the price may have increased by several times. The fact that in another locality under study, the wood-carving production centered on the village of Ban Thawai in northern Thailand, the price differentials between producer and local shops were similar, shows that the situation in Dan Kwien was not exceptional. Moreover, in both localities the principal value added was in finishing rather than in the manufacture of the raw product.

The steep increase in the price of local products, even before they entered the marketing channels proper, did not preclude further considerable increases as the products moved through the marketing channels themselves. The bulky, heavy, and easily breakable products are not easy to move, and particularly to export; packing and transport costs add considerably to marketing expenses, in addition to the markups at each link in the channel.

While shopowners on the market, rather than the village potters, were the principal local beneficiaries of the development of Dan Kwien pottery, some potters have realized that they need to learn to finish their products, and to achieve direct access to the market, in order to increase their share of the profits of the pottery business. By skipping the entrepreneurs on the local crafts market and selling their wares directly to outsiders, some of them have achieved this objective. Despite the failure of the 'Art Center,' villagers were thus gradually winning greater direct access to the market.

Postscript: Dan Kwien in the late 1990s

Production and marketing

In the course of the six years which passed since the original study on which this chapter is based was conducted, the Dan Kwien market underwent several significant changes, though not a complete transformation. Some of these reinforced the trends which were already noted in the original study; others point in new, and sometimes reverse directions. I have continued the study of Dan Kwien throughout the years 1993–1998, keeping in touch with developments and conducting periodic surveys of the market. In this update I shall present the principal changes which characterize this period.

The most conspicuous change is the considerable expansion of the market and its increased heterogeneity (Table 9.2).

In the course of five years, 1992–1997, the number of establishments on the market more than doubled, from 44 in 1992 (Table 9.1, lower

Type of Establishment	Location		Total
	South Bank	North Bank	
Workshop (including shop)	2	2	4
Shop (Dan Kwien products only)	28	7	35
Shop (Mainly Dan Kwien products)	16	3	19
Shop (Mainly outside products)	19	2	21
Stalls (Dan Kwien pottery only)	6	–	6
Total crafts establishments	71	14	85
Restaurants and eating places	5	2	7
Packaging materials	1	–	1
Total other establishments	6	2	8
Total	77	16	93

Table 9.2 Composition of the Dan Kwien Crafts Market, 1997.

section), to 93 in 1997. Perhaps more significant than the mere expansion in the number of establishments is their progressive heterogeneization: only about half of the establishments carried exclusively Dan Kwien wares, while more than 20% carried exclusively products from other localities: mainly pottery from elsewhere in Thailand and ceramics from Vietnam, but also textiles and a variety of souvenirs from other places; another 20 percent offered a mix of local and outside products. There was also a marked increase in the number of restaurants and eating places: in 1992 only one such establishment was found on the market; in 1997 there were seven.

In early 1998 a further significant expansion of the market took place: a local landowner has cleared a field at the back of the more developed south bank of the market and built close to forty stalls around an inner yard. At my last visit most of these have already been occupied or were in the process of occupation, mostly by local villagers selling Dan Kwien wares.

In terms of the geography of the market this is an important new development: while throughout the 1990s the market grew lengthwise, in a 'ribbon-pattern' along the Korat-Chokchai road (Ch. 8), this new complex breaks that pattern: like the emergence of the new markets in the woodcarving village of Ban Thawai (Ch. 10), it broadens, rather than extends the shopping area.

Despite the considerable growth of the Dan Kwien market and the concomitant expansion in the production of Dan Kwien pottery, no significant structural changes in the organization of the production

212

processes have taken place in the course of the 1990s. Acharn Viroj, who has returned to Dan Kwien in the 1970s to revive the local pottery production, took up a teaching position in another city, and closed his workshop on the market (though his family still maintains a shop). The three other large workshops expanded their production considerably, employing up to one hundred workers and office staff. New production machinery, such as grinders, clay mixers and slip-cast machines were purchased in the hope that they would facilitate and speed up production; new gas kilns were purchased to achieve a more efficient firing of the pots. One of the workshops modernized and computerized its office procedures and opened spacious show-rooms for its wares. This workshop also printed an attractive catalogue (as did another of the major workshops). However, despite these innovations, no significant restructuring of the production process has occurred – though its operations are now much bigger than they have been in the early 1990s, the methods of production and its organization did not change substantially: it remains a craft workshop, rather than becoming an industrial enterprise. Indeed, a Japanese visitor remarked in the course of his visit to the workshop, that its front has a modern appearance, but the back, the working area, reminded him of Japan two hundred years ago. Neither did the other two big workshops initiate a transition to a more industrial mode of operation. There may be various reasons for this persistance of habitual methods, but a significant one appears to be related to the background of the owners of all the workshops: it is in art rather than in technology. Lacking technological experience, they purchased expensive but inappropriate machinery, or failed to use it efficiently: machinery often remained idle, while old manual methods prevailed. In particular, manually rotated wheels are still used by the potters even in the biggest workshop; only in 1997 did some potters in Dan Kwien begin to introduce simple power-driven wheels. Dan Kwien thus lags behind some other, smaller and in other respects more tradition-bound pottery producing villages, such as Muang Koong in Chiang Mai province, or Tung Luang in Sukhothai province, where power-driven wheels have been already introduced several years ago.

Similarly, the bulk of the pottery produced in the big workshops is still fired in wood-burning kilns, while the use of gas-burning ones was up to recently only at an experimental stage. Breakage in wood-burning kilns continued to be high, and many pots have still to be manually repaired prior to painting.

In the course of the 1990s occurred a marked shift in local pottery products. There was a considerable decline in the production of pottery

Figure 9.6 Garden Furniture in Light Colors (1996).

in 'Dan Kwien glaze', the blackish sheen which was the hall-mark of the local style at the outset of commercialization. The decline was caused by several factors: the considerable growth of exports further reduced the importance of 'markedness', of Dan Kwien products, as they came to be seen as relatively cheap garden furniture for suburban homes. Among the domestic as well as foreign public, the dominant trend throughout the decade was towards painted pottery in increasingly lighter, conspicuous and sometimes contrasting colors (Fig. 9.6); black is not a popular color. Finally, the production of the blackish glaze by the habitual methods is more difficult and costly than the production of ordinary pottery, and involves a higher percentage of breakage.

214

However, one of the major local producers has nevertheless attempted in the late 1990s to revive the style, albeit by an innovative production process. The blackish glaze was commonly achieved by the use of the 'reduced oxygen' method of firing pots, made of local clay, in wood-burning kilns. The alternative method, evolved after some experimentation, is based on the use of a mixture of local clay with clay from another locality, fired in a gas-burning kiln. The pottery produced by this new method closely resembles the original Dan Kwien glaze ware (compare Fig. 9.7 to Plate 10), while breakage is minimal. If proven economically viable, this line of production will constitute a unique case of reproduction, by modern technologies of a 'traditional' local pottery style – a mild form of 'staged authenticity' in MacCannel's (1973) sense.

In the course of the 1990s, Dan Kwien products achieved a wide national and international reputation. A yearly Dan Kwien pottery exposition and sale was held in the luxurious River City Shopping Complex from 1993 onwards (Amatyakul 1996). Dan Kwien pottery was described in touristic publications (e.g. Fang 1995) and in the promotional literature on northeastern Thailand. Dan Kwien products were found in tourist shopping areas and on local markets throughout the country. Nevertheless, the fastest expanding domestic market for Dan Kwien products were the new Thai urban and suburban middle classes, rather than foreign tourists. With growing prosperity and suburban expansion, prior to the financial crisis of 1997, Thais purchased considerable quantities of decorative pots and garden furniture, whether as tourists passing through the Dan Kwien market, or from outlets in urban shops and markets.

However, the most significant development in the marketing of Dan Kwien pottery in the course of the 1990s, was the consolidation of exports: the two big producers, who started to export in the early 1990s, succeeded to expand significantly their export activities, despite the constraints of low quality and absence of standardization of products mentioned above. By the mid-1990s exports became the principal market for Dan Kwien pottery, with importers, chain-stores and department stores in Europe, North America and Australia ordering large quantities of wares, some produced according to specifications and models supplied by the foreign firms. At the peak, one of the big producers was exporting up to two large containers of pottery a month. In an effort further to promote his exports, this producer spent a considerable sum of money for a booth at a major international garden furniture exposition in Europe, though with little success. In fact, the

Figure 9.7 Pottery in Blackish 'Dan Kwien Glaze', Reproduced by Novel Method (1997).

scope of orders from abroad has begun to decline substantially by the late 1990s as cheap pottery from China, Vietnam and Indonesia flooded the world market; major foreign firms shifted their orders to producers in those countries, where they were offered more favorable conditions than the Dan Kwien producers were willing to offer. Dan Kwien, like other crafts villages (Ch.12), is currently experiencing a 'handicrafts squeeze'.

The process of heterogeneization

With the expansion of the market for Dan Kwien pottery during the economic boom in Thailand in the mid-1990s, the rate of innovation of products, styles and ornamentation, which has been rapid in the early 1990s slowed down somewhat. The principal innovations consisted of new kinds of garden furniture, such as fountains (Plate 11), which sold well to the burgeoning Thai middle class. The principal emphasis was given to the mass production of standardized wares, rather than of innovative products or unique creations. Especially noticeable was the virtual disappearance of eathenware figurative sculptures, which were one of the major innovations of the early stages of commercialization of Dan Kwien pottery.

In the course of the 1990s, the potters in the villages surrounding the market gradually acquired the skills of finishing and painting their own products: middlemen and shop-keepers from various localities in Thailand increasingly placed their orders directly with the villagers,

216

thus skipping the intermediaries of the Dan Kwien market, even as more and more locals from the villages acquired booths on the expanding market.

While the rate of innovation in earthenware products declined, the process of heterogeneization took a new turn, largely unrelated to the local crafts traditions: the production of so-called 'sandstone' reliefs and statuary (Fig. 9.8). Earthenware reliefs, assembled of separately fired tiles, have been made in Dan Kwien for some years, mostly on orders from Buddhist temples or public institutions. But 'sandstone' sculpture production was a new technique: resembling antique sandstone statuary, the new 'sandsone' objects made in Dan Kwien, are in fact not at all sculpted from stone; rather they are concrete castings made from a mixture of cement and sand. The owner of the biggest workshop on the market, initiated their production and hired several Thai artists to draw the designs of the reliefs.

Since Dan Kwien is located on the tourist route to major Khmer archeological sites in northeastern Thailand, the motifs for the sandstone sculptures were initially taken from Khmer classic art and mythology. Later on Thai, Hindu and even antique Greek and Roman mythological motifs were added; recently motifs from 'traditional' Thai rural life (Fig. 9.8) and folklore were introduced, some of them resembling the reliefs carved on northern Thai teak furniture. The reliefs and statuary are purchased primarily by upper-middle and upper class Thais; some are even exported, despite their considerable weight.

Though a single entrepreneur presently produces the bulk of sandstone reliefs and statuary, some local pottery producers already started to follow his lead and began to cast smaller 'sandstone' objects. The tendency to copy any successful innovation, common in Dan Kwien pottery production for a long time, is thus already emerging in this new field – though it is doubtful whether many local producers will be able to enter it, since it demands considerable investments.

Conclusion: The Dynamics of Change in Dan Kwien in the Course of the 1990s

In the course of the 1990s, the Dan Kwien market underwent considerable additional heterogeneization; however, this came about mainly through the increased introduction of products from other localities, rather than from the further heterogeneization of local products. The market gained popularity with mainly domestic tourists, who were the principal customers of the local retail business; however,

Figure 9.8 'Sandstone' Relief of Stylized Northeastern *kaen* Players (1997).

production became increasingly oriented to the wholesale, and especially to export markets. These markets cater to a highly mixed clientele, only a part of which can be defined as 'touristic'; as local producers increasingly concentrated on the production of garden furniture, their principal clients became members of the growing Thai urban and suburban middle-class and their counterparts in countries importing Dan Kwien products. The recently emerging 'sandstone' sculptures served a similar purpose in the homes and compounds of upper class Thais. The growing specialization, in response to an expanding market, in the production of 'garden furniture' reduced the rate of innovation, and hence of heterogeneization of local pottery production. With the growing emphasis on large objects, the economic importance of smaller and cheaper wares, such as earthenware jewelry, declined. This decline, in turn, reduced the choice of locally produced pottery for visiting tourists, and particularly for those coming from abroad, who are constrained by considerations of bulk and weight from purchasing larger objects.

Dan Kwien pottery production thus went through a circle in the last quarter of a century: from the initial production of functional pottery for a limited local public, through a brief period of production of everyday functional objects for a wider audience, and a longer period of production of 'marked' decorative objects mainly for a domestic and foreign tourist public, to a growing emphasis on the production of a new class of functional objects, garden furniture, for a non-touristic domestic and, through exports, foreign clientele. In the process, the 'markedness' of Dan Kwien pottery declined in importance, as the producers responded to the tastes and preferences of increasingly more remote customers, who are little concerned about the origin or 'authenticity' of the objects which they purchase. Though it is necessary for the objects to be decorative to attract the buyers, their decorations have been adapted to appeal to an ever more remote customer public, while moving away from the earlier style of Dan Kwien pottery, which endowed the place with its reputation. In the light of this principal trend of change, the recent reproduction by new methods of pottery in the blackish 'Dan Kwien glaze' can be seen as a nostalgic return to an 'original tradition' even though, as we have seen above, this 'tradition' was itself invented only a few decades ago.

Dan Kwien is undergoing a process of disassociation between the various stages of production and marketing, resembling that found in Ban Thawai (Ch. 10). While local clay was considered the main factor endowing Dan Kwien pottery with its distinct character, clay from other localities is increasingly mixed with the local clay, to increase its pliability. In sandstone production, the raw materials are wholly extraneous to the locality. The gradual introduction of machinery and new types of kilns, while improving production methods, will eventually disassociate them from the inherited local techniques. The heterogeneization of the market by outside products disassociates it partly from local production; and the market demand for 'unmarked' decorative and functional objects, disassociates local products from earlier styles identified with the locality. Like Ban Thawai carvings, Dan Kwien pottery, and even more its 'sandstone' sculpture, could well be produced anywhere – the pottery is losing its intrinsic links with the locality; it is becoming 'de-placed'.

To an outsider, the future of Dan Kwien pottery production looks rather bleak. The financial crisis of 1997, combined with growing competition in the export market, hit Dan Kwien hard. In early 1998 production of pottery stopped nearly completely, as Thai customers abruptly ceased purchasing non-essential goods, even as orders from abroad contracted significantly, owing to the 'handicraft squeeze'. Dan Kwien market was at a standstill. The locals, however, apparently entertained a rosier picture of the future – the fact that all the newly built booths were soon rented out to local shop-keepers, indicates that the locals perceived the crisis as only a temporary setback, which will not affect the growth of the market and the prosperity of Dan Kwien in the long run. The considerable decline in the rate of the Thai currency, which lost about 60 per cent of its value could indeed help to revive exports, as Thai products become cheaper in dollar terms. The domestic market, however, on which the great majority of shop-keepers in Dan Kwien depend, may still take a considerable time to recover.

Notes

1 This chapter reports the findings of a longitudinal study of the commercialization of Dan Kwien pottery, conducted intermittently in the years 1991–1998, within the framework of a broader study of commercialization of Thai folk arts. The initial stage of the study was supported by a grant from the Horowitz Institute for Research on Developing Countries at Tel Aviv Univeristy. The later stage, from 1994 onwards, was supported by a grant of the Netherlands-Israel Research Program. The support of these institutions is hereby gratefully acknowledged. Thanks are also due to Ed McGrath for his kind assistance during fieldwork in Dan Kwien.

2 The production process, as described in some technical detail by Quain (1983), remained virtually unchanged in the early 1990s:

Reddish brown clay, rich in iron oxide, is collected from the banks of the Moon River, and after washing and sieving, is mixed with sand from the same river; 3 parts clay – 1 part sand.

The wheels on which the pots are thrown are made simply from a disc sawn from a log of teakwood, which spins freely on a pivot of hardwood which is tuck into the ground. The wheel itself is only 2 or 3 inches above ground level. Six of these wheels are placed in a row. The potter, sitting on the ground, with an assistant turning the wheel by hand, starts throwing on the first wheel: the clay at this stage, is very soft. He then starts throwing on the next wheel, and so on, returning to the first wheel when the clay is firm enough to proceed further.

When the throwing is completed the pots are stored in a large shed until leather hard and ready for decoration . . .

The circular shaped kilns are about 16 ft. in diameter by 6 ft. high, (internal size), with fire-hole and chimney at opposite sides. A wall is built from fire-hole to flue, supporting the roof and dividing the kiln in two parts. A raised shelf is built inside the kiln and the pots are placed on this shelf for firing. The fire area itself is about 6 ft. square.

The firing takes about five days, in separate phases as follows. The first phase takes about 40 hours using large pieces of firewood; then medium sized firewood is fed to the fire for 8 hours; then 12 hours using still smaller firewood to raise the temperature to the maximum which is very critical. Overfiring will cause severe bloating, while underfiring will fail to produce the dark 'saltglaze' look which makes the pots so attractive. The fire-hole is then closed, leaving only a small opening, and reduced firing still goes on for about three days. The fire-hole is then re-opened to allow cooling, and the pots removed. (Quain, 1983:10)

10

FROM BUDDHA IMAGES TO MICKEY MOUSE FIGURES

The Transformation of Ban Thawai Carvings [1]

The village of Ban Thawai is a major center for carvings and other craft products in northern Thailand. In this Chapter I present and analyze the dynamics of change in the production and marketing of crafts in the village as a process of continuous disassociation between components which at an earlier stage tended to be closely associated. I will argue that this process is a consequence of the growing integration of the village into wider regional, national and international frameworks. While this integration helped the expansion and diversification of craft production and marketing in the village, some contemporary developments may transform the character of the village.

The Model

In order to create a point of reference, in relation to which the process of disassociation could be described, I propose a somewhat schematic model of craft production in rural areas of the Third World – including Thailand – in the period preceding commercialization. The model comprises six principal components:

(1) *Materials*; the materials for craft production are typically locally available; they may be either collected, or grown, by the artisans themselves, or bartered or bought on local or regional markets.

(2) *Knowledge, skills and technologies*; craft production is typically based on informally acquired and transmitted native knowledge, skills and technologies, passed within the household, or from master artisans to apprentices. Though knowledge, skills and technologies are not necessarily locally invented, but may have been borrowed from other localities or cultural groups, they are typically well-integrated into local tradition.

(3) *Designs and decorations*; the designs of objects and their decorations will typically reflect wider ethnic or regional styles, though they may also feature some distinctive local traits.

(4) *Work force*; artisans are typically local, while employees and apprentices are either local or come from near surroundings of the locality.

(5) *Production process*; all or most stages of the production process are performed locally by the artisans themselves, or with the assistance of employees and apprentices.

(6) *Distribution and consumption*; most ordinary craft products are intended either for self-use, or for barter or sale to households or shops in the locality itself or in the surrounding region; fine crafts have in the past been sent as tribute to rulers or traded in remote urban centers; but even in such cases, the members of the elites who acquired them still constituted an 'internal audience' (Graburn 1976b:8), sharing the basic cultural premises of the producers.

Folk crafts in the era preceding commercialization were not static and unchanging. However, the process of change was slow, and innovations – whether independently invented or borrowed from the outside – tended to be integrated into the prevailing style, so that no acute 'gradients' appeared, dividing one stylistic period from another, and no marked differences between the style of one artisan and another could be usually noted.

In this chapter I shall use this model as a point of reference, to which the process of disassociation between the components of the model could be referred. Such a process can be found to some extent in most craft-producing villages in northern Thailand; I shall illustrate it here through an extended case study of Ban Thawai, where it is particularly pronounced.

Ban Thawai

Ban Thawai is located about 15 km. west of the major urban center of northern Thailand, Chiang Mai. Its traditional economy was based on irrigated sticky-rice cultivation. Contrary to the popular image (Yee 1992), Ban Thawai was not one of the traditional 'craft villages' (Gallagher 1973), since the villagers began to engage in woodcarving only in the 1960s. However, the village is now a major center for the production, finishing and marketing of carvings and other craft products of northern Thailand. It is popular with Thai and foreign

Figure 10.1 Buddha Image Carved of Old Teak (1995).

visitors and businessmen, and has acquired a reputation as a tourist attraction (Emmons 1992). From the village, great quantities of carvings are exported abroad.

In the early 1990s, the village consisted of about 200 households, around 150 of which were in some way engaged in craft production; crafts were the principal source of employment and income for the local population, although most craft producing villagers continued to cultivate rice, mainly for their own consumption.

The spatial structure of craft production and marketing in Ban Thawai has been described, on the basis of data for 1991, in Chapter 8. Since 1991, however, some important changes have taken place in this structure; especially significant is the emergence of two markets in the area of the village, which will be discussed below.

Figure 10.2 Burmese Style Buddha Image, Decorated in Pattern of Curved Embossed Lines (1991).

When the production of carvings was initiated in the village, it approximated in most respects the model presented above, although it did not reflect it completely. During the subsequent period, up to the present, a continuous process of disassociation between the components of the model has occurred, transforming the nature of craft production and marketing in the village.

In the following section, this process will be described in some detail, on the basis of information collected in the village in the course of repeated visits and surveys between the years 1991 and 1996.

The Process of Disassociation in Ban Thawai

In the promotional materials, Ban Thawai carvings are often presented as deeply rooted in local and northern Thai traditions. Thus, an article on the village in a tourist publication claims that 'The skills of these humble craftsmen [Ban Thawai carvers], women and children are not learned from specialist schools . . . The skills they picked up and developed are from their fathers, who, in turn, drew from their fathers. This has gone on for generations . . .' (Yee 1992:20).

In fact, unlike artisans in some traditional Thai 'craft villages' (Gallagher 1973), such as the nearby pottery village of Muang Koong or the basket weaving village of Ban Pha Bong in the district of Saraphi in Chiang Mai province (Ch. 12), the villagers of Ban Thawai did not in the past engage in carving as a local specialization, though some of them may have known how to carve such items as temple gables and similar ornaments, as did villagers in many other northern Thai localities. In fact, the origins of figurative carving in Ban Thawai are extraneous to the village, and rooted in the trade of Buddha images along the Thai-Burmese border. In the late 1960s, some Ban Thawai villagers were employed by an antique shop in Chiang Mai in the restoration of such images, which often reached the city in a state of considerable disrepair. As they acquired the necessary skills, the villagers began to produce copies of Burmese Buddha images, and of other religious statuary in that shop (cf. Emmons 1992). However, they soon left the urban workshop and relocated into the village, producing there the same objects on their own account in simple workshops, located mostly within their household compounds. According to informants, all members of the first generation of carvers in the village learned their trade in that Chiang Mai antique shop; they later transmitted their skills to their offspring and other villagers. This is sometimes recognized even by writers of promotional material: seeking to compromise the historical recency of Ban Thawai carving with the desired image of a traditional 'craft village', one of them states that '. . . the present Thawai people are the descendants of master sculptors which made their mark 20 years ago' (*Exports from Thailand* 1990:40).

The 'base-line' from which my analysis departs will be the late 1960s or early 1970s, when the production of figurative carvings in Burmese style started in the village. I shall examine in detail the transformation of craft production and marketing, in terms of the components of the model outlined above, during the following three decades, and especially during the five years of my study of the village.

Figure 10.3 Gilded Figurine of a Traditional Thai Musician (late 1970s) (Author's collection).

(1) *Raw materials*

Burmese Buddha images were carved from teak wood. The early Ban Thawai carvings were similarly made of teak. At the time teak was found in the surrounding forests; however, the intensive exploitation of teak forests made the material increasingly scarcer and more expensive. Eventually, the authorities prohibited the cutting of teak trees, and the use of teak for carvings. Consequently, Ban Thawai carvers turned to other, cheaper but also coarser and less finely grained kinds of wood, especially the raintree (*ton chamcha*), popularly known as 'monkey-pod', which abounded in the surrounding region. The vast majority of Ban Thawai carvings are presently made of raintree wood. However, as the production of carvings expanded, raintrees also began to disappear from the area. Raintree wood, and in particular big trunks needed for the carving of large objects such as elephants, had to be brought in from ever more distant areas: at first, from provinces adjoining Chiang Mai province, later from some more remote northern provinces, such as Tak, and eventually from far-away regions, particularly the North-East (Isan) – at distances of up to 1,000 kilometers from Ban Thawai.

The origin of the raw materials for the carvings was thus gradually disassociated from the resource base of the village and its surroundings. With growing scarcity of the wood and distance of its origin from the village, its price increased progressively. This led to an intensification of its use, which, in turn, influenced the size and kind of carvings: since a tree consists of a voluminous trunk and branches of ever-smaller size, intensification of the use of the wood was reflected in the production of ever larger numbers of increasingly smaller objects, so that virtually all the wood was utilized. An extreme example of this process is the recent appearance of 'pencils', made of small finger-thick branches of the tree.

Another consequence was the employment of other kinds of wood: on the one hand, of softer and less valuable, but cheaper and more easily available varieties, which, however, can be used only for the carving of relatively simple, small objects; and on the other hand, of recycled old teak wood, especially of old agricultural implements, such as mortars, animal feeding troughs, boats and carts (kwien), which the villagers have discarded as they modernized their technology and life style. The old teak wood has been used, often to considerable effect, for the carving of large, finely chiselled objects (Fig. 10.1), including religious statuary and reliefs with mythological themes. Since trading in old teak wood is permitted by law, some dealers and workshop owners have openly accumulated large amounts of this material, probably in anticipation of its exhaustion in the future.

The huge expansion in the mass production of carvings in Ban Thawai, and other northern Thai carving villages, has – perhaps unexpectedly – substantially contributed to an emergent ecological problem: the gradual disappearance of trees near settlements and the deforestation of northern Thailand. Though perhaps a minor factor in view of the large-scale destruction of Thai forests, destruction caused by the use of wood for carving may have increased in relative importance after the ban on logging concessions in 1989, since raintrees and other low-quality woods were not protected by the ban (Charasdamrong 1991a:8).

To ameliorate the growing scarcity of wood, some carving villages in the near-by Mae Tha district of Lamphun province have begun to

Figure 10.4 Relief with Ramakien (Thai Ramayana) Theme (1992).

Figure 10.5 Sculpture of Luang Pho Koon (center) a Venerated North-eastern Monk (1995).

plant raintree saplings, in order to assure themselves of a supply of raw materials in the future; the trees will be ready for cutting in about a decade. No such initiative was taken in Ban Thawai – possibly because, as we shall see below, the actual carving takes place ever less in Ban Thawai, as the villagers tend to acquire raw carvings from other localities, and especially those in Mae Tha district, and specialize in the finishing and marketing of the products. Moreover, since land is becoming ever scarcer and more expensive owing to the penetration of urban land uses into the area of the village, it may also become increasingly hard to find the necessary land for a substantial plantation of raintrees.

(2) *Knowledge, Skills and Techniques*

Contrary to the assumption of the model, the knowledge, skills and techniques for the production of carvings have not emerged locally, and have not been slowly absorbed from others in the past, but as we saw above, were acquired relatively recently through the employment of villagers in a shop in Chiang Mai. However, the knowledge, skills and technologies so acquired were part of an artisan tradition, albeit a Burmese one. This is not exceptional, but rather a specific instance of a historical process of cultural exchange between northern Thailand and Burma. In Chiang Mai the villagers learned how to carve Buddha images and other religious statuary from teak, and lacquer, gild and ornament them in a specific style, consisting of patterns of curved, embossed lines, often inlaid with pieces of glass (Fig. 10.2). This is, from our perspective, the 'base-line' from which the process of disassociation in the domain of knowledge, skills and techniques has started, as Ban Thawai carvers opened up to new influences and ideas, and experienced pressures to adapt to new market demands. On the one hand, new skills were acquired, as carvers learned to produce an extraordinary variety of objects, and developed a facility to reproduce them from a sample or even a picture; also, new finishing styles were added to the Burmese style used at the 'base line'. On the other hand, however, several simplifications were introduced into the production process; these reduced the level of skill needed for making some of the products. Machinery was introduced into some stages of production; in particular, electric saws are now frequently used to cut the wood into approximate forms before carving, and the roughly carved objects are also frequently polished by machines rather than rubbed down by hand as before. Moreover, some finishing styles, such as the painting of carvings with industrial paints rather than with *lac* (a natural paint) are cheaper, simpler and demand less skill than the older elaborate lacquering, gilding and ornamentation in the Burmese style. The simplifications made it possible to employ growing numbers of laborers, many of them young girls, on low wages, in the mass production and decoration of carvings.

Some of the more elaborate techniques of decoration may thus fall into disuse and be eventually forgotten. However, most carving skills

Figure 10.6 Figures of Burmese Dancers (1992).

are still well preserved, and loss of skills, as occurred in some more traditional craft villages, has not yet become a problem. Skills are transmitted informally between generations, or from master carvers to apprentices. No formal training of local carvers takes places within the village or in handicraft training centers, such as those belonging to the Queen's SUPPORT Foundation (SUPPORT 1985, Davis 1987).

(3) *Designs and decorations*

Ban Thawai carvings, which at the 'base line' consisted of Buddha images and religious statuary decorated in Burmese style (Fig. 10.2), underwent a rapid process of 'heterogeneization' (Ch. 9). In the early 1970s the Thai authorities prohibited the export of Buddha images,

Figure 10.7 Sculpture of Tiger in Shop in Market (1996).

thereby disposing carvers to look for other lines of production. The owner of the antique-shop in Chiang Mai had already at an early stage asked a local artist to devise new designs for carvings, such as various animals and fishes; these were later adopted by Ban Thawai carvers and produced in the village. Some of the new designs are related to the northern Thai cultural heritage: one of the most popular products in the 1970s and 1980s were sets of musicians, playing different Thai instruments. These came in several sizes, and were at first decorated in Burmese style (Fig. 10.3), but later painted in a variety of colors and hues (Plate 12). The expansion of the export market spurred on the process of heterogeneization: as Ban Thawai acquired a reputation as a source of relatively cheap carvings of good quality, orders were received for new products, samples or drawings of which were supplied by intermediaries or exporters; most of these were utterly unrelated to Thai cultural traditions. The variety of local products was already considerable when I started my study of Ban Thawai; it accelerated in the next five years, and at present defies exhaustive classification. I shall, therefore, only briefly outline a typology of the principal carving styles observed in the village in the course of my study. These will be presented in accordance with their relative affinity to Thai, Burmese or other regional traditions (i.e., their 'orthogeneity,' see Shiloah and Cohen 1983), as against their lack of connection to these traditions and origination in other, especially Western models and influences (i.e., their 'heterogeneity,' see Ch. 9). Five main styles can be distinguished along this spectrum:

(1) *'Classicist'*: This style draws from the ancient traditions, originating far beyond the 'base line,' of Thai, Burmese, Khmer, Chinese or Indian art; products in this style are mostly copies of old religious or mythical images, made mostly from teak wood (Fig. 10.1). New compositions in this style, predominately large teak-reliefs are also common (Fig. 10.4). A 'neo-classicist' variation of this style consists of precise copies, from photographs, of portraits of popular contemporary Buddhist monks, such as Luang Pho Koon (Fig. 10.5).

(2) *'Traditionalist'*: This style continues the artistic tradition, prevalent at the 'base line'; it consists of the production of Burmese-type Buddha figures and other Buddhist images such as dancers or worshippers (Fig. 10.6), as well as some related objects, such as sets of lotus flowers, leaves and pods for Buddhist altars.

(3) *'Neo-traditionalist'*: A style which is based on local, mostly northern Thai or Chinese popular culture and draws its themes from it: carved in this style are animals figuring in popular religious customs, such as elephants or tigers (Fig. 10.7), sets of musicians, reliefs (Fig. 10.8) and mirror frames in flowery designs, and a variety of artificial flowers (which probably evolved from the lotus set mentioned above).

(4) *'Local-innovative'*: A new style, which depicts the local life and environment, without being intrinsically related to local cultural traditions. In this style are produced images of Thai, Chinese or hill tribe men, women and children, mostly in simplified ethnic attire, in different pursuits or postures, such as carrying baskets or *wai*-ing (a

Figure 10.8 Bird and Flower Relief (1995).

posture of respectful salutation), and a variety of figurines of house animals, such as pigs and chickens, birds and various kinds of fish.

(5) '*Extraneous-innovative*': a new style (or family of styles), unrelated to any past religious traditions, or local culture, life or environment. This style, or styles, is adopted from outside sources and is primarily expressed in copies of various objects from Western or Asian models, such as dogs, ducks, frogs with umbrellas, masks, golf players (Fig. 10.9) and characters from Disney films (Fig. 10.10–10.11). In the 1990s, the production of 'Western' style statuary became widespread: cowboy busts and heads, busts and full-size figures of Amero-Indians proliferated; one of the more extreme instances is the figure of a half-naked Apache, with a shield and spear, wearing jeans and shoes (Fig. 10.12).

Probably not all Ban Thawai carvings could be subsumed under one or another of these styles; the typology also does not comprise other local products, such as decorated basketware and furniture. Even with these limitations, it reflects well the staggering variety of Ban Thawai carving styles.

It should be noted that even as new innovative stylistic types have emerged, the older ones have not been given up. Thus, Buddha images in Burmese style are still produced, besides Amero-Indian busts and Mickey Mouse figurines. However, in recent years a trend away from the older 'traditionalist' and 'neo-traditionalist' styles towards the innovative styles, especially that based on extraneous models and

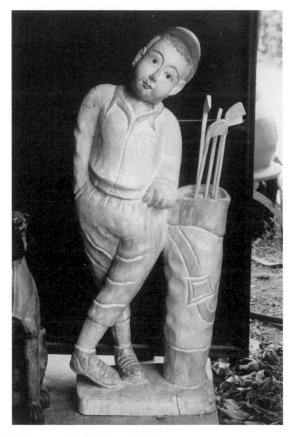

Figure 10.9 Figure of Golf Player (1993).

influences has taken place. Ban Thawai carvings have thus become increasingly 'heterogenetic,' unrelated to either the local or the wider regional cultures. This trend is not unique to Ban Thawai; it can be found in many other Thai craft villages and has been documented by myself for Dan Kwien pottery (Ch. 9). A contrary, but weaker, heterogenetic trend is also observable in Ban Thawai: the increased production of carvings in the 'classicist' style, harking back to ancient stylistic models, which – unlike work in the 'traditionalist' style – are also unrelated to any continuously vital regional style.

Such a duality of opposing trends, one harking back, the other looking ahead, can be observed elsewhere in Thailand – for example, in

Figure 10.10 Disney-film Figurines (1992).

contemporary 'Sukhothai' pottery; it is also found in the tourist arts of other Third World countries (cf. Cohen 1992c:20–21).

The expansion of the production of Ban Thawai carvings was accompanied by constant innovations of designs. This is partly a consequence of changing demand on the world market; but it is probably also due to competition between producers – the innovators having, at least for a short time, an edge on the market; however, they lose that advantage as others copy their innovative designs (Ch. 9).

Changes also took place over time in the decoration and ornamentation of Ban Thawai products. The curved embossed pattern with glass inlays, dominant at the early stages of production, is still used – sometimes, indeed, incongruously, on objects unrelated to local traditions, such as on a pair of kangaroos (Fig. 10.13). Another early technique of decoration is purposely produced 'cracked paint', which endows the object with an appearance of antiquity. However, as mass production expanded, objects were increasingly more simply decorated: by the mid-1990s most were only painted in a variety of hues, or partly painted and partly merely varnished (Plate 13). The fact that the same objects are made in different sizes, and often decorated in a variety of styles increases considerably the heterogeneity of Ban Thawai carvings.

(4) *Labor force*

The extent of disassociation in the domain of the labor force has in Ban Thawai been relatively minor. The bulk of the labor force employed is still local: the great majority of the owners of carving enterprises are locals, or individuals who married into local families; only in a few cases did outsiders settle in the village expressly in order to establish a woodcarving workshop – even though one of the finest craftsmen in the village is an outsider from another northern Thai district. Employees of local enterprises – mostly girls and young women engaged in the decoration of carvings – are either of local origin or inhabitants of adjoining villages. There was no significant influx of an outside labor force into local craft production. In contrast to some other craft-producing villages in the Chiang Mai area, such as the basket-weaving village in the Saraphi district (Ch. 12), inter-generational continuity in Ban Thawai workshops is relatively high, sons continuing in the steps of their fathers. This continuity is due to the relatively high profitability of Ban Thawai crafts, in comparison with alternative employment opportunities.

This relatively high profitability, however, is due to an increasing division of labor between Ban Thawai and other craft-producing villages. Owing to the advantageous location of the village, the villagers have succeeded in retaining the more profitable stages of production, while externalizing the less profitable ones to other localities. The continuity in the local labor force has, therefore, been a consequence of this externalization: instead of bringing in workers from the outside, work was delegated to outside producers. The stages of the productive process have thus been disassociated from one another.

(5) *Production process*

At the 'base-line', Ban Thawai carvers have been executing all the main stages of the production process by themselves: they cut the wood

Figure 10.11 Mickey Mouse Figure (1996).

blocks, carved the objects, decorated and marketed them. Though Ban Thawai is still known as the 'carving village' (Emmons 1992), the part of the locals in the production process has, in fact, gradually contracted over the years: though some of the villagers still engage in carving, most work-shops by the mid-1990s specialized in the finishing processes, while acquiring the raw, semi-finished carvings from elsewhere – particularly from several localities in the district of Mae Tha in the adjoining province of Lamphun, and from the more remote village of Ban Lùk in Lampang province. Workshop owners in Ban Thawai usually order large quantities of such raw carvings from individual carvers or from carving enterprises in those localities, and paint and decorate them in their own village.

237

The favorable location of Ban Thawai and the growing demand for its products made this specialization possible. Being located in the vicinity of the city of Chiang Mai, Ban Thawai is easily accessible to visitors and buyers from both Thailand and abroad. As ever larger quantities of their products were ordered by local distributors and exporters, Ban Thawai producers gradually delegated the less profitable stages of production to carvers in more remote, less accessible villages, which had few direct outlets to the market and in which wages were lower; they themselves concentrated on the latter, more profitable finishing and marketing stages. By buying semi-finished products from elsewhere, they also rid themselves of the need to tie up their capital in large stores of raw materials, particularly raintree wood. Rather, they enjoyed a high turn-over of capital by ordering and purchasing semi-finished carvings according to market demand, and finishing them quickly for sale. The carvers in those more remote villages until recently lacked some of the skills and, particularly, the necessary market contacts, to finish the products according to clients' demands, and market them directly. This state of affairs is changing, and will probably change even more in the future, as the carving villages in the Mae Tha district become more easily accessible to outsiders with the recent completion of a hard-surface road through the area.

(6) *Distribution and Consumption*

Ban Thawai carvings were from the outset not intended for a local audience: since their origins are extraneous to the village, the carving products were oriented exclusively to an external audience. Villagers of the region do not tend to purchase Ban Thawai carvings for their own use. Ban Thawai differs in this respect from traditional crafts villages, such as the potters' villages of Dan Kwien (Ch. 9) in northeast Thailand or Tung Luang in Sukhothai province, in which products for local use still constitute a significant part of production.

Ban Thawai, and the road leading to the village from Chiang Mai, constitute the principal marketing area for carvings in northern Thailand, and increasingly also for other kinds of craft products (Ch. 8). The marketing establishments in that area range from simple shacks and shops to huge production-cum-marketing compounds and modern touristic craft centers. The clientele is equally varied and ranges from local and foreign tourists buying a few souvenirs to distributors, shopkeepers from major Thai cities and exporters who buy or order great quantities of woodcarvings at wholesale prices.

Figure 10.12 Figure of Apache Indian (1995).

The extent and importance of Ban Thawai as a crafts marketing center grew considerably in the early 1990s. In the course of my study I undertook several surveys of the business establishments in Ban Thawai itself and along the routes to the village (Ch. 8). The results of these surveys are summarized in Table 10.1.

The data in the table are divided according to the principal areas in which craft products are marketed: the village of Ban Thawai, and the access road leading from the district town of Hang Dong to the village.[2]

In 1991, virtually all craft-trading establishments in the area of the village of Ban Thawai were located in a 'ribbon' pattern either along a track just before the entrance into the village proper or along the main street of the village itself (Ch. 8). In the period between 1991 and 1994 this pattern changed: the establishments came to be concentrated in two markets, rather than strung out along a ribbon. The main market was established in front of the village, and is now composed of several rows of shops, grouped on both sides of the track leading into the village; the track itself was upgraded into a hard-surface road in 1995. This market was constructed on land owned partly by the owners of two of the major craft enterprises in Ban Thawai. A second, smaller market, however, emerged along a *klong* (canal) in the village itself. It had originally been put up temporarily in 1994 for a village fair, but was left in place after the fair, and has become a permanent – and expanding – feature of the village. These ecological changes had also some structural consequences.

With the concentration of marketing in the markets, the ribbon of shops along the main street of the village virtually disappeared; only the big compounds of two of the largest craft-producing and marketing enterprises remained in their previous locations on the street, in the immediate vicinity of the market at the entrance to the village. In the majority of cases, however, a separation took place between the location of the production and marketing activities.

Up to the early 1990s both production and marketing was concentrated in household compounds along the main street of the village. In 1991 there was in most cases no clear separation between these two kinds of activities. The finished products were mostly put on shelves or merely assembled on the floor in front of the working area. There existed only few 'shops' in the sense of spatially demarcated areas in which products are intentionally displayed in order to attract the attention of potential customers. With the emergence of the two markets, marketing was separated from the households in which production takes place; some minor finishing activities, however, are conducted in the stalls and shops in the new markets. Most workshops along the main street ceased to serve as outlets for sale, although many owners maintain their own shops on the new markets. However, the sphere of marketing has been increasingly penetrated by outsiders: with the opening of the market at the entrance of the village, many shops were established by people from other localities. Some are from nearby villages and towns, but others hail from the city of Chiang Mai, from other provinces and even from Bangkok. They sell both, Ban Thawai products and craft products from other areas. However, outsiders are found in the market at the entrance to the village; they have not yet penetrated the smaller market along the *klong* in the village itself.

The craft-selling establishments along the access road from Hang Dong to Ban Thawai (see Table 10.1) have from the outset differed from those in the village proper in several respects: Many of them are

Figure 10.13 Pair of Kangaroos Decorated in Pattern of Curved Embossed Lines (1992).

relatively large, export-oriented enterprises, owned by people from outside the village; they display large quantities of carved products in simple, elongated huts which serve as storage-cum-showrooms. These enterprises cater primarily to middlemen and businessmen, rather than to tourists and other individual customers. While some of them employ their own carvers, most purchased raw carvings from other localities and engage on the premises primarily in finishing the products.

In 1991 the craft establishments within the area of the village as well as on the access road to it were homogeneous in character: the great majority engaged exclusively in the sale of wood carvings (Table 10.1). During the five years between 1991–96 the crafts business in both areas underwent considerable expansion and heterogeneization: In the area of the village, the number of craft-selling establishments tripled, from 77 to 224; the increase was much smaller along the access road – only about half as many again – mainly because some of the smaller establishments moved from the road to the big new market at the entrance to the village. The expansion in the number of establishments was accompanied by a rapid diversification of the products sold in them: whereas in 1991 woodcarvings were virtually the only merchandise sold, in 1996 the majority of the establishments carried some other crafts, either exclusively or in addition to carvings.

As a consequence, the number of enterprises selling only carvings declined and in 1996 constituted a minority in both marketing areas: in the village area, their number peaked in 1994 at 118 and fell to 92 in 1996; on the access road their number almost halved between 1991 and 1996 – from 41 to 22 (Table 10.1). The total number of establishments selling carvings, including those which also sell some other products, however, increased in the village area substantially, from 76 to 156; while on the access road their number declined slightly, from 43 to 41. Indeed, several large enterprises on the road closed shop up to 1996. This decline may well indicate the increased importance of the new craft markets as the magnet attracting customers, at the expense of the establishments along the ribbons.

The greatest increase in both areas during the 1991–1996 period occurred in the number of establishments selling other kinds of crafts, such as furniture, antiques, textiles and clothing or pottery. From virtually none in 1991 their number increased to 68 in 1996 in the village area, and from 5 to 21 on the access road. There were also in 1996 nine establishments in the village area selling basketware only; it should be noted, however, that the finishing of basketware is an important side-line of many wood-carving establishments in Ban Thawai. While the raw baskets are made elsewhere, they are painted and decorated in the village in the same styles as the wood-carvings (Ch. 12).

Finally, there was also a considerable increase in the number of service establishments in the village: from none in 1991, their number reached 28 in 1996. Some of these are auxiliary services, such as paint stores and packing and transporting enterprises; others are personal services, especially small restaurants and drink stalls, serving locals, employees on the market and visitors.

The retail and wholesale sectors of the crafts market are not segregated in Ban Thawai, even though some specialization exists: larger establishments generally focus upon the wholesale and export

Type of Product	Ban Thawai			Hang-Dong-Ban Thawai Access Road			Total		
	1991	1994	1996	1991	1994 (no data)	1996	1991	1994 (no data)	1996
Woodcarvings only	75	118	92	41		22	116		114
Woodcarvings and other crafts	1	9	64	2		19	3		83
Total Woodcarvings	76	127	156	43		41	119		197
Furniture			25	1		5	1		30
Antiques			1	1		11	1		12
Textile and Clothing		4	11						11
Pottery and Ceramics		2	11	1		2	1		13
Carved Flowers	1	1	4	1		1	2		5
Basketry		4	9	–		–	–		9
Various crafts	–	3	7	1		2	1		9
Total other crafts	1	14	68	5		21	6		89
Total crafts	77	141	224	48		62	125		286
Services and Non-craft shops	–	5	28	2		5	2		33
Grand Total	77	146	252	50		67	127		319

Table 10.1 Development of Craft and Other Business Establishments in Ban Thawai and on Its Access Road, 1991–1996

business, but also sell single pieces to individual buyers. However, in a more abstract sense the dynamics of the two sectors has been different. The on-going diversification of products is characteristic primarily of the retail sector: as Ban Thawai acquired a reputation as the 'carvers' village' and growing numbers of local and foreign tourists came to shop there, locals who previously dealt only in carvings found it profitable to diversify their wares. Others, particularly outsiders, added further diversity by opening shops selling other kinds of crafts. As in the case of the pottery village of Dan Kwien, the growing reputation for a specific type of crafts has – somewhat ironically – created a growing market for different other kinds of crafts.

The wholesale sector, however, underwent a different dynamics: it remained on the whole homogeneous, specializing in selling carvings to an expanding national and international market. Indeed, Ban Thawai is probably the main center of the national wood-carving market; its products can be encountered in souvenir and tourist shops in many remote corners of the world. But no other craft products except locally ornamented basketware are marketed wholesale, either in the village area or on the access road. Ban Thawai as a distribution center thus developed in two directions: it attracted to itself crafts from other localities to be marketed to visitors to the village in small quantities; while its own principal products, wood-carvings, are distributed on an expanding world-market to a growing number of far-away clients.

Conclusion

Despite appearances, Ban Thawai became a 'carvers village' only in the recent past. Woodcarving was not a traditional occupation of the villagers, and the carvers never catered to a local audience; their products were from the outset commercialized and destined for an external audience. In this respect, the initial stage of the dynamics of woodcarving in the village failed to reflect the model proposed at the beginning of this article. In other respects, however, the initial stage reflected the model fairly closely.

In the body of this chapter, the process of gradual disassociation between the components of the model, relative to that stage, was described in some detail. In 1996 little was left of the integrated production and marketing of carvings in a 'traditional' Burmese style, characteristic of the beginnings of woodcarving in the village. The various stages of the production process have been divided between different localities, the kinds of objects and their styles have changed

244

enormously and the local crafts market became increasingly diversified, in terms of both products as well as of the origins of the shop-owners.

While a similar process of disassociation is found in other 'craft villages' in Thailand, as, for example, in the pottery village of Dan Kwien (Ch. 9), it appears to be more pronounced in Ban Thawai than in most other 'craft villages'. I shall attempt in this concluding section to clarify the factors which intensified this process.

The location of Ban Thawai within the metropolitan catchment area of Chiang Mai appears to be the key for the explanation of the difference. Chiang Mai is the principal tourist destination of northern Thailand and the regional crafts center. Its 'night market', in which a wide variety of crafts and other products are displayed, is itself a major tourist attraction.

Ban Thawai is close enough to the city to be easily accessible, but has at least until recently been remote enough not to be swallowed by its metropolitan expansion. Unlike some villages nearer to the city, it has therefore preserved its identity. Local carvers, who had in fact initially learned their trade in the city, could easily keep abreast of the trends and fashions on the urban crafts market. Much of the production of the village was at the early stages marketed through enterprises located in Chiang Mai. Later on, however, businessmen and intermediaries began to approach the producers of Ban Thawai directly, and some eventually located their own businesses along the access road to the village, as did also some packing and transporting agencies. In the area of marketing and dispatch of products, Ban Thawai thus gradually achieved some degree of autonomy from Chiang Mai.

The combination of accessibility and autonomy engendered developments in two directions, both of which accelerated the process of disassociation: expansion of marketing in the locality, on the one hand, and integration of its products into ever wider local and international markets, on the other.

The growing reputation of Ban Thawai as a carving village brought growing numbers of customers – tourists, middlemen, agents and shopkeepers – to the village. The increased demand at the local level led to structural changes: production was separated from marketing; the earlier ribbon-pattern of small workshops along the main street of the village, in which carvings were both produced and sold, virtually disappeared; in its place, two markets emerged in the area of the village. The markets, in turn, engendered further developments: local shopkeepers diversified the scope of products offered by introducing crafts produced in other localities. The disassociation between production and marketing culminated in the penetration of one of the markets by outsiders, who opened shops selling a variety of merchandise completely extraneous to the locality. In 1995, the village became more easily accessible with the improvement of the access road from the town of Hang Dong, occasioned by the hosting of the SEA Games by the city of Chiang Mai. Easier access brings more visitors to the village; their growing numbers, in turn, giving impetus to further market diversification.

The contrary process of the growing penetration of Ban Thawai carvings into expanding markets encourages the process of disassociation in a different direction: it has led to a loss of 'markedness' of local products. Individual visitors, especially ethnic or cultural tourists (Keyes and van den Berghe (eds.) 1984), tend to seek products which are 'marked' – even if not necessarily strictly 'authentic', they have to bear some recognizable marks relating them to the local ambience. However, as the market expands and reaches new, increasingly more remote audiences, such as mass tourists and, through exports, customers in farther-off locations – as it did in the case of Ban Thawai – the importance of the ethnic and cultural marks of the products declines, since potential clients are less knowledgeable and less interested in them; rather, they tend to seek attractive, well-made decorative or functional objects at comparatively low prices. The feedback from the market to the producers induces them to adapt products, styles, materials and production methods and organization to the changed circumstances, thus engendering or intensifying the process of disassociation. Mass production of unmarked, relatively cheap products, in a variety of styles – iconically embodied in the Mickey Mouse figures – is the ultimate outcome of the process of market expansion.

This transition to mass production has been facilitated by the background of Ban Thawai woodcarving and by the governmental policy towards it. The fact that the village has not been one of the traditional 'craft villages' may have facilitated the process of disassociation and the adaptation of Ban Thawai producers to the expanding crafts market. Although, in a broad sense, the local carvers engaged at the outset in a 'traditional' craft activity – carving of Buddha images and other religious statuary – they did not work within an ingrained local tradition and had no local clientele. They were, therefore, probably more prepared to adopt innovations than artisans in 'craft villages', who grew up within a strong, established local tradition.

246

The initiation, expansion and heterogeneization of Ban Thawai craft production proceeded spontaneously and did not receive governmental encouragement or support. The village has not been included in the Queen's project, SUPPORT, nor in any other governmental craft promotion project. Nonetheless, governmental decisions and policies did have some impact upon the direction in which craft production developed in Ban Thawai and upon the process of disassociation described above. The governmental prohibition of the export of Buddha images gave an early impetus to the diversification of products. The prohibition of the cutting of teak trees and of the use of teak for carvings, induced the carvers to use cheaper and more abundant varieties of woods, especially the raintree. This change in the basic raw material was a crucial step towards the mass production of cheaper carvings. Finally, the decision of the authorities to construct a 'cultural center' in front of the village encouraged the establishment of the big new market there – which prospered, though the 'cultural center' remained closed.

As we have seen, by the mid-1990s, Ban Thawai was already a major craft center of northern Thailand and may well eventually become the western counterpart of the well known 'umbrella village' of Bo Sang ('Amethyst' 1991), a major tourist attraction on the so-called 'Handicraft Road' to the east of Chiang Mai (Ch. 8). Its very success, however, is gradually changing its character.

Perhaps the most significant and paradoxical outcome of the growing reputation of Ban Thawai as the 'carvers' village' is that fewer and fewer locals actually engage in carving. Rather, as the market for Ban Thawai products increased, locals concentrated increasingly in the more profitable finishing and marketing stages of production, relegating the earlier stages to other localities. Ban Thawai thus came to occupy the top position in a regional hierarchy of craft villages (Ch. 8). However, mass wood carving in the region as a whole is threatened by the growing scarcity of its basic raw material.

Ban Thawai and the villages which supply it with rough carvings are major consumers of wood; the mass production of carvings is one of the factors in the gradual denudation of northern and northeastern Thailand (Charasdamrong 1991a). Wood is now imported from remote sources. As the once abundant kinds of wood, especially the raintree, becomes generally ever scarcer and more expensive, the mass production of carvings, particularly of large ones, such as elephants, may become seriously affected.

As pointed out above, Ban Thawai, though easily accessible from the city of Chiang Mai, has preserved its distinctiveness. But there are signs that the village is becoming ever more integrated into the metropolitan region of Chiang Mai. The wave of urban expansion is hitting the immediate surroundings of Ban Thawai: along the access road to the village from the district town of Hang Dong, three housing estates were under construction in early 1996, on what used to be rice fields. Ban Thawai may thus gradually lose its distinctive rural character, and its inhabitants may become ever more drawn into the urban economy. The younger generation will probably be ever more attracted to employment in the encroaching urban area, as are the inhabitants of other villages within the metropolitan area of Chiang Mai. Local owners of craft workshops will, therefore, have to compete with urban wages; the increase in wages, combined with the growing costs of raw materials, will make Ban Thawai carvings more expensive and hence less competitive on the world craft market.

Locals might therefore tend to give up gradually the production of carvings, including its finishing stages, which are at present their chief specialty. Indeed, in the more peripheral carving villages there is a growing tendency for producers to finish their carvings themselves, rather than sell them in a 'raw' state to Ban Thawai workshops. Ban Thawai craft persons can be expected to concentrate ever more on the marketing of crafts and other products imported to the local markets from elsewhere, rather than engage in production themselves. The reality of Ban Thawai will then become ever more remote from its image as the 'carvers' village'. Ironically, this growing discrepancy between image and reality would be largely a consequence of the very success of Ban Thawai as a woodcarving center: for it is its reputation which attracts to the village visitors and other potential customers in the first place – and thus helps it to make the transition to a marketing center, on which diverse crafts and other wares are taking up an ever increasing part of the market. The transition which Ban Thawai faces will not be exceptional: other northern Thai 'craft villages', such as San Khampaeng, are at a more advanced stage of the same transition and have already lost much of their distinctive character; while Bo Sang, the 'umbrella village' (Suvapiromchote 1988, *Sawaddi* 1993), is also undergoing a similar rapid change, as the production of umbrellas and other *saa* (mulberry tree bark) paper products is being displaced by the marketing of a wide variety of other wares (Ch. 8). The process of disassociation thus seems to lead to an eventual transformation of the character of successful craft-producing villages, in the course of which the very traits on which their distinctive identity has been established gradually vanish. This, however, appears to be less an exceptional case than an instance of a broader process found in other touristic localities. Many resorts, for example, have built their reputation on the natural amenities which they offered, but their very success has so badly damaged those amenities that their current propensity depends on the offer of a variety of contrived attractions, unrelated to their initial function (cf. Cohen 1995:23–24). Such similarities between apparently very different localities should be given more systematic attention in the comparative study of the dynamics of tourist destinations.

Notes

1 This chapter is based on material collected within the framework of a broader project on the commercialization of Thai crafts funded, in part, by a grant from the Netherlands-Israel Research Project, whose support is hereby gratefully acknowledged.
2 In Chapter 8 which deals with the development of 'craft ribbons' along the roads in Thailand, I dealt with the pattern of craft marketing in Ban Thawai, and along the roads leading to it from the city of Chiang Mai, in terms of a 'ramified' ribbon, composed of four sections: (1) The main road from the city of Chiang Mai to the district town of Hang Dong; (2) The access road from Hang Dong to the track leading into the village of Ban Thawai; (3) The track leading from the access road to Ban Thawai; and (4) the main street of Ban Thawai itself. The first section is not dealt with here, since it is not directly relevant for present purposes. The last two sections are combined in Table (1) under 'Ban Thawai', owing to changes in the ecology of craft marketing in the area of the village.

11

REHABILITATIVE COMMERCIALIZATION
The Revival of Ban Namon Weaving

Introduction

The vitality of a local culture is an important factor influencing the direction of the development of local craft production, once it undergoes a process of commercialization. In an earlier article I have attempted to distinguish different types of commercialization of ethnic crafts (Cohen 1989), one of which I called 'rehabilitative commercialization': this was defined as the revival of a declining ethnic craft, by an external, sponsoring agency, destined for a new, external public. Such an agency will typically be concerned with the preservation of local skills and artistic traditions, though it seeks to adapt them to the tastes and preferences of a novel public. In that earlier article I claimed that this was a relatively benign form of commercialization, since in its absence the craft would probably not survive the penetration of the local economy and society by industrial products through external market forces, but would just die out. I argued that this type of commercialization may not only keep alive a moribund craft, but also revive half-forgotten techniques, as well as lead to the initiation into the craft of new producers, who have not been previously involved in production for a local audience (Cohen 1989:164).

The question arises, what are the dynamics of such a revived craft in the long run? Does it remain 'orthogenetically' bounded, namely stylistically faithful to the revived tradition, in the face of pressures to accommodate production to the tastes and preferences of the novel public? Or does it undergo a process of growing 'heterogeneization', a radical stylistic change, despite the initial intention of the sponsoring agency to preserve its distinctive traditions? Those sponsoring the revival of a declining craft have often been confronted by the dilemma

250

whether to insist on the preservation of its distinctive style in face of a limited or declining market demand, or to yield to pressures to introduce new and alien stylistic elements, more germane to the tastes of the consumers of an expanding market. Some choose a conservative strategy, priorizing highly skilled artisans who produce high-quality 'traditional' crafts, for a relatively limited market; others opt to safeguard or enhance the income of a wider circle of producers, even by compromising cultural and aesthetic considerations (cf. Ch.3; Cohen 1992b). Moreover, the sponsoring agency is usually able to control the production and marketing process only in the first stages of commercialization; independent, private intermediaries and business-men usually begin to place orders with producers and to market local products once the craft was successfully revived, either complementing the work of the sponsoring agency, or even supplanting it.

The channels through which the marketing of the craft products expands and the nature of the new, external publics reached by them, have a crucial influence upon the extent of heterogeneization of local craft products. The development of wholesaling and especially exports of local crafts, which are only successful if a broad, international public, often uninformed about the local culture, is targeted, tends to generate pressures for heterogeneization, as feed-backs from the markets and demands for custom-made products induce local artisans to introduce new products and adopt new styles, unrelated to their cultural background (Chs. 9–10). In the absence of such developments, local production may tend to stay within orthogenetic boundaries, but at the price of a relatively modest size of the market.

The suggested relationship between the production and marketing of a revived craft will be examined on the example of the weaving village of Ban Namon, located in *tambon* (sub-district) Hua Tung, *amphoe* (district) Long of Phrae province in northern Thailand. Though weaving is common throughout the district, it is most widespread in *tambon* Hua Tung; Ban Namon is the village in which the revival has begun.

There exists an extensive literature on Thai textiles, including many descriptions of northern Thai weavings (Conway 1992: 134–155; Howard 1994: 157–205). However, much of this literature relates primarily to old or traditional techniques, objects and uses of textiles, while paying only scant attention to the processes of change which these textiles underwent in recent decades. Indeed, no systematic research of the process of commercialization of the textile production

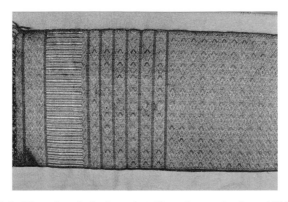

Figure 11.1 Silver-threaded *pha sabai* (from Pranom's shop, 1998; author's collection) (detail).

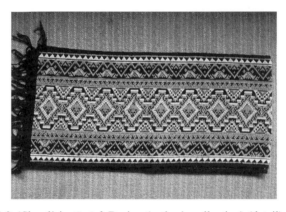

Figure 11.2 'Shawl' in *tin jok* Design (author's collection) (detail).

of any lowland Thai community have as yet been conducted. The present case study is thus a first attempt to deal with this topic.

The study of Ban Namon was one of a series of case studies of craft villages in northern and northeastern Thailand, within the context of a research project on the commercialization of Thai crafts. The dynamics of craft production in this village will therefore be compared primarily to that of the other craft villages in the project, specializing, respectively, in pottery, wood carving and basketry (Chs. 8–10,12); but some attention will also be paid to parallel processes in some other weaving villages.

Ban Namon

Amphoe Long in which Ban Namon is located in one of five principal lowland localities in Thailand in which the weaving of *tin jok*, a broad, richly ornamented band attached to the tubular skirt (*pha sin*) of the traditional woman's costume has been revived and commercialized. The other such localities are the village of Had Siew (Wisudthiluck 1992, Rosenfeld and Mabry 1982, Sukphisit 1988) in Sukhothai province, Mae Chaem (Na Renunakhon 1993, Ekachai 1992), a remote district in Chiang Mai province, the district of Lablae (Rosenfeld and Mabry 1982) in Uttaradit province, and the *tambon* of Ku Bua (Lualamai 1989, Phondee 1993) in Ratchaburi province. I have paid brief visits to all these localities, but have not systematically studied the dynamics of commercialization of their products. My impression, however, is that its dynamics in many respects are quite similar to those of Ban Namon weavings.

Amphoe Long is a relatively remote district; the town of Long is connected to the city of Phrae, about fifty kilometers away, by a narrow and twisting road. The *tambon* of Hua Tung is one of a chain of small villages stretching along a country road through a little plain, a few kilometers from Long town. Ban Namon, one of the nine villages comprising the *tambon,* consists of about 300 households. Its population belongs to the principal northern Thai ethnic group, the Yuan (Hanks 1983, Prangwatthanakun and Cheesman 1987: 69), commonly known as *khon muang* (people of the town). The village was in the past a rather inaccessible place, but can now be relatively easily reached from a road linking the district towns of Long and Wang Chin, which passes just beyond the village. However, the village is not a popular destination for foreign, or even domestic tourists, as are some of the principal craft villages in the Chiang Mai area, or even those in the immediate vicinity of Phrae city (Ch. 8).

The staple food grown by the villagers is sticky rice, as it is in other northern Thai villages. In the off-season, villagers plant onions, tapioca and corn as cash-crops. Some villagers own citrus orchards. However, subsistence crops, especially rice, are still the basis of the local agriculture. Weaving, practiced in almost every household, is an important source of supplementary income; as women, and even a few men, engaged increasingly in weaving, agricultural production may have been somewhat affected. However, unlike in some other craft villages, such as the carving village of Ban Thawai (Ch. 10) or the pottery village of Dan Kwien (Ch. 9), where agriculture is not practiced

253

any more save for subsistence rice-production, in Ban Namon and the surrounding villages, weaving does not dominate the local economy.

Tin jok Weaving in Ban Namon

Before Siam was opened to the world in the course of the nineteenth century, and industrial products began to penetrate ever deeper into the countryside, the weaving of silk and cotton for clothing and other household uses was a highly specialized craft in northern Thailand. However, though common, it was not a ubiquitous activity; weaving was concentrated in the relatively low-lying districts (Bowrie 1993a:147), probably because their inhabitants were able to grow their own cotton and silk worms. Mastery of the more complex weaving techniques, such as supplementary wefts, was limited to a few villages in each area (Bowrie 1993a:148). Clothing styles and designs differed considerably by region and the ethnic origin of the population (Conway 1992) as well as by class (Bowrie 1993b). Many of the more specialized weavers of northern and north eastern Thailand belonged to various ethnic minorities, which have migrated into the territory of con-temporary Thailand or were forcefully resettled by the rulers from newly conquered remote areas to thinly populated, more central ones. Weavers would supply the needs of the royal household and aristocracy, trade or barter their products in local markets or produce them for the use of their own household.

Industrial textiles and ready-made clothing have gradually displaced home-woven garments in more accessible areas of the country, as they did most other craft products. However, unlike some other crafts which virtually died out, weaving, like pottery, survived, particularly in the more remote areas of the north and northeast of the country (Warren and Tettoni 1994:91). In many villages in those areas, women of the older generation continued up to the present to weave their distinct garments, especially tubular skirts (*pha sin*), worn nowadays mainly on festive occasions. While in some localities they still grow their own silk worms, most women at present use industrial, rather than home-grown, silk and cotton yarn.

Ban Namon is one of those villages which has specialized in the past in some of the more complex types of cotton weaving, and particularly in the making of *tin jok* with distinctive local designs (*Sun watthanatham* B.E. 2538 [1995]).

Tin is an old Lao and Thai word for the leg; *jok* means in the Lao language to slip something in and out (Sintujarivatr, 1972:16). A *tin jok*

Figure 11.3 New Monochromatic *tin jok* with Three Bands of '*tin jok*' (Pranom's shop, 1993) (detail).

is '. . . a piece of cloth [made] to cover the legs, which is made by slipping threads in and out of the loom [i.e. by supplementary weft weaving]' (Sintujarivatr, 1972: 16). The *tin jok* is woven separately and attached to the bottom of the *pha sin* to cover the lower part of the woman's legs. According to Conway, '*jok* is woven in silk or cotton in a variety of colors and patterns, including stylized birds, plants and flowers and abstract patterns of squares, diamonds, hooks, hexagons and zig zags, and may contain gold and silver threads. *Jok* is sometimes woven in brilliant yellow cotton, possibly an attempt by village weavers to imitate the golden thread worn by the wealthy' (Conway 1992: 141). Indeed, on the old *tin jok* of Long district, the yellow color frequently predominated (*Sun watthanatham* B.C. 2538[1995]: 18–20; Plate 14).

Tin jok were in the past extensively woven and worn by ethnic groups originating in contemporary Laos, especially the Phuan, a Thai people who inhabited the flat areas of the plateau to the east and northeast of Vientiane (see map in Chazee 1995:92). In the course of the 19th century and especially during the 1830s, the Siamese kings initiated a policy of depopulation of the Phuan State, resettling a large number of the Phuan people on the right (western) bank of the Mekong river (Smuckarn and Breazeale 1988: 9–69), including the districts of Sri Satchanalai (in which Had Siew is located) and Lablae in Uttaradit province. These localities were well known for their *tin jok*. The old Phuan *tin jok* 'display extraordinary patterns, some requiring up to a thousand shed sticks [for discontinuous supplementary weft weaving]' (Prangwatthanakun and Cheesman 1987:25).

The Phuan were the chief exponents of *tin jok* weaving in Thailand, but the custom of weaving and wearing *tin jok* was also wide-spread in Yuan areas (Phondee 1994:106–7), as it was in *amphoe* Long, possibly under Phuan influence.

Tin jok weaving in *amphoe* Long declined in modern times, but did not completely die out. The basic weaving skills were still occasionally transmitted by the older weavers to members of the younger generation. A young woman of Ban Namon, Pranom Thapang, acquired in the course of the 1970s the skills of *tin jok* weaving from one of her aunts. In 1979, on the occasion of Queen Sirikit's visit to the village, Pranom, who by then was already a highly skilled weaver, presented to the Queen a *tin jok* which she had woven. Impressed by her work, the Queen asked Pranom to pass her skills to other village women and ordered that the amount of 2000 baht (about US $100 at the rate current at the time) be given to her for the purchase of raw materials for the weavers. The Queen promised to buy all the locally woven cloth (probably through her SUPPORT Foundation; see SUPPORT 1992: 248–254). Consequently, Pranom organized a housewives producers group (*klum mae ban*) which initially consisted of twelve weavers. Pranom also began instructing the women in her village and in the surrounding area in weaving techniques and designs. She herself continued to acquire knowledge of new designs and colors on her frequent visits to the royal Phuping palace, north of Chiang Mai, where she went to sell the weavings of her *klum* (Sukphisit 1990b).

The Commercialization of Ban Namon Weaving

The revival and initial commercialization of *tin jok* weaving in Ban Namon was sponsored by the Queen. The Queen and her foundation seem to have encouraged rural craft development in accordance with three principal, potentially conflicting goals: they sought to preserve inherited handicraft traditions, as well as to provide a supplementary source of income to rural artisans. While opposed to radical innovation, the Queen and her foundation approved some adaptation of the styles and forms of products to the new market demands, but did not encourage radical stylistic innovations. They also required fine, high-quality products, which would enhance the reputation of Thai artistry at home and abroad; such products feature prominently in the shops and publications of the foundation (e.g. SUPPORT 1992).

The Queen and her foundation helped to organise the artisans in local housewives producers groups (*klum mae ban*), loose cooperative bodies, which would advance loans to their members to purchase raw materials, control the quality of their products, and market them; they would also provide instruction to the members on ways to improve their products and to adapt them to current market demands.

The *klum* were managed by a chairwoman (*hua na*), usually the most skillful local artisan; sometimes a president (*pathan*), often a prominent local person, was also nominated.

In Ban Namon, Pranom became the chairwoman of the local weavers *klum*. From the first twelve members, the *klum*, at its peak in the 1980s, expanded to about 170 weavers. However internal conflicts alienated some of the members, and in 1988 the *klum* fell apart; though it still exists officially, it in fact ceased to operate a long time ago. During the period of my research, which started with a preliminary visit in 1991 and extended to 1998, Pranom still claimed to be the head of her *klum*, though she in fact operated as a private entrepreneur.

The Queen's foundation, though it continued to purchase high-quality products from Pranom, did not interfere with this process of privatization. After it had sponsored the revival of the local weaving industry, the foundation had in fact little impact on the industry's further development. It did not regulate and enroute it along prescribed routes, as did the NGOs which sponsored the commercialization of hill tribe crafts (Ch. 3).

The fate of the womens' *klum* in Ban Namon is just one instance of a general trend which I observed in many craft villages in northern Thailand. Womens' *klum* have been frequently established by various sponsoring agencies to facilitate the production and marketing of various local crafts; however, insofar as these efforts succeeded, internal tensions inevitably arose in the *klum*, mostly between the chairperson and the members; these tensions eventually led to the disintegration of the cooperative framework and the privatization of production and marketing of the craft. One source of tension was the favoritization by the person in charge of the *klum* of members of his or her own extended family in the distribution of production orders. Thus, in the basketry village of Ban Pha Bong in Saraphi district of Chiang Mai province, most of the still active members of the basket weaving *klum* belonged to the president's extended family; they were allocated the bulk of the orders, while other members abandoned the *klum* (Ch. 12). Another common source of tension is the retention by the chairwoman of part of the proceeds of sale of the members' products, allegedly for the operational expenditures of the *klum*; since profit margins in the crafts business tend to be very low, producers often

Figure 11.4 Old *pha sin*, with *tin jok*, Consisting of a Single Row of 'Squares', Encased in Rows of Smaller Designs (Collection of Wat Saleng, Long district) (detail).

prefer to sell their products by themselves, rather than through the *klum*, thus saving this expense.

The most important tension leading to the disintegration of the *klum*, however, which was apparently also the decisive one in the case of Ban Namon, derives from the inherent ambiguity in the role of the chairwoman: she is mostly not only a manager, but also herself a major producer and trader in craft products. The chairwoman was usually given a sum of money to start the activities of the *klum*, either by the Queen's foundation or by some other public agency. The money was intended to serve for loans to members for the purchase of raw materials. She was also given the task to market the members' products. However, she was not precluded from employing other artisans on her own account, or trade privately in their products. Some chairwomen probably also used the money allocated to the *klum* to develop their private business. Hence, a gradual shift often occurred in their activities, as they turned market contacts, acquired in their role as chairwomen of the *klum*, into sources of private profit.

Pranom's career exemplifies this transition. She became head of the *klum* owing to her exceptional weaving skills and her personal relationship with the Queen and members of her entourage. At the outset, Pranom would impart her skills to other women in the village and its surroundings, who then joined the *klum*; she then marketed their products for them. However, with the proliferation of weaving skills in the village and its surroundings, Pranom began increasingly to purchase the products of weavers who were not members of the *klum*, and to resell them for personal gain. Her conduct provoked tensions between herself and the other members of the *klum*, which eventually led to the dismissal of Pranom as chairwoman of the *klum*. Another woman was appointed chairwoman in her place, but new conflicts regarding financial matters emerged, leading eventually to the cessation of all activities of the *klum*. This does not, however, prevent Pranom to continue to refer to the women from whom she purchases weavings for her shop, as members of her *klum*.

As Pranom accumulated some capital, she began to hand out work to weavers, taking back their products and paying them what in fact amounted to a piece-wage for their work. She thus became an entrepreneur, managing a putting-out system of weavers working for her at their homes. As the system became routinized, Pranom would hand the weavers a sample of the desired design, a bundle of heddles, and yarn in the appropriate colors. This method was also adopted by several other local shop-owners who hand out work to weavers.

In the early 1990s, about one hundred women worked for Pranom, but she continued to teach weavers in ever remoter localities; thus, she helped to introduce weaving into several villages of *amphoe* Wang Chin, adjoining Long district; recently she even began teaching some Karen hill tribe women in a remote village in *amphoe* Long to produce *tin jok*, even though *tin jok* is completely alien to their culture. It appears that Pranom disseminated her weaving skills not merely altruistically, but also in order to prepare a potential labor force which will supply her shop with its products; according to local villagers, Pranom tends increasingly to assign orders to women from outside her village, probably because their work is cheaper than that of the longer-established weavers of Ban Namon itself. The women of Ban Namon have a choice of working for several competing shop-keepers in *tambon* Hua Tung; in other localities, however, there are no craft shops, and the weavers are therefore probably more dependent of Pranom as a source of orders. In any case, the proliferation of weaving skills throughout the area tends to keep the remuneration of weavers low, and especially of those who are able to weave only the routine, simpler designs; according to Pranom, such designs can be woven by many weavers. However, among about one hundred *tin jok* designs woven in the area, there are some highly complex ones, including such which only a single woman is capable to weave; the remuneration received by weavers of those designs tends to be correspondingly higher.

Pranom herself continues up to the present to weave high-quality and innovative pieces, particularly for special occasions, such as public competitions, at which she was several times awarded first prizes.

As Pranom's business expanded, her home, in which her shop is located, underwent several transformations. In the early 1990s there were still some looms in the compound around her house, at which local women wove fine weavings, using silver and gold thread. The front room of her house served at the time as a simple shop, with wares stored on shelves. Pranom's prize-winning weavings were kept in a cupboard at the back of the room. By 1994 this room became a show-room: some old local *tin jok* and the growing number of Pranom's prize-winning pieces and other personal mementos were more prominently displayed. Selected products were exposed in the room, while the bulk of other wares was moved into an adjoining storage room. In 1996 a poster of a recent local *tin jok* fair, featuring a weaving by Pranom, adorned the entrance to her shop. By then, Pranom already acquired a national reputation, through several articles in both Thai and English, with photos of herself and her work, which were published in the press. The wares in the showroom were tagged 'Pranom' (without any further details) in Thai and English. In 1998, finally, the front room ceased to serve as a show-room, and was given a solely symbolic role: its entrance was occupied by a traditional Thai house altar, on which stood out a large photo of King Chulalongkorn (Rama V), the veneration of whom recently became a popular urban cult in Thailand (Vaananen 1993: 18–20). Significantly, however, no tags with Pranom's name were any more attached to the products in the shop – possibly a sign of her failure to penetrate the foreign tourist or export markets.

Figure 11.5 Old *tin jok* with Several Rows of 'Squares', Encased in Rows of Smaller Designs (Collection of Wat Saleng, Long district)

In the course of less than two decades, Pranom, a young local girl whose work attracted the Queen's attention, became in turn the chairwoman of a housewives *klum* and a business woman running a successful private enterprise, with growing national reputation as a master-weaver. Several other women in Ban Namon and the adjoining village of Hua Tung, mostly seamstresses who previously served the local villagers, followed Pranom's example, and began to deal in local weavings: like Pranom, they use to hand out samples of weavings, yarn and bundles of heddles to weavers in the village and its vicinity, and keep a small stock of local products for sale in their shops. But the scope of their operations is much smaller than Pranom's. These shop-keepers seek to compete with Pranom by offering their wares at lower prices than hers, but the quality of their wares also tends to be lower.

Pranom remains by far the most successful of the traders in local weavings. However, her success notwithstanding, there are some significant limitations to the expansion of Pranom's business, and especially to her ability to penetrate new marketing channels; these limitations, in turn, constrain the process of change in the style of local weavings.

Pranom, though successful in business, remained essentially a peasant woman, whose marketing activities, though they grew in scope, are conducted namely through traditional channels: from early on, and up to the present, Pranom participated in fairs and various other craft-markets, where she demonstrated her weaving skills and sold her own

261

and other weavers' products. Some of these venues are related to festivals and other festive occasions in the provinces; others take place in urban settings, such as the annual fair of Kaset Sart University, or the periodic craft sales in the luxurious River City complex in Bangkok. Except River City, the principal visitors of these venues are rural or urban Thais, rather than foreign tourists.

The marketing and promotion of Ban Namon weavings in the village and the region as a whole is underdeveloped. Few domestic tourists visit the village or the *tambon* of Hua Tung. A few foreign tourists visit Pranom's shop, but rarely the other local establishments. The principal clients of Ban Namon shops are middlemen and shop-keepers from urban centers and other localities. A few shops in Long town and on the access roads to the district display Ban Namon weavings. However, in contrast to some villages in the vicinity of Phrae (Ch. 8), no craft-shop ribbons, which could attract significant numbers of tourists, emerged along these roads. Even in the city of Phrae, which is becoming a popular destination of mostly domestic tourism, Ban Namon weavings are not much in evidence: *tin jok* is part of the attire of the female staff in one of the major local tourist hotels and *tin jok* skirts and other Ban Namon products are sold in one or two boutiques. The local authorities have also done little to promote Ban Namon weavings. In the mid-1990s two *tin jok* fairs took place, but the practice was discontinued when a new district chief was appointed to *amphoe* Long. School-teachers in *tambon* Hua Tung have to wear *tin jok* skirts once a week, but this practice is probably intended more to bolster local pride and cultural identity than to promote local products.

Ban Namon products are found in various localities outside Phrae province. Thus Had Siew, itself a center of revitalized *tin jok* production, also serves as an important outlet for Ban Namon weavings. The village is located in the vicinity of the archeological site of Sri Satchanalai, and serves as a stopping place for tourists visiting the site. A local shop-owner in Had Siew has collected a large number of old *tin jok* skirts from all parts of northern Thailand and established a small museum adjoining his shop, which attracts passing visitors; he is a major purchaser of Ban Namon weavings, which are apparently sold in his shop as if they were local Had Siew products. Shopkeepers in Ban Namon claim that their products sell better in Had Siew than they do in their own village, since more tourists pass through that locality. However, Sri Satchanalai is, like Phrae, only a minor destination on itineraries of foreign tourists, and attracts predominantly domestic Thai tourism.

In the major tourist centers of Thailand, Ban Namon weavings are found primarily in fashionable shops catering to a local clientele, rather than in tourist-oriented establishments and markets. They do not figure prominently in such popular tourist shopping areas as the Chatuchak weekend market in Bangkok or the night bazaar of Chiang Mai. Foreign tourists and other foreigners probably do purchase some Ban Namon products, but they are not the principal clients for these wares.

The revival of Ban Namon weaving was successful because local production was re-oriented to an external clientele; however, owing partly to the nature of the marketing channels for these products, and partly to a growing interest in hand-made textiles among the Thai urban public, it was the latter, rather than foreign tourists or other foreigners, which provided their main clientele. The principal customers for hand-made cotton weavings, including those of Ban Namon are the older urban middle and lower-middle classes, who tend to wear 'traditional' costumes, especially fine *pha sin*, on festive occasions; and the new middle and upper-middle classes, who recently developed a taste for the use of hand-made 'traditional' textiles as material for modern fashions or for their ornamentation. High class Thais in contrast generally prefer silk cloth to cotton (Bowrie 1993b); indeed, designers of Thai *haute-couture* use primarily silk for their creations, which adorn the pages of such elite-oriented publications as *Silk Magazine*. Some designers, however, do occasionally employ fine cotton-weavings for the ornamentation of their costumes, including *tin jok* from various localities, among them *amphoe* Long. Ban Namon weavings thus eventually reached into the highest rungs of Thai fashion, even though its predominant clientele remain the Thai middle classes.

In contrast to Thai silk, Thai hand-woven cotton products did not generally gain much popularity among foreign tourists. Insofar as foreign tourists purchase Ban Namon products, they appear to be less interested in 'original' *tin jok* and prefer other products, ornamented by *tin jok* designs, which have been adapted to their tastes and needs. However, foreign tourists seem to be relatively little exposed to Ban Namon products, owing to the nature of the channels through which these products are marketed.

Finally, Ban Namon products do not yet reach any foreign markets. Neither Pranom nor any other shop-keeper in the village engages in exports. Pranom claims that she does not know how to deal with exports and that she lacks the linguistic skills for this kind of business; nor does anyone else in the locality possess such skills. In that respect the local shop-keepers resemble other small dealers in craft villages,

Figure 11.6 Silver-threaded *pha sin* Consisting of Five Bands of *tin jok* (Pranom's shop, 1992).

whose business grew from traditional roots, and who experience difficulties in adapting it to the demands of the export market. In Dan Kwien, only two entrepreneurs, both urban Thais who have settled there and initiated the large scale commercialization of the local pottery, eventually turned to exports – but only one of them possesses an export license, while the other exports through his agent in Bangkok (Ch. 9). None of the pottery producing villagers in Dan Kwien engages in exports. In Ban Thawai, several packing companies, managed by outsiders to the village, provide assistance to the local entrepreneurs in the conduct of their voluminous export business in woodcarvings (Ch. 10). The shop-keepers of Ban Namon did not establish any links to agents or exporters, nor have any foreigners or other outsiders to the village, to the best of my knowledge, as yet initiated the export of Ban Namon weavings.

In conclusion, it appears that, though *tin jok* weaving is a source of significant supplementary employment for the women of Ban Namon and the surrounding villages, the present marketing channels for Ban Namon products are of limited potential, so that the products did not yet reach some major groups of potential clientele. In that Ban Namon hardly differs from other centers of *tin jok* production, all of which appear to be marketing their products along similar channels. The limited market in turn appears to support a certain conservatism in the form and design of Ban Namon products, as of those of other *tin jok* producing localities, in sharp contrast to the rapid transformation of the products of some other craft villages, such as Ban Thawai and Dan Kwien, which penetrated the tourist and export markets on a massive scale.

Continuity and Change in Ban Namon Weavings

The 'rehabilitative commercialization' of Ban Namon weaving has been accomplished without major stylistic discontinuities between the past and the present. Some changes, however, have been introduced in the products, partly under the influence of the initial sponsoring agency, the Queen's foundation, and partly on the initiative of local weavers, and particularly Pranom, the master-weaver.

Tin jok was, and remains, the distinctive product of Ban Namon. However, it has never been, nor is it as present, the only locally woven article. In the past, a wide range of different kinds of weavings have been produced by local women; most of these are not made any more, even as some new products have been introduced to suit the tastes and needs of an external clientele.

In the past, the villagers planted their own cotton, spun the yarn and dyed it in natural dyes. Two kinds of cotton fibres were in use: from shrubs and from tall, tree-like plants. The latter served for the preparation of heavy blankets which at present are not made any more while ordinary cotton was used for clothing, including *tin jok* skirts, and for various ceremonial articles, such as the *pha sabai*, a long and narrow cloth (Conway 1992:189), still worn by women on ritual and festive occasions.

At present, weavers do not grow their own cotton any more, but purchase industrially produced and dyed cotton yarn. The *tin jok* now is the only one of the various traditional weavings which is still regularly produced. The local women do not even weave the tubular skirts to which the *tin jok* is attached, but purchase them on the market. The *pha sabai* is still occasionally made, sometimes with gold or silver thread (Fig. 11.1). However, more common is an adaptation of the *pha sabai* to a new purpose: a shorter and narrower piece, which is sold as a 'shawl' (Fig. 11.2). This and other new products are oriented to the external market, and are not commonly used by the local population.

Here I shall deal primarily with the dynamics of change in the designs of the principal commercialized Ban Namon product, the *tin jok*. I shall then turn briefly to the ornamentation of the other contemporary weaving products, which has been primarily derived from the *tin jok* designs.

Tin jok is produced by one of two techniques of supplementary weft. The more complex of these techniques, *jok* in the narrow sense, is the discontinuous supplementary weft, '. . . which is achieved by using a stick, porcupine quilt or the fingers to pick out certain warp yarns into which a special supplementary weft yarn is threaded while still in the loom' (Prangwatthanakun and Cheesman 1987:25). This technique is still used by the weavers of Tambon Ku Bua in Ratchaburi Province and in Mae Chaem district of Chiang Mai province. A simpler technique is the continuous supplementary weft, called in Thai *khit* in which '. . . the pattern has been thought out and put into the warp by means of . . . a system of string heddles extra [i.e. in addition to] the heddles used for plain weave' (Prangwatthanakun and Cheesman 1987:29). It is significant that 'The use of heddles for [continuous] supplementary weft patterns is a labor-saving device which has resulted in the simplification of designs, previously picked out by hand and limitless in combination, the designs now being restricted to the number and order of heddles' (Prangwatthanakun and Cheesman 1987:29). In Ban Namon, the discontinuous supplementary weft technique is not generally in use any more, though a few women specializing in some complex designs may still be using it; the continuous supplementary weft is presently the dominant technique.

Most, though not all, designs on commercial Ban Namon *tin jok* are based on designs which have been used by the local women at the 'baseline', namely in the period preceding commercialization. The design on most of the old *tin jok* consists typically of several narrow rows of small repetitive motifs, such as couplets of 'birds' (*nok*), 'swans' (*hong*) or 'rosettes', on both sides of a wider central row of 'squares' (*khom*) (Phondee 1994:107), in fact romboids, within which various further motifs are embedded. In *amphoe* Long most of the

266

Figure 11.7 Broad Woven Shawl, Decorated with *tin jok* Designs at Both Ends (Author's Collection).

motifs in the rows and within the 'squares' were given distinctive names (*Sun watthanatham* B.E. 2538 [1995]:16–26). Permutations between different types of rows and 'squares' engendered in the past a wide variety of designs in local *tin jok*. The abbot of Wat Saleng, a Buddhist temple in the vicinity of Ban Namon, sought to preserve this variety by establishing a collection of old *tin jok*, made by village women in the surroundings of the temple. Some of these old weavings have served as samples for the commercial *tin jok* presently woven by the women of Ban Namon.

The yarn of the older *tin jok* in the collection of Wat Saleng was dyed in natural colors, but for the more recent ones industrial yarn was already used, even though the weavings were not yet commercialized.

The dominant color in the old *tin jok* is a brilliant yellow (Plate 14; Conway 1992:141); this is still the predominant color of *tin jok* presently produced in some areas of northern Thailand, such as Mae Chaem (Na Renunakhon 1993:89).

The designs on the commercialized *tin jok* closely resemble, in their general appearance and in many of the details, those of the 'baseline'. Indeed, some of the designs have been carefully copied from the old *tin jok* in Wat Saleng's collection. However, there are also some significant simplifications and adaptations.

In the past the making of *tin jok* was free of commercial considerations; and since the prestige of a woman depended on her skill at weaving, the women spent considerable time in the weaving of their *tin jok*. With commercialization, considerations of efficiency, in the sense of time spent on weaving as against remuneration, became uppermost in the weavers' minds. Since weavers are ordinarily paid by the number of pieces produced, and not by the time invested, they prefer to produce designs which are easily and quickly made. The finer points in the execution of such pieces are often left out, as large numbers of the same design are routinely, and sometimes carelessly, produced. However, while run-of-the-mill, cheap *tin jok* predominate, some pieces, especially those woven partly or wholly of silver or gold thread (Fig. 11.3) are carefully executed in no less complex designs than in the past. However, the weavers specializing in such work receive a much higher remuneration than those weaving ordinary *tin jok*.

The principal stylistic adaptations introduced into commercialized Ban Namon *tin jok* are changes in the colors and color combinations on the designs. There is a decline in the dominance of yellow on the *tin jok*, and some reduction in the use of multiple, strongly contrasting colors, common on the older *tin jok*; some new *tin jok* are almost monochromatic (Fig. 11.3). Darker colors often dominate to an extent not common in the past. Such an amelioration in color contrasts, and the replacement of bright by muted colors has also been observed in commercialized Hmong embroideries (Ch. 3), reflecting their adaptation to the tastes of Western customers.

As commercial production of *tin jok* progressed over the years, the desire to create more distinctive and attractive pieces for the new, external audience, led to attempts to re-design the *pha sin*, the traditional skirt. The initiative was again taken by Pranom. The old *pha sin* of Long district consisted of a tubular skirt usually woven in a pattern of simple, parallel horizontal lines, to which was attached a *tin jok* along whose center ran one or several rows of 'squares' (Figs. 11.4–11.5).

Pranom spectacularized the *pha sin* by multiplying the numbers of *tin jok* on it and reducing the plain part of the *pha sin*. Thus, the skirt on Fig. 11.3 is decorated with three, rather than the ordinary one, *tin jok* bands; eventually, the plain part disappears completely, the whole skirt consisting of five repetitive bands of *tin jok* (Fig. 11.6).

The changes in *tin jok* and *pha sin*, though introduced for commercial purposes, are primarily 'orthogenetic'. However, Pranom, who initiated the revival of traditional weaving in Ban Namon and its surroundings, also spearheaded in the last few years an incipient heterogeneization of the local weaving designs. Pranom copied textile designs of some other localities in Thailand, such as those of Lablae, in the nearby province of Uttaradit, and from other *tin jok* producing localities. Instructors from the Queen's foundation also taught local weavers in Pranom's house some of the refined designs of the Yuan people of Ku Bua, in Ratchaburi province, and even of the very popular silk-weavers of Chonnabot in northeastern Thailand (Angsanakul 1989). Pranom recently even adapted some designs of the Kachin people of Burma to local weaving techniques; indeed, she claims to be able to adapt any design to local techniques, and then weave it herself or ask one of the skilled weavers working for her to produce it. Copying of Lablae or Ku Bua designs can hardly be considered 'heterogeneiza-tion', since they are based on basically the same traditions of *tin jok* weaving as those of Long district; the adaptation of designs outside this tradition, like those of Chonnabot or of the Kachin, signifies a tendency to heterogeneization. However, such heterogenetic designs are not yet commonly produced; in Pranom's shop only a few such weavings are usually found, while the other shops in the village do not carry them at all. The situation in Ban Namon hence differs sharply from that in Dan Kwien (Ch. 9) or Ban Thawai (Ch. 10), where a considerable and increasing part of production became unrelated to local traditions, and is made on order, according to specifications, or from samples provided by foreign clients.

However, while designs changed little in Ban Namon, some new products have been developed in order to expand the market and to attract new kinds of clients. Most common is the narrow 'shawl' mentioned above; it is ornamented by a *tin jok* design, running along its length (Fig. 11.2). Broader shawls, with designs derived from those on the *tin jok*, but running along their breadth at both ends, are also commonly made (Fig. 11.7). A related product is a length of cloth of indeterminate function, offered by local shopkeepers as material for a shirt; it is usually decorated with three rows of 'squares' (Fig. 11.8).

Figure 11.8 Woven Cloth with Multiple *tin jok* Design (author's collection).

I surmise that these products are more suitable for a foreign audience than unadulterated *tin jok*, for which they can hardly find much use in their customary life styles. Local weavings, particularly the *tin jok*, were also sometimes used innovatively, in a manner which I called elsewhere 'secondary elaboration' (Ch. 4). At first, local seamstresses decorated clothing in a modern urban cut, like jackets or vests, by patches of *tin jok*. More recently, as pointed out above, Thai fashion designers also introduced local *tin jok* as decorations into Thai *haute couture*; their creations were featured on models in national fashion shows, and in fashion magazines and books.

Finally, locals are also decorating a variety of utilitarian objects, such as ladies' bags, shoulder bags, picture frames, cushion covers and even tissue paper containers, with locally woven cloth, patterned with elements of *tin jok* designs (*Sun watthanatham* B.E. 2538 [1995]:27–29). While the patterns on this cloth are orthogenetic, the objects themselves are completely foreign to the local culture. Most of them have in fact been originally introduced into Thai crafts by foreign NGO's, which sponsored the decoration of various utilitarian objects with the embroideries of hill tribe, primarily Hmong, refugees from Laos in the late 1970s and early 1980s (Chs. 2–3). The production of similar objects, decorated in various local patterns, then spread to other, non-tribal weaving areas in northern and north-eastern Thailand, and eventually also to Ban Namon and its surrounding. However, in Ban Namon, these objects do not constitute an important component of the local craft production for an external clientele.

Discussion and Conclusions

Within the analytic framework of different types of commercialization of ethnic crafts (Cohen 1989), the case of Ban Namon approximates most closely that of 'rehabilitation': although the weaving of *tin jok* in the village and its surroundings has never stopped completely, it was moribund: two decades ago only some older women still possessed the necessary weaving skills, and with their demise, the weaving of *tin jok* would have probably died out were it not for the efforts of an external sponsoring agent, the Thai Queen and her foundation, to revive it. In contrast to some other instances of rehabilitative commercialization, as for example, that of the tribal refugees form Laos (Cohen 1989:164–5; Ch. 3), in Ban Namon the sponsors merely initiated the rehabilitation, by enjoining Pranom, the young master-weaver, to teach the craft to other local women, and by setting up a local housewives' weaving group (*klum mae ban*). However, except for purchasing some high-quality products from Pranom, and occasionally providing an instructor to teach local weavers some new designs, the foundation was not much involved in the process of commercialization of Ban Namon weaving; in particular, it did not help to develop new markets for local products. Consequently, the marketing of the weavings underwent privatization: the *klum* gradually disintegrated, as Pranom, its chairwoman, increasingly engaged in private trading. Several local shop-keepers also began to deal in weavings on a smaller scale. The marketing of the weavings became the private business of Pranom and the other shop-keepers, with only some of the finer products reaching the foundation's shops.

Even though the sponsoring agent did not intervene much in the process of commercialization and its privatization, the style of Ban Namon weaving remained on the whole within the confines of orthogenetic changes. This relative conservatism can be attributed to the predominantly traditional character of the marketing channels through which the weavings were marketed and to the kind of external audience primarily reached by them – the urban Thai middle classes, who are the principal clients of Ban Namon weavings. The tastes and preferences of this audience appear to be, in cultural terms, rather conservative, and are certainly closer to the weavers' cultural traditions than are those of various potential foreign audiences. With growing economic prosperity the market represented by this domestic audience expanded, so that increasing numbers of weavers in the village and its surroundings were able to sell their products, without introducing major innovations into them. Local weaving could therefore preserve its

271

'orthogenetic' character, since there was little incentive to access new, especially foreign audiences, along other, more modern marketing channels.

Ban Namon is not conveniently located to attract foreign tourists. Nor is *amphoe* Long a tourist destination, and will hardly be able to gain a place on the tourist map in the future, especially since the *tin jok* festival, held twice in the mid-1990s, has been discontinued. Even in the city of Phrae, an emerging tourist center, Ban Namon weavings are not much in evidence; neither are they prominently displayed on tourist markets or shopping areas of major destinations of foreign tourism. While foreign tourists do purchase some Ban Namon products, they constitute, in my estimate, only a minor segment of the market for the village's wares.

Ban Namon products are not exported in commercial quantities. In fact, it appears that their export potential has not even yet been tested.

The minor role of foreigners in the market for Ban Namon weavings, and especially the absence of exports, constrains the scope of the market, and hence also the volume of products which can be sold at current prices. However, the constraints also inhibit external pressure for far-reaching heterogeneization of designs, of the kind found in Dan Kwien or Ban Thawai, where foreigners often place orders for products made from samples which they supply, according to their specifications (Chs. 9–10). Such attempts at heterogeneization of designs as did take place in Ban Namon, particularly on the initiative of Pranom, remained marginal and exploratory, and did not affect the essentially 'orthogenetic' nature of the bulk of local production. Local weavers did also not compete with one another in the invention of innovative products which would endow them for a while with a degree of 'monopolistic' power on the market, as they frequently do in Dan Kwien. However, unlike in Ban Pha Bong (Ch. 12), this lack of spontaneous innovativeness did not bring about a decline of the craft, since the domestic market expanded enough to absorb the routinely made weavings. It appears also that local weavers are not too eager to increase production significantly, since weaving is mainly a supplementary source of income for village women, while agriculture remains the main source of subsistence. Unlike Dan Kwien or Ban Thawai, neither Ban Namon nor any other village in its surroundings became a 'craft village', in the sense that weaving supplanted agriculture, even though the latter seems to have been somewhat neglected as weaving became a progressively more important source of income. This reflects on the declining profitability of agriculture, since weaving in itself is not a very profitable occupation. It is difficult to estimate the economic returns on weaving, since, as a cottage industry, it is not an employment at which women work continuously for a whole working day. However, by my reckoning, weavers of ordinary designs do not earn more than 100 baht (US$ 4.00 before the devaluation of 1997) in a full work-day. Indeed, some younger women do not want to engage in weaving, owing to its low returns, and are looking for other employment alternatives. This unwillingness of the younger generation to engage in crafts, owing to the relatively low income of rural artisans in comparison with the new opportunities which the burgeoning Thai economy has opened to rural people before the current financial crisis, is also noticeable in other villages in my study (Ch. 12). However, the economic conditions in Thailand changed radically with the bust of the economic boom in mid-1997. With growing unemployment, it is becoming ever harder for young rural people to find employment outside their villages; they may thus fall back upon craft production at least as a temporary expedient. Moreover, some villagers who had emigrated to the cities, have lost their jobs and returned to their villages. A few women who returned to Ban Namon and the surrounding area, apparently began to engage again in weaving. The number of weavers may thus increase in the near future, even as the market for Ban Namon products will probably contract: the Thai middle and higher classes, presently the principal clientele of Ban Namon weavings, have been hard hit by the financial crisis, and hence their demand for such relative luxuries as hand-woven textiles can be expected to decline. In early 1998 shop-keepers in Ban Namon still reported good sales, even though Pranom already felt some slowdown in demand. Despite the sharp decline in the value of the Thai currency, the local shop-keepers have not raised their prices, in order to preserve the volume of sales. Under conditions of inflationary pressures caused by the crisis, the returns to both producers and sellers will thus decrease in real terms.

Owing to the decline of Thai currency, the prices of Thai products have concomitantly declined sharply in dollar terms; this should encourage tourism and exports. Overall demand by foreigners for Thai crafts can thus be expected to increase significantly. However, it is questionable whether the small local entrepreneurs of Ban Namon will be able to take advantage of this overall increase in demand; the marketing of Ban Namon weavings has until now been conducted primarily along the more traditional channels, with which the local village women who became shop-keepers were familiar and to which they had easy access. None of them has made serious attempts to tap the potential tourist and export markets directly; nor have outside agents attempted to initiate exports of Ban Namon wares. I have noted above that the absence of such attempts has helped to preserve the basically orthogenetic character of the local commercialized weavings; the opening of these new markets would probably involve an adaptation of the products and designs to the tastes and preferences of a foreign audience and therefore lead to a growing heterogeneization of the products. Under present conditions, the viability of Ban Namon weaving may well depend upon such an adaptation. However, local shop-keepers are not prepared for this exigency. In early 1998, none of them was actually aware of the impending shift in the potential market for their products; while the prevailing dire economic situation makes it improbable that an outside entrepreneur will take the initiative and burden the risks to initiate such a shift.

Notes

1 This chapter reports the findings of a longitudinal study of the commercialization of Ban Namon weavings, conducted intermittently in the years 1991–1998, within the framework of a broader study of commercialization of Thai folk arts. The initial stage of the study was supported by a grant from the Horowitz Institute for Research on Developing Countries at Tel Aviv University. The later stage, from 1994 onwards, was supported by a grant of the Netherlands-Israel Research Program. The support of these institutions is hereby gratefully acknowledged.

12

THE DECLINE OF BASKETWARE IN A NORTHERN THAI CRAFT VILLAGE[1]

Introduction

A world-wide decline of folk-crafts has accompanied the penetration of industrial products into ever more remote localities, affecting presently every corner of the world. The renewed interest in crafts in the last decades (Graburn (ed.) 1976, Cohen 1992) derived mainly from the revival of craft production for a new 'external' public (Graburn 1976b), served by the export and tourist markets, whose tastes and uses for folk crafts are very different from those of the traditional local clientele of craft producers. Consequently, recent anthropological research has focused primarily on those crafts which preserved their vitality, or which were recently revived, or even newly invented. Those crafts which suffered a decline – and which represent the majority of crafts of the pre-industrial world – were rarely, if ever, systematically studied (cf. Graburn 1976b:5). Indeed, I am aware of only one detailed case study of the decline of a folk craft – African ritual sculpture under the influence of European missionary activity and colonial rule (Biebuyck 1976). The dearth of research on this subject therefore calls for a more systematic investigation of the factors which influence the different fates of crafts – in particular, the factors which cause some crafts to survive or even undergo a revival, while others decline or even disappear.

The comparative study of commercialized crafts conducted by myself in several craft villages in northern and north-eastern Thailand serves this task well. Specifically, the study enables us to juxtapose the case study of decline of basketware production in one of the northern villages, to the relative success of others in surviving, and even prospering, in the production and marketing of crafts on the tourist and export markets (Ch. 9–10).

275

Basketware in Ban Pha Bong[2]

Ban Pha Bong is located in the Saraphi district of the Chiang Mai province in northern Thailand, about 15 kilometers northeast of the city of Chiang Mai, the principal urban center of northern Thailand. The district as a whole is changing rapidly under the metropolitan influence of the neighboring major city. Though Ban Pha Bong is located at some distance from the main traffic routes through the district, it is also undergoing rapid urbanization, both physically and functionally. Ban Pha Bong is a fairly well developed village with paved streets, fenced gardens, and some modern houses intermingled with the older, often spacious and well kept wood habitations; its external appearance approaches that of a suburban settlement. The wave of urban expansion of Chiang Mai recently began to penetrate the area of the village – two model houses for the first housing estate, located at the fringes of the village, have already been constructed.

Most village households still engage, at least partly, in agriculture. They grow rice, primarily for their own consumption, and tend longan (*lamyai*) orchards, as do most of the other villages in the district; the fruit is the principal source of agricultural income for the villages. However, the younger labor force is already well integrated into the urban economy: many males work in the city and its surroundings, mostly in the construction industry. Some engage in trade, primarily in agricultural products. The urban economy has also penetrated directly into the village: several locally owned sewing factories employ village women in the production of large quantities of standard clothing on orders from outside enterprises.

The district of Saraphi was a 'traditional' basketware producing area, with a region-wide reputation for the quality of its work. In the past, basketware production has been largely oriented to the needs of wet rice agriculture and fishing for local consumption. One of the principal items produced in Ban Pha Bong was the *krabung*, a rice basket used for measuring and carrying rice (Plate 15; see also Kanokpongchai (ed.) 1991:114–16); the villagers also made a variety of utensils for trapping or keeping live fish, such as the long-necked fish trap *kra-joo* and the duck shaped fish container *khong-ped* (Kanok-pongchai (ed.) 1991:161,192). These products were usually sold or bartered in the surrounding region by itinerant traders. The basic raw materials were rattan (*wai*) and bamboo (*mai phai*) which grew in the environs of the village. However, local demand for 'traditional' basketware has in recent times considerably declined. The decline is

Figure 12.1 An Adapted Traditional Basket, Woven in the *lai khad* ('polished') Design.

Figure 12.2 An Adapted Traditional Fish Container Woven in the *lai song* (double-layered) Design.

due to the substitution of industrial goods for basketware, as well as to changes in the agriculture of the region: with the transition from wet rice cultivation to *lamyai* orchards, the basis on which local basketware production rested has been largely destroyed. Moreover, even in rice cultivation, farmers tend to substitute plastic bags for the *krabung* baskets, so that local demand for them has virtually disappeared.

A similar decline of demand for utensils used in rice production has also occurred elsewhere in Saraphi district: thus, the village of Don Keo has in the past specialized in the production of the *kooh*, a very big rice-

277

threshing basket (Kanokpongchai (ed.) 1991:152). However, demand for this basket has disappeared in recent years, as threshing machines were substituted for manual threshing; the production of the *kooh* has therefore virtually stopped (Chinvarakorn 1997). An attempt by villagers of Don Keo to produce miniatures of the *kooh* for sale to tourists has also failed, since tourists showed little interest in them; consequently no threshing baskets of any size are at present produced in that village.

While Ban Pha Bong was similarly affected by a decline in local demand, unlike in Don Keo, basket-weaving has not stopped. From the 1960s on, local products begun to be adapted to the growing external urban and tourist markets. However, it is important to note that most of the local basketware did not reach these markets in their 'raw', unadorned form, but underwent further embellishment elsewhere. Indeed, in contrast to Don Keo, basketware production in Ban Pha Bong remained for some time fairly vital, ever after local demand decreased. However, in recent years a gradual decline of local basketware production can be noted. In the following pages I shall describe the dynamics of change in the local basketware production and examine the factors behind its gradual decline.

The Commercialization of Ban Pha Bong Baskeware Production

The commercialization of basketware production in Ban Pha Bong took place within a changing ecological and economic context. This affected the conditions of production and hence the profitability of basket-weaving.

At the 'base line', the period proceeding commercialization for the external market, the most important raw materials, rattan and bamboo, were abundant in the surroundings of the village. With the expansion of the *lamyai* orchards, more and more land came under cultivation; rattan bushes and bamboo clumps were uprooted, and these basic raw materials became ever scarcer. While in the past bamboo was cut by the basket weavers themselves, at present it has to be bought from itinerant traders, who bring it in from more remote, less intensely utilized areas. As bamboo became scarce in the region as a whole, its price gradually rose: a bundle of bamboo sticks (*mat*), which some years ago sold for 3–4 baht (about 12–16 cents US at the rate prior to the 1997 devaluation), sold by the mid-1990s for about 30–40 baht (US $1.20–1.60). Since the price of locally made baskets has increased at a much lower rate, basketware production became ever less profitable. Moreover, poorer

Figure 12.3 A Basket Produced in the District of Phanat Nikhom for the Tourist and Export Market (author's collection).

Figure 12.4 An Elderly Ban Pha Bong Woman Weaving a Basket.

producers, especially the elderly women, found it hard to purchase the increasingly more expensive raw materials.

Rattan, presently used mainly for finishing the edges of baskets woven from bamboo, is not found in the region of Ban Pha Bong anymore. This material is purchased mainly from Ang Thong, a far-off province in the central plain; however, though Ang Thong is also a major center of basketware production, the rattan used there is imported from Malaysia rather than locally collected. Because of its high price, some producers in Ban Pha Bong use cheaper, but less durable materials to finish their products.

Thai basketware is distinguished by a great richness of weaving patterns (Nutcherinphon B.E. 2525). However, only a small number of relatively simple patterns such as several versions of *lai khad* ('polished' design, Nutcherinphon B.E. 2525: 9, 18–22) and *lai song* (double-layered design, Nutcherinphon B.E. 2525: 12, 30–34) have been used by the majority of basket weavers in Ban Pha Bong (Fig. 12.1–12.2).

Some members of virtually every household still possess the basic skills for the production of simple, unadorned, functional baskets in these patterns. However, most types of the traditional baskets are not made anymore; but a few have been adapted, in various ways, to the new market demand.

As in the past, basket-weaving skills are transmitted from mother to daughter within the household. However, many women of the younger generation show no interest in the craft and have failed to acquire even the basic skills, while those who have acquired them, often do not use them; with disuse, they will probably be forgotten, and certainly not transmitted to their offspring. Neither are new weaving designs, more attractive to the external public than the traditional ones, learned and adopted by the local basket-weavers.

The Queen's foundation, SUPPORT (SUPPORT 1985, 1992), organizes formal training courses for practitioners of about a dozen crafts, in which techniques and designs adapted to the changing market are taught; its program includes the weaving of 'refined basketware' (Warren and Tettoni 1994:145–7). But unlike basket-weavers of the district of Phanat Nikhom, who make fine baskets (Fig. 12.3) or the makers of *yan lipao* basketware of northern Thailand (SUPPORT 1992:304–10), the basket-weavers of Ban Pha Bong have not been invited to participate in such courses. As the president of the local basketware producers' group (*klum*) rather diffidently explained, the quality of local traditional basketware is not high enough to elicit such an invitation. Ban Pha Bong basketware producers are thus left with their own simple and declining skills; these are hardly a sufficient basis for a successful transformation of production in response to changing market conditions.

Figure 12.5 The President of the Ban Pha Bong Basket Producers *klum* (group) at Work.

In Ban Pha Bong, as in most Thai villages, basket-weaving is predominantly a women's occupation (Fig. 12.4). The local workforce consists primarily of elderly women, most of them beyond the age of fifty, and a single male master-weaver, who is also the president of the basketware producers' group (*klum*) (Fig. 12.5). In contrast to most of the women, he works full-time in basketware.

Basket-weaving is a household occupation. The elderly women usually work alone; they are sometimes assisted by their daughters or daughters-in-law in the evenings, when these return home from other employment. Men, mostly husbands, sometimes assist the weavers by cutting up the bamboo sticks, which are then stripped into thin straps for weaving. Some men also assist in the finishing of the baskets, like cutting rough edges, sewing or glueing them; but the weaving itself is done only by the women. No hired help is employed by anyone in the village.

It is hard to estimate the number of women employed in basket-weaving in the village, since some weaving is done, at least occasionally, in most of the households. Only a few women, however, engage in basket-weaving as their principal occupation. Even those do not engage in the craft on a steady, full-time basis. Rather, they weave baskets when they are free of other household chores, the intensity of their work depending on the size and urgency of orders. They do not store products for sale.

Income from basket-weaving is low, even by northern Thai village standards; measured in terms of return to work hours, it is lower than in

281

virtually all other northern Thai village crafts. Even if a woman devotes a full working day to basket-weaving, her daily income does not usually reach more than 70 baht (US $2.80). In comparison, even relatively unskilled carvers or potters in craft villages usually earn at least 100 baht (US$4.00) a day, and skilled craftsmen reach several times that amount.

The producers' group was formed in 1987 to help basketware weavers receive more orders and to provide them with raw materials. A warehouse was constructed with the support of the government in the vicinity of the present president's compound. Members contributed 100 baht (US$4.00) each for a revolving fund for the purchase of raw materials. The president receives the orders, and is supposed to distribute them among the members, provide them with raw materials, deliver the finished products and pay off the producers. The products are slightly marked up to cover the maintenance and operation costs of the group. Any remaining profits are to be divided among the members once a year.

However, the group has few members, and their numbers are declining: in 1992 there were 38 members, though many more women in the village produced basketware; in 1995 only 24 members remained; the number of active members was even smaller, and many of these belonged to the president's extended family. The president usually fills the smaller orders by himself; if he receives a larger one, he distributes it primarily among the members of his family. Members who have left the group complain about inequities in the distribution of profits, and claim that by working on their own, they receive more money for their work, and get paid more promptly then they did as members of the group.

The group's president claims in response that the group suffers from the competition of individual basket-weavers, whose work is cheaper but of lower quality than that of the group's members. For example, they do not use the relatively expensive rattan, but rather a cheaper substitute to finish the edges of their baskets. Nevertheless, the group is losing business to individual producers.

The experience of the basketware producers' group in Ban Pha Bong is altogether similar to that of similar producers' groups in other craft villages, where such groups have been established through outside, mainly governmental initiative. Soon after their establishment they tend to suffer from squabbles among members, exploitation by the president of his or her position, decline in active membership and, eventually, disintegration. Many textile weavers groups in northern Thailand have

Figure 12.6 An adaptation of the *krabung*, Produced for the Tourist or Export Market.

in fact become inactive, while their presidents developed an often thriving private business, handing out raw materials to producers, and collecting and selling their products. However, this stage has not yet been reached in Ban Pha Bong. Considering the low profitability of local basketware it is doubtful that such a private business will emerge in the future.

In contrast to the processes of far-reaching heterogeneization of products in the more successful craft producing villages in Thailand, in Ban Pha Bong the products and their designs have changed relatively little in comparison with the 'base-line'. Virtually all products destined for the market were modelled on types of baskets which the villagers have been producing at the 'base line'; they underwent merely 'orthogenetic' changes (Shiloah and Cohen 1983), mere adaptations to their new, different purposes: in the past they were functional objects, but now their purpose became primarily decorative. Various traditional utensils, such as the *krabung* (Plate 15), fish traps and fish containers (Ngamsit 1982; Kanokpongchai (ed.) 1991:104–7, 160–1, 182–193) have been adapted to make vases, baskets and other decorative items for the tourist and export markets (Fig. 12.6–12.8). Villagers did not evolve entirely new products on their own initiative, but they are

283

sometimes asked to make copies from models supplied by outside entrepreneurs. However, such requests are rare, and do not usually lead to the initiation of a new product into the repertoire of local basketware weavers. In this respect, Ban Pha Bong differs substantially from some more developed craft producing villages, such as Dan Kwien and Ban Thawai (Ch. 9–10), which thrive on 'heterogenetic' products (Shiloah and Cohen 1983), the models for which were initially given to them by outsiders.

The Ban Pha Bong basket-weavers have little incentive – and often also lack the necessary capital – to stock up their products; even the producers group's warehouse stores relatively few items. Most of the production is done on outside orders; and since there are usually insufficient orders to employ the available workforce, many of the basket-weavers are underemployed. Underemployment, in turn, keeps prices and incomes low since most of the elderly women have no alternative source of gainful employment and are therefore willing to work for very low returns. Younger women, however, tend to move into more remunerative jobs, giving up basket-weaving as an occupation.

Ban Pha Bong products are not 'marketed' in a strict sense, but are mostly produced to order. A few local middlemen order small quantities from producers – both members and non-members of the producers' group. Here some vestiges of the old marketing system are preserved: the middlemen still occasionally sell baskets at regional fairs to a local clientele, thus resembling the itinerant traders of an earlier era.

The bulk of Ban Pha Bong products, however, is ordered by outsiders and is eventually intended for a new, external public – although they are not sold to it in their 'raw' state as locally produced, but undergo considerable further elaboration. The principal purchasers of Ban Pha Bong basketware are woodcarving workshops in Ban Thawai (Ch. 10). These workshops order baskets – sometimes in large quantities – from the producers group, the middlemen, or directly from the producers, and paint, lacquer and decorate them in styles resembling those on the locally produced woodcarvings (Fig. 12.9–12.10). The decorated items are then sold on the tourist or export markets. Measured in terms of investment of time, money and materials, the decoration of Ban Pha Bong baskets is a much more profitable activity than the weaving of baskets.

Ban Pha Bong basket-weavers are very much aware of this difference; indeed, some years ago they attempted to decorate their baskets by themselves, instead of selling them in their 'raw' state, thereby improving the profitability of their craft. However, the quality

284

Figure 12.7 Another Adaptation of the *krabung* for the Tourist or Export Market.

of their work was considerably inferior to that of Ban Thawai decorations: they simply painted the baskets in a reddish-brown color, but neither lacquered nor decorated them with those elaborate designs which make the Ban Thawai baskets so attractive to both Thai and foreign buyers.

In Ban Pha Bong, several explanations were offered for the failure of the local basket-weavers to decorate their products by themselves; some claimed that there was no market for decorated baskets in the village, because tourists did not regularly visit it – while Ban Thawai shopkeepers preferred to purchase 'raw' baskets and decorate them by themselves. Others claimed that the locals did not have the means to purchase the equipment and raw materials necessary for decorating the baskets. A typically Thai suggestion was that locals did not like to paint their baskets because paints exude a bad smell (cf. Cohen 1988b). But the most likely explanation is that local producers – mostly elderly women without formal training – do not possess the knowledge and

Figure 12.8 A Flower Vase, Adapted from the *kra-joo*, a Traditional Fish Trap.

Figure 12.9 A Small Ban Pha Bong Basket in its 'Raw' and Undecorated Form (right) and After Undergoing Decoration in Ban Thawai (left).

skills necessary to decorate basketware of a marketable quality. Such knowledge and skills are in fact found in Ban Thawai, since the woodcarvers in that village learned to decorate Buddha images and other religious statuary in a Burmese style at the incipient stage of commercialization, and applied that style – in a simplified manner – to the decoration of baskets (Ch. 10). As the president of the basketware producers' group in Ban Pha Bong put it, the people of Ban Thawai have a 'good head' (*hua dee*) for decorating baskets, while his own people do not.

A relatively new source of orders for Ban Pha Bong basketware are urban enterprises in the Chiang Mai area, which use them as receptacles in packaging their products, such as strawberries, small dolls or toys. Such establishments tend to order large quantities of tiny, simple and cheap baskets. Thus, in 1992, the producers' group received an order for 80,000 small baskets, at 1.70 baht (7 cents US) per unit. An urban doll producer regularly orders small bamboo trays for his dolls, at about 5.00 baht (20 cents US) per unit. In 1994, for example, he ordered 4,500 such units, and in 1996 – 500. The president of the producers' group distributes such orders between its members, for whom they became one of the principal sources of employment. Ironically, however, despite the common complaint of insufficient orders, the elderly women often find it hard to supply the required quantities on time. With little organization of production and no quality control, the producers' group is ill-suited for reliable large-scale production of standardized items.

The Retreat from Basketware

Basketware in Ban Pha Bong is a declining occupation. All three generations of women in the village tend gradually to retreat from it and turn to more remunerative occupations.

The retreat is most pronounced in the present generation of young and middle-aged women. Though most of them possess the basic basket-weaving skills, and many had engaged in basket production in the past, in recent years they have turned to other kinds of employment. Basket-weaving is a low-prestige occupation in their eyes and they engage in it, if at all, only during their spare time and then mostly to help elder female members of the household to fill orders, rather than engaging in it on their own account. Many of these women find employment in sewing in the village itself. Most work in the sewing factories, each of which employs about twenty women. These factories

Figure 12.10 A Ban Pha Bong Basket Decorated in Ban Thawai (author's collection).

produce simple standardized garments in large quantities on orders from urban entrepreneurs. In addition, those women who have been able to purchase an electric sewing machine, work for such enterprises at home (cf. Parnwell et al. 1990). They are paid on a piece-rate basis and earn about 100 baht (US$4.00), or more, a day. Their income from sewing is significantly higher, and more regular, than they could have earned from weaving baskets. The children of these women, in turn, show no interest in basketware, and do not ordinarily acquire even the basic skills of the craft.

The low remuneration and prestige of basket-weaving have thus confined the craft to the elder generation of women in the village, for whom it has become a 'residual occupation,' virtually the only way of making some income, however meager. However, an alternative source of employment, even for the elderly women, has emerged in the last few years – the production of hand-made toothpicks. Many of the older women have turned away from basket-weaving and turned to toothpick-making. This new employment opportunity was provided by an urban entrepreneur, who supplied producers with the simple machinery and tools needed for making toothpicks (Fig. 12.11) and purchased all their production, packaging and marketing it in the city of Chiang Mai (cf. Parnwell et al. 1990).

The women received 3.00 baht (about 8 cents US) for a packet of 100 toothpicks. Workers ordinarily made about fifty packets in the course of a full working day, thus earning about 150 baht (US $6.00) a day; but they had to supply the raw material – bamboo – by themselves. Workers claimed that toothpick making is simpler than basket-weaving and earned them a more regular income. They also needed much less raw material than in basket-weaving. Though toothpick makers were generally elderly women, a few men also began to engage in this new occupation. Some younger women, who used to weave baskets, were also enticed into this simpler, but more remunerative work. However, at the outbreak of the economic crisis in 1997, the urban entrepreneur abruptly cancelled his orders.

The retreat from basketware in Ban Pha Bong thus embraces the whole spectrum of generations: the girls of the younger generation refuse to engage in the craft and do not even acquire its basic skills; the generation of their mothers, though possessing these skills, do not practice them as an occupation; and even the generation of the older women, the principal producers of basketware, have begun to turn away from it, many preferring the making of tooth-picks to weaving baskets, as long as there was a demand for the former.

Discussion

The decline of local demand for the 'traditional' basketware products of Ban Pha Bong has deflected local production to the growing tourist and export markets. However, production for these markets is presently in decline, and may stop completely in the next generation, as skills fail to be transmitted, owing to loss of interest in basket-weaving as an occupation. The question therefore emerges, why did basket-weaving decline in Ban Pha Bong while other commercialized crafts thrived or remained viable in other northern Thai villages?

Attempting to answer this question, we have to start with a general observation: the commercialized craft production in Thailand, as a whole, came under pressure from a variety of sources: a situation which

Figure 12.11 A Ban Pha Bong Woman Making Toothpicks.

I propose to call 'handicraft squeeze' has developed. Up to the late 1990s, Thailand was a rapidly developing country (Pongpaichit and Baker 1996); its development was accompanied by rising labor costs. This had two consequences for craft production: on the one hand, less developed countries competed successfully with Thai crafts on the world market – for example Philippine basketware was generally cheaper than that produced in Thailand. On the other hand, workers were enticed away from rural occupations, including crafts, to more remunerative employment in manufacturing and services. Indeed, urban occupations are penetrating the villages (cf. Parnwell et al. 1990), especially those located within the metropolitan orbit of big cities, such as Ban Pha Bong. Concomitantly, raw materials for crafts also become commodities, and consequently ever more costly, as we have seen in the case of rattan and bamboo in Ban Pha Bong.

290

The 'handicraft squeeze' was caused precisely by the combination of these contrasting influences: while raw materials became more expensive and alternative employment for artisans more remunerative, the pressure of the world market depressed the prices of craft products; the profitability of crafts was thereby reduced – a state of affairs which was in Ban Pha Bong reflected in the falling income of basket weavers.

The 'handicraft squeeze' however, also affected the Thai craft market as a whole; how come, then, that some villages were able to cope with it and others were not? Why did it affect Ban Pha Bong basketware to a greater degree than Ban Thawai woodcarving or Dan Kwien pottery? The main reason seems to be the inability of Ban Pha Bong basket-weavers to respond to the changing circumstances of their work: while the ecological and economic context of basketware production in Ban Pha Bong has changed significantly in the last few decades, the local products underwent only a modest change. The artisans in the village were unable to adapt their products to the changing conditions, as have the woodcarvers of Ban Thawai or the potters of Dan Kwien.

Although the village was an important source of basketware for the area at the 'base-line', the weaving patterns commonly known to the producers were relatively simple and of a limited variety. The villagers appear to have had few if any opportunities to learn other patterns, more attractive to the new, outside audience. The techniques of basket-weaving remained virtually unchanged; the products merely underwent some 'orthogenetic' adaptation, but there was no significant hetero-geneization. Ban Pha Bong baskets thus remained 'authentic,' in the sense of maintaining a continuing resemblance between current products and those at the 'base line'. In particular, the basket-weavers failed in their single attempt at a more radical innovation – to paint or decorate their baskets, in order to make them more appealing to the new customers and thus liberate themselves from dependence on Ban Thawai, where the profitable work of embellishing the 'raw' Ban Pha Bong baskets is accomplished. The continuity in techniques and forms of production and lack of innovation – which should have attracted the more authenticity-seeking customers – proved to be a drawback on the mass crafts market.

If the quality of Ban Pha Bong 'traditional' basketware were at a level with, for example, the 'fine' southern Thai *yan lipao* basketware or mat-weaving (cf. Peetathawatchai B.E. 2519), or of the '*ka-pok*' or *khit* basketware of Isan (northeast Thailand) (SUPPORT 1992; Fang 1994), Ban Pha Bong basket-weavers might have been invited to participate in training courses of the SUPPORT Foundation. There they could have acquired new weaving and finishing techniques, thereby becoming better able to cope with the 'handicraft squeeze.'

However, Ban Pha Bong basketware was not distinguished enough to attract the attention of sponsoring institutions; and since local basket-weavers were unable to accomplish the adaptation of local production to the new circumstances by themselves, basketware production could not go but downhill. As the younger generation abandoned the craft, it became a 'residual occupation', the preserve of the elderly generation – and even they have began to turn away and embraced toothpick making instead. To all appearances, Ban Pha Bong basketware appears to be doomed to extinction, save for the unlikely exigency that an outside agency will undertake the difficult task of sponsoring its revival.

Conclusion

In an earlier chapter (Ch. 10) I proposed the idea that in the wake of commercialization of a 'traditional' rural craft, a process of disassociation tends to take place between the various components of the production and marketing process, which have previously been closely associated. According to the model proposed there, at the 'base line', namely in the period preceding commercialization, all components of the production process tend to be closely associated: both materials and workers are of local origin, knowledge and skills are part of a local or regional culture, transmitted informally between parents and children or masters and apprentices; the products are predominately functional and their designs and ornamentation are part of a local or regional tradition (although they might have originated elsewhere); they are mostly used, bartered or sold locally or in the nearby region. In the course of commercialization, the components of this process tend to become gradually disassociated, as raw materials originate elsewhere, new skills are acquired, outsiders enter production, and products, designs and ornamentation become adapted to an expanding market, consisting of an external audience, which does not share the cultural background and lifeways of the producers. I have documented this process in a case study of the woodcarving village of Ban Thawai, in the district of Hang Dong, to the west of Chiang Mai. In that village, a far-reaching disassociation has taken place between the components of the process, accompanying a significant expansion of production for the tourist as well as the world-wide export markets (Ch. 10). A similar process took place in another highly successful craft village, the pottery village of Dan Kwien in northeast Thailand (Ch. 9). In the course of the process of disassociation, the products undergo a radical 'hetero-geneization' and are often changed to such an extent that all similarity with the products at the 'base line' virtually disappears. This is ironic since it is often precisely the original attractiveness of the products at the 'base line' which puts the process of disassociation into motion. Insofar as those products were seen as culturally 'marked' and authentic, the adaptation of production to changing market conditions, while preserving the craft's viability, leads to a loss of that markedness and authenticity. This is particularly the case when large-scale demand in the export market overshadows the demand of the tourist market.

In Ban Pha Bong, however, only a partial process of disassociation has taken place, and even this was of relatively limited scope. The source of raw materials was disassociated from production, and so were the ultimate consumers of the products, who do not share any more the producers' culture. However, the products themselves were only to a limited degree disassociated from their original cultural background – they merely underwent 'orthogenetic' changes (Shiloah and Cohen 1983), but not heterogeneization: the raw materials, techniques of production and basket-weaving patterns remained virtually unchanged in comparison to the 'base-line'. The form of the products was only slightly adapted to their new functions. Most importantly, the producers failed to evolve or learn novel techniques of painting and decorating their products, without which they could not reach their ultimate clientele, and therefore remained dependent on orders from artisans in another village, who painted and decorated their products. This state of affairs kept their incomes low and induced producers and their offspring to look for other lines of work. The basketware of Ban Pha Bong may perhaps appear more authentic than the products of some other craft villages, but, unfortunately, its authenticity had done little to help it sell.

Our analysis leads to a somewhat ironic conclusion: in many cases of commercialization of crafts, a growing gap tends to emerge between the style of local craft production at the 'base line' and the preferences and demands of the new markets. The gap grows as the export market for mass products overshadows the tourist market. This circumstance, in conjunction with changes in the local ecological and economic contexts, engenders the process of disassociation and accompanying heterogeneization of products, which enables a craft to survive and even to prosper. In the course of that process, however, the craft is transformed, losing much of its initial markedness and presumed authenticity. However, if by choice, or by force of circumstances as is the case in Ban Pha Bong, that process does not occur, the craft may well face the threat of gradual decline and eventual disappearance.

Notes

1 This chapter is based on materials partly collected within the framework of a research project on the commercialization of folk crafts in northern Thai villages, under a grant from the Netherlands-Israel Research Program, whose support is hereby gratefully acknowledged.
2 Ban Pha Bong is, strictly speaking, a sub-district (*tambon*) composed of several adjoining villages (*mooban*); basketware is presently produced primarily in two of these, Moo 3 and Moo 4; the following presentation relates primarily to those two villages.

REFERENCES

Abrams, A. 1970 'With the Meo Tribesmen in Thailand' *The New Leader*, July 6;8–10,

Abrams, A. 1971a 'Marching into Misery', *Far Eastern Economic Review*, 72(17), April 24: 1971:21–24.

Abrams, A. 1971b 'Laos' Meo Tribesmen: A Nation of Refugees', *The New Leader*, June 14:9–10.

Abrams, A. 1974 'Times have Changed but the CIA Stays On', *Asia Magazine*, Oct. 20:22–27.

Adams, M.J. 1980 'Structural Aspects of East Sumbanese Art' *in* J.J. Fox (ed.):*The Flow of Life: Essays on Eastern Indonesia*. Cambridge, Mass.: Harvard University Press, pp. 208–220.

Almagor, U. 1983 'Colors that Match and Clash', *Res*, 5.49–73.

'Amaranth' 1990 'Metallic Earthenware of Dan Kwien', *Hotel Information News*, No. 13:28–32.

'Amethyst' 1991 Chiang Mai's Colorful Bo Sarng Umbrellas: Setting a Handicraft Route in Motion', *Kinnaree*, 8(5):42–51.

Amatyakul, S. 1996 'Show Promotes Unique Earthenware Products', *Bangkok Post*, Feb. 17:31.

Angsanakul, P. 1989 'Masters in the Art of *Mudmee* Silk Making', *Bangkok Post*, June 24: 21.

Angsanakul, P. 1997 'In Search of Thailand's Woven Heritage', *Bangkok Post, Outlook*, Jan 11:8.

Arin, 1992 'Silk Brocades of Lanna', *Kinnaree*, 9 (9):86–91.

Aspelin, P.L. 1977 'The Anthropological Analysis of Tourism: Indirect Tourism and Political Economy in the Case of the Mamainde of Mato Grosso, Brazil', *Annals of Tourism Research* 4 (3):135–60.

Bangkok Post 1992 'Kaysone Phomvihane, 1920–1992: An Underground Guerilla Who Became President', *Bangkok Post*, Nov. 23:4.

Barnard, B. 1984 'Is it Authentic? The Tourist Arts of Southeast Asia', *UFSI Reports (Asia)* No. 14.

Barney, G.L. 1967 'The Meo of Xieng Khouang Province' *in* P. Kunstadter (ed.): *Southeast Asian Tribes, Minorities and Nations*, Princeton. N.J.: Princeton University Press, Vol. 1, pp. 271–293.

295

Barry, A 1985 'Laotian Needlework Comes to America', *New York Times*, August 29.
Becker, H.S. 1974 'Art as Collective Action', *American Sociological Review*, 39 (6):767–776.
Becker, H.S. 1978 'Arts and Crafts', *American Journal of Sociology* 83:862–889.
Beier, U. 1968 *Contemporary Art in Africa*, London: Pall Mall Press.
Bekker, S. 1978 'Bronze Casting: Thailand's Living Tradition', *Sawaddi,* July–August:24–28.
Bellion, W. 1991 'The Aftermath of Conflict: Hmong Story Cloth – The Threads of War at the Richmond Art Center', *Artweek*, Sept. 5:14.
Ben-Amos, P. 1977a 'Pidgin Language and Tourist Arts', *Studies in the Anthropology of Visual Communication*, 4 (2):128–139.
Benyasut, M. 1990 *The Ecology of Phanat Nikhom Camp*. Bangkok: Chulalongkorn University, Institute of Asian Studies Indochinese Refugee Information Center (IRIC), Occasional Paper Series, No. 001.
Bernatzik, H.A. 1947 *Akha und Meau: Probleme der angewandten Völkerkunde in Hinterindien*. Innsbruck: Wagner'sche Univeritäts Buchdruckerei.
Berry, B.J.L. 1963 *Commercial Structure and Commercial Blight*, Chicago: University of Chicago, Department of Geography, Research Paper No. 85.
Bessac, S. 1988 *Embroidered Hmong Story Cloths*. Missoula, Montana: University of Montata, Contributions to Anthropology, No. 9.
Bewig, J. 1978 *Chinesische Papierschnitte*. Hamburg: Museum für Völkerkunde.
Bhanthumnavin, K. 1972 'Overcoming the Problem of Resettling Hill Tribes', *Southeast Asian Spectrum*, 1(1):23–34.
Bhruksasri, W. 1989 'Government Policy: Highland Ethnic Minorities' *in* McKinnon and Vienne (eds.), pp. 5–31.
Biebuyck, D.P. 1976 'Decline of Lega Sculptural Art' in: *Graburn* (ed.), pp. 334–349.
Binney, G.A. 1968 'The Social and Economic Organization of Two White Meo Communities in Northern Thailand'. Washington D.C.: Advanced Research Projects Agency (mimeo).
Bowie, A.K. 1993a 'Assessing the Early Observers: Cloth and the Fabric of Society in 19th Century Northern Thai Kingdoms', *American Ethnologist*, 20(1):138–158.
Bowie, A.K. 1993b 'Trade and Textiles in Northern Thailand: A Historical Perspective', *in* S. Prangwatthanakun (ed.) *Textiles of Asia: A Common Heritage*, Chiang Mai: Center for the Promotion of Arts and Culture, Chiang Mai University, pp. 180–200.
Boyer, R. McD. 1976 'Gourd Decoration in Highland Peru' *in* Graburn (ed.), pp. 183–196.
Brown, I. 1980 'Government Initiative and Peasant Response in the Siamese Silk Industry, 1903–1913' *Journal of the Siam Society*, 68(2):34–47.
Brown, S., 1979 'The Origins of Thai Silk', *Arts of Asia*, 9(5):91–100.
Brunnstrom, D. 1991 'Kaysone: A Durable Revolutionary' *Bangkok Post*, August 16:4.
Business Review 1986 'Getting Ready for "1987 Visit Thailand Year"', *Business Review*, 14 (166):51–79.

REFERENCES

Butler, R.W. 1991 'West Edmonton Mall as a Tourist Attraction', *Canadian Geographer*, 35 (3):287–295.
Butler-Diaz, J. 1981 *Yao Design in Northern Thailand* (rev. ed.), Bangkok: The Siam Society.
Camacrafts 1984 *Camacrafts; Handcraft from Northeast Thailand* [commercial catalogue], [Bangkok: Camacrafts].
Campbell, M., N. Pongnoi and Ch. Voraphitak 1978 *From the Hands of the Hills*, Hong Kong: Media Transasia.
Cannon, A. 1982 'Of Pots and Potters', *Sawaddi*, Sept.–Oct.:30–34, 37.
Catlin, A. and S. Beck 1981 *The Hmong: From Asia to Providence, Rhode Island*, Providence, RI: Roger Williams Park Museum, Center for Hmong Lore.
Chagnon, J. and R. Rumpf, 1983a 'Decades of Division for the Lao Hmong,' *Southeast Asian Chronicle*, No. 91: 10–15.
Chagnon, J., and R. Rumpf, 1983b 'Search for 'Yellow Rain'', *Southeast Asian Chronicle*, No. 90: 3–17.
Chan, S. (ed.) 1994 *Hmong Means Free*, Philadelphia: Temple University Press.
Charasdamrong, P. 1971 'Government Combats Red Subversion Among Hilltribes', *Bangkok World*, June 19.
Charasdamrong, P. 1991a 'Where Have All the Trees Gone?', *Bangkok Post*, Oct. 20:8–9.
Charasdamrong, P. 1991b 'Woodcarver Laments End of an Era', *Bangkok Post*, Oct. 20:9
Chatman, S. 1983 *Story and Discourse*, Ithaca, NY: Cornell University Press.
Chauvet, J.M. 1984a 'Asia's Forgotten Army', *Bangkok Post*, Oct. 7:15.
Chauvet, J.M. 1984b 'Three Weeks with the Lao Rebels', *Bangkok Post*, Oct. 7.:15.
Chazee, L. 1995 *Atlas des ethnies et des sous-ethnies du Laos*, Bangkok: Laurent Chazee.
Chiangmai Travel Holiday 1991 'Royal Blue Denims', *Chiangmai Travel Holiday*, Aug. 16:16,24
Chindarsi, N. 1976 *The Religion of the Hmong Njua*, Bangkok: The Siam Society.
Chinvarakorn, V. 1997 'Silent Witness of Days Gone By', *Bangkok Post, Outlook*, Sept. 3:4.
Chudhavipata, W. 1986/7 'The Craft of Mat Making' *Thailand Illustrated*, 5(2):28–32.
Chuenprapanusorn, B. 1988 'Korat, Gateway to the Northeast', *Kinnaree*, 5(9):44–49.
Chunpraseri, Ch. 1988 'Pat [Fan]' *Lae Siam*, 1(4):54–59 (in Thai, summary in English).
Clair, J. 1977 *Marcel Duchamp, catalogue raisonné*, Paris: Musée National d'Art Moderne.
Clark, C. 1991 'A Craft for Kings', *JewelSiam*, 2(1):44–47.
Cohen, E. 1979 'The Impact of Tourism on the Hill Tribes of Northern Thailand', *Internationales Asienforum*, 10(1/2):5–38.
Cohen, E. 1982a 'Jungle Guides in Northern Thailand: The Dynamics of a Marginal Occupational Role', *Sociological Review*, 30(2):234–266.

297

Cohen, E. 1982b 'Marginal Paradises – Bungalow Tourism on the Islands of Southern Thailand', *Annals of Tourism Research*, 9(2):189–228.

Cohen, E. 1982c 'Refugee Art in Thailand', *Cultural Survival Quarterly*, 6(4):40–42.

Cohen, E. 1983 'Hill Tribe Tourism', in McKinnon and Bhruksasri (eds.), pp. 307–325.

Cohen, E. 1988a 'Authenticity and Commoditization in Tourism', *Annals of Tourism Research*, 15:371–386.

Cohen, E. 1988b 'The Broken Cycle: Smell in a Bangkok *soi* [lane]', *Ethnos*, 53(1–2):37–49.

Cohen, E. 1989 'The Commercialization of Ethnic Crafts', *Journal of Design History*, 2(2–3): 161–168.

Cohen, E. 1991 *Thai Society in Comparative Perspective*, Bangkok: White Lotus.

Cohen, E. 1992a 'Pilgrimage Centers: Concentric and Excentric' *Annals of Tourism Research*, 19(1):33–50.

Cohen, E. 1992b 'Policy Options for Tourist Art Development', *World Travel and Tourism Review*, 2:175–176.

Cohen, E. 1992c 'Tourist Arts', *Progress in Tourism, Recreation and Hospitality Management*, 4:3–32.

Cohen, E. 1992d 'Who are the *chao khao*? "Hill Tribe" Postcards from Northern Thailand', *International Journal of the Sociology of Language*, No. 98: 101–125.

Cohen, E. (ed.), 1993 'Tourist Arts', *Annals of Tourism Research*, 20(1):1–215 (Sp. Issue).

Cohen, E. 1995 'Contemporary Tourism – Trends and Challenges', in R. Butler and D. Pearce (eds.): *Change in Tourism*, London: Routledge, pp. 12–29.

Cohen, E. 1996 '*Thai Tourism: Hill Tribes, Islands and Open-ended Prostitution*', Bangkok: White Lotus.

Comber, L. 1969 *Chinese Magic and Superstitions in Malaya*, 4th (rev.) edition, Singapore: Eastern University Press.

Conway, S. 1992 *Thai Textiles*, London: British Museum Press.

Cooper, R.G. 1978a 'Dynamic Tension: Symbiosis and Contradiction in Hmong Social Relations', *in* J. Clammer (ed.): *The New Economic Anthropology*, London: Macmillan, pp. 138–175.

Cooper, R.G. 1978b 'Unity and Division in Hmong Social Categories in Thailand', *in* P.S.J Chen, and H.D. Evers (eds.) *Studies in ASEAN Sociology*, Singapore: Chopman Enterprises, pp. 297–320.

Cooper, R.G. 1984 *Resource Scarcity and the Hmong Response*. Singapore: Singapore University Press.

Cooper R.G. et al. 1991 *The Hmong*. Bangkok: Artasia Press.

Crystal, E. 1983 'Hmong Traditions in the Crucible of Social Change', *in* Dewhurst and MacDowell (eds.), pp. 3–15.

Cultural Survival Quarterly 1982 'Ethnic Art: Works in Progress' *Cultural Survival Quarterly*, 6(4):1–42 (Sp. Issue).

Cultural Survival Quarterly 1987 'Militarization and Indigenous People', *Cultural Survival Quarterly*, 11(3): 1–58, 11(4):2–64. (Sp. Issues)

Davies, R.L. 1974 'Nucleated and Ribbon Components of the Urban Retail System in Britain', *Town Planning Review*, 45(1):91–111.

REFERENCES

Davies, R.L. 1984 *Retail and Commercial Planning*. London: Croom Helm.

Davis, B. 1987 'SUPPORT, A Queen's Foundation for Her People', *Sawasdee,*, August 16: 10–15.

Davis, N. 1975 'A Thorny Problem for Thailand', *Far Eastern Economic Review*, 90(43):20–22.

de Beauclair, I. 1970 *Tribal Cultures of Southwest China*, Taipei: Oriental Cultural Service.

Deitch, L.I. 1977 'The Impact of Tourism Upon the Arts and Crafts of the Indians of the Southwestern United States', *in* V.L. Smith (ed.). *Hosts and Guests*, Philadelphia: University of Pennsylvania Press, pp. 173–182.

Dennys, N.B. 1968 [1876] *The Folklore of China*, Amsterdam: Oriental Press.

Dewhurst, C. 1985 'Life at Ban Vinai', *The Nation,* Jan. 6:19.

Dewhurst, C.K. and M. MacDowell 1983 'Michigan Hmong Textiles', *in* Dewhurst and MacDowell (eds.), pp. 15–25.

Dewhurst, C.K. and M. MacDowell (eds.) 1983 'Michigan Hmong Arts: Textiles in Transition', Michigan State University, The Museum, *Folk Culture Series*, 3(2):1–74.

Dhuravatsadorn, L.B. 1923 'The White Meo', *Journal of the Siam Society*, 17: 153–189.

Diran, R.K. 1997 *The Vanishing Tribes of Burma*, London: Weidenfeld and Nicholson.

Donnelly, N.D. 1986 'Factors Contributing to a Split Within a Clientelistic Needlework Cooperative Engaged in Refugee Resettlement', *in* Hendricks, Downing and Deinhard (eds.), pp. 159–173.

Donnelly, N.D. 1994 *Changing Lives of Refugee Hmong Women*. Seattle: University of Washington Press.

Dowing, D.T. and D.P. Olney (eds.) 1982 *The Hmong in the West* Minneapolis, Minn.: University of Minnesota, Center for Urban and Regional Affairs, Southeast Asia Refugee Project.

Dunnigan, T. 1982 'Segmentary Kinship in an Urban Society: The Hmong in St. Paul-Minneapolis', *Anthropological Quarterly*, 55(3): 126–134.

Ekachai, S. 1992 'Weaving in and out of Debt', *Bangkok Post*, May 14:25,42.

Eliade, M. 1971 *The Myth of the Eternal Return*, Princeton, N.J.: Princeton University Press.

Elkan, W. 1958 'The East African Trade in Woodcarvings', *Africa*, 28(4): 314–323.

Embroidered History 1987 *Embroidered History: Hmong Story Cloths*, Long Beach, CA: Long Beach Museum of Art.

Emmons, R. 1992 'The Carvers of Tawai', *Thailand Traveler*, June: 18–24.

Enwall, J. 1995 *A Myth Became Reality. History and Development of the Miao Written Language*, Stockholm: Institute of Oriental Languages, Stockholm University, 2 Vol.

Everingham, J. and J. Burgess 1973 'Long Wait in the Mountain', *Asia Magazine*, Aug. 19:3–6.

Exports from Thailand 1990 'This Shop Sells Quality', *Exports from Thailand*, 1(6):40–41.

Fang, S. 1994 'The Artifice of Bamboo Handicraft', *Bangkok Post, Horizons*, July 14:5.

Fang, S. 1995 'Going Pottery in Korat', *Thailand Traveller*, 5(39):44–49.

Finch, J. 1982 'Laos: Stitching as Language among the Hmong in America', *Craft International*, 1(4):33–37.

Flower Cloths 1981 *Flower Cloths: Art of the Hmong*, Eugene, Ore: University of Oregon Museum of Art.

Fournier, M. 1987 'Hmong Stories and Story Cloths', *The World and I*, Sept. 1987: 615–29.

Freeman, J.M., H. Nguyen and P. Hartsell 1985 'The Tribal Lao Training Project', *Cultural Survival Quarterly*, 9(2):10–12.

Gallagher, B.M. 1973 'Craft Villages of Northern Thailand', *Arts of Asia*, 3(3):48–55.

Garrett, W.E. 1974 'No Place to Run: The Hmong of Laos' *National Geographic*, 145(1):78–111.

Garrett, W.E. 1980 'Thailand Refuge from Terror', *National Geographic*, 157(5):633–641.

Geddes, W.R. 1970 'Opium and the Miao: A Study in Ecological Adjustment', *Oceania*, 4(1):1–11.

Geddes, W.R. 1976 *Migrants of the Mountains: The Cultural Ecology of the Blue Meo (Hmong Njua) of Thailand*, Oxford: Clarendon Press.

Getz, D. 1992 Tourism Planning and Destination Life Cycle, *Annals of Tourism Research*, 19(4):752–770.

Getz, D. 1993a 'Planning for Tourism Business Districts', *Annals of Tourism Research*, 20(3):583–600.

Getz, D. 1993b 'Tourist Shopping Village: Development and Planning Strategies', *Tourism Management*, 14(1):15–26.

Gittinger, M. and H.L. Lefferts 1992 *Textiles and the Thai Experience in Southeast Asia*, Washington D.C.: The Textile Museum.

Godfrey, S.K. 1982 'Americans Help to Preserve and Sell the Craftwork of Their Laotian Neighbors', *The Craft Report*, July: 8–9.

Goldman, A.Y. 1995 *Laotian Embroidery: Migration and Change*, Bangkok: White Lotus.

Gombrich, E.H. 1964 'Moment and Movement in Art', *Journal of the Warburg and Courtauld Institutes*, 27:293–306.

Graburn, N.H.H. 1967 'The Eskimos and Airport Art', *Trans-action*, 14(10):28–33.

Graburn, N.H.H. 1969 'Art and Acculturative Processes', *International Social Science Journal*, 21:457–468.

Graburn, N.H.H. 1976a 'Eskimo Art: The Eastern Canadian Arctic', *in* Graburn (ed.), pp. 39–55.

Graburn, N.H.H. 1976b 'Introduction: Arts of the Fourth World', *in* Graburn (ed.) pp. 1–32.

Graburn, N.H.H. (ed.) 1976 *Ethnic and Tourist Arts*, Berkeley: University of California Press.

Graburn, N.H.H. 1984 'The Evolution of Tourist Arts', *Annals of Tourism Research*, 11:393–419.

Graham, D.C. 1961 *Folk Religion in Southwest China*, Washington D.C.: Smithsonian Press.

Graham, W.A. 1954 [1920] 'Pottery in Siam', *in The Siam Society Fiftieth Anniversary Publication*, Vol. I: 1904–1929, Bangkok: The Siam Society, pp. 99–130.

REFERENCES

Greenwood, D.J. 1992 'Tourism as an Agent of Change: a Spanish Basque Case', *Ethnology*, 11(1):80–91.

Gunn, G.C. 1983 'Resistance Coalitions in Laos', *Asian Survey*, 23(3):316–340.

Hafner, J.A. 1985 'Lowland Lao and Hmong Refugees in Thailand: The Plight of Those Left Behind', *Disasters*, 9(2):83–91.

Hahn, C. 1990 'Picturing the Text: Narrative in the Life of the Saints', *Art History*, 13(1)1–33.

Hamilton, J.W. 1976 *Pwo Karen: At The Edge of Mountain and Plain*, St. Paul: West Publishing Co.

Hamilton-Merritt, J. 1980 'Poison Gas War in Laos', *Reader's Digest*, October 1980.

Hamilton-Merritt, J. 1982 'The Poisoning of the Hmong', *Bangkok Post*, March 1.

Hamilton-Merritt, J. 1993 *Tragic Mountains; The Hmong, the Americans and the Secret Wars for Laos, 1942–1992*, Bloomington, Ind.: Indiana University Press.

Hanks, L.M. 1983 'The Yuan or Northern Thai', in: J. McKinnon and W. Bhruksasri (eds.), pp. 101–111.

Hearn, R.M. 1974 *Thai Government Programs in Refugee Relocation and Resettlements in Northern Thailand*. Auburn, NY: Thailand Books.

Hendricks, G.L., B.T. Downing and A.S. Deinard (eds.) 1986 *The Hmong in Transition*. New York: Center for Migration Studies of New York, Inc., and Southeast Asia Refugee Studies of the University of Minnesota.

Henninger, D. and M. Hoelterhoff 1982 'The Art of a People on the Run', *Wall Street Journal*, Sept. 29.

Heritage B.E. 2532 'Mother of Pearl Inlaid Doors, a Unique Aspect of Thai Artistic Identity', *Heritage*, Sept.: 27–38.

Herring, K.R. 1985 'Umbrellas', *Sawaddi*, Sept.-Oct.:38–41.

Hirschfeld, L.A. 1977 'Art in Cunaland: Ideology and Cultural Adaptation', *Man* 12:104–123.

Hmong Art 1986 *Hmong Art: Tradition and Change*, Sheboygan, WI:John Michael Kohler Arts Center

Hoagland, L. 1985 The Chitralada Shops, *Loookeast*, 16(9):13–18.

Holiday Time in Thailand 1978 'The Wonderful World of Thai Woodcarving' *Holiday Time in Thailand*, 18(5):12–16.

Holiday Time in Thailand 1988: Thailand Arts and Crafts Year '88-'89', *Holiday Time in Thailand*, 28(4):38–41.

Howard, M.C. 1994 *Textiles of Southeast Asia: An Annotated and Illustrated Bibliography*, Bangkok: White Lotus.

Hubert, A. 1985 '*L'alimentation dans un village Yao de Thaïlande du nord*, Paris: Centre National de Recherche Scientifique.

Hudson, R. 1973 *Hudson's Guide to Chiang Mai and the North*, Chiang Mai: Hudson Enterprises.

Ihde, D. 1979 *Experimental Phenomenology*. New York: Putnam & Sons.

Jansen, A.C.M. 1989 '"Funshopping" as a Geographical Notion: the Attraction of the Inner City of Amsterdam as a Shopping Area', *Tijdschrift voor Economische en Sociale Geografie*, 80 (3): 171–183.

Jansen, K. 1991 'Thailand: The Next NIC?', *Journal of Contemporary Asia*, 21(1): 13–30.

301

Jansen-Verbeke, M. 1991 'Leisure Shopping: A Major Concern for the Tourist Industry', *Tourism Management*, 12(1):9–14.

Johnson, A.D. and Ch. Johnson 1981 *Six Hmong Folk Tales Retold in English*, St. Paul, Minn.: Macalester College.

Johnson, Ch.R. (ed.) 1981a *The Woman and the Tiger: A Hmong Folk Tale in Hmong and Beginning ESL*, St. Paul Minn: Macalester College, Linguistics Department.

Johnson, Ch.R. (ed.) 1981b *The Orphan and Ngao Zhua Pa: A Hmong Folk Tale in Hmong and Beginning ESL*, St. Paul, Minn.: Macalester College, Linguistics Department.

Johnson, Ch.R. 1982 'Hmong Myths, Legends and Folk Tales: a Resource for Cultural Understanding' *in* Downing and Olney (eds.) pp. 86–98.

Johnson, Ch. (ed.) 1985 *Dab neeg hmoob: Myths, Legends and Folktales from the Hmong of Laos, St. Paul*, Minn.: Macalester College.

Johnson, Ch.R. 1988 'The Greening of I-Sarn', *Business Review*, 16(193):11–12.

Jules-Rosette, B. 1984 *The Message of Tourist Art*, London: Plenum.

Kaalund, B. 1979 *The Art of Greenland*, Berkeley, Cal.: University of California Press.

Kacha-Ananda, Ch. 1992 'The Religious Life of the Yao People of Northern Thailand: Some Introductory Remarks', in: A.R. Walker (ed.): *The Highland Heritage*, Singapore: Suvarnabhumi Books, pp. 293–314.

Kampe, K. 1997 'Introduction: Indigenous Peoples of Southeast Asia', in: D. McCaskill and K. Kampe (eds.) *Development and Domestication: Indigenous Peoples of Southeast Asia*, Chiang Mai: Silkworm Books, pp. 1–25.

Kandre, P. 1967 'Autonomy and Integration of Social Systems: The Iu Mien ("Yao" or "Mien") Mountain Population and their Neighbors', in Kunstadter, P., (ed.) *Southeast Asian Tribes, Minorities and Nations*, Princeton, N.J.: Princeton University Press, Vol. 2, 583–638.

Kanokpongchai, S. (ed.) 1991 *Museum of Folk-Culture,* Bangkok: Muang Boran Publishing House.

Kanomi, T. 1991 *People of Myth*, Kyoto: Shikosha Publishing Co.

Kanwerayotin 1992 'The Dying Craft of Candle-making', *Bangkok Post*, Aug. 16:29.

Kasemani, Ch. [B.E] 2527 Ban Meo [The Hmong House], Chiang Mai: Tribal Research Center (in Thai) (mimeo).

Katz, L. 1991 'Thai Folk Pottery', *Ceramics Monthly*, 39, Sept:28–35.

Kent, W.E., P.J Shock and R.E. Snow 1983 'Shopping: Tourism's Unsung Hero(ine)' *Journal of Travel Research*, 21(4):2–4.

Kerdphol, S., 1976 'Government Policy is Leading to Disaster in the Hills', *Bangkok Post Sunday Magazine*, Jan. 1:9–10.

Kerdphol, S., 1986 *The Struggle for Thailand: Counter-Insurgency, 1965–1985*, Bangkok: S. Research Center Co.

Keyes, Ch.F. and P. van den Berghe (eds.) 1984 'Tourism and Ethnicity', *Annals of Tourism Research*, 11(3):333–501 (Sp. Issue).

King, A.W. 1988 'Muang Koong: A Unique Pottery Village', *Saen Sanuk*, 8(9):44–47.

Kinnaree 1991 'Chiang Mai's Colorful Bo Sarng Umbrellas: Setting a Handicraft Route in Motion', *Kinnaree,* 8(9):42–51.

302

REFERENCES

Kulick, E. and D. Wilson 1996 *Time for Thailand: Profile of a New Success*, Bangkok: White Lotus.
Kunstadter, P. 1983 'Highland Populations of Northern Thailand' *in* McKinnon and Bhruksasri (eds.), pp. 15–45.
Kunstadter, P. and E.C. Champman 1978 'Problems of Shifting Cultivation and Economic Development in Northern Thailand, *in* Kunstader et al.(eds.), pp. 3–23.
Kunstadter, P., E. Champman and S. Sabhasri (eds.) 1978 *Farmers in the Forest*, Honolulu: University Press of Hawaii.
Lacey, B. 1982 'Ethnic Colors Explode Market', *Detroit News*, Oct. 3.
Lao 1985 *Lao*, No publisher [in Laotian].
Larnlua, A. 1990 'A Village of Homemade Brassware', *Bangkok Post*, March 16:28.
Layton, D.H. 1968 'Heavenly Trousers', *Suwaddi*, 6(4). 10–14, 26–27.
Layton, R. 1991 *The Anthropology of Art*, Cambridge: Cambridge University Press (2nd Edition).
Lee, G.Y. 1982 'Minority Policies and the Hmong' *in* M. Stuart-Fox (ed.) *Contemporary Laos*, St. Lucia, Queensland: University of Queensland Press, pp. 199–219.
Leesuwan, V. 1981 *Thai Cultural Heritage*, Bangkok: Ministry of Education, The Office of the National Culture Commission.
Leiper, N. 1990 'Tourist Attraction Systems', *Annals of Tourism Research*, 17 (3): 367–384.
Leitch, T.M. 1986 *What Stories Are*, University Park and London: Pennsylvania State University Press.
Lemoine, J. 1972a 'L'initiation du mort chez les Hmong: I. Le Chemin', *L'Homme*, 12(1): 105–134.
Lemoine, J. 1972b *Un Village Hmong Vert des Haut Laos*, Paris: C.N.R.S.
Lemoine, J. 1983 'Yao Religion and Society', *in* McKinnon and Bhruksasri (eds.), pp. 195–211.
Lemoine, J. and C. Mounge 1983 'Why Has Death Stalked the Refugees?', *Natural History*, 92 Nov:6 19.
Lessing, G.F. 1979 [1766] *The Laocoon and Other Prose Writings of Lessing*, W.B. Ronnfeldt (ed.), London.
Levi-Strauss, C. 1963 *Structural Anthropology*, Harmondsworth: Penguin.
Lewis, P. and E. Lewis 1984 *People of the Golden Triangle: Six Tribes of Thailand*, London: Thames and Hudson.
Lindsay, R. 1969 'How "Mao" the Meo?', *Far Eastern Economic Review*, 63(5):182.
Linklater, L. 1988 'Chiang Mai's Umbrella Magic', *Lookeast*, 19(7):34–37.
Lobe, Th. and D. Morell 1978 'Thailand's Border Patrol Police: Paramilitary Political Power', *in* L.A. Zurcher and G. Harries-Jenkins (eds.) *Supplementary Military Forces: Reserves, Militias, Auxiliaries*, Beverly Hills, CA: Sage, pp. 153–178.
Lohitkul, Th. 1990 Phu Thai Dam, *Thailand Illustrated*, 8(24):18–23.
Long, L.D. 1993 *Ban Vinai: The Refugee Camp*, New York: Columbia University Press.
Lookeast 1988 'Thai Art of Metal Casting', *Lookeast*, 19(11):43–47.
Loshak, D. 1989 'Space, Time and Edward Munch', *Burlington Magazine*, 131(1033): 273–282.

Lualamai B.E. 2532 *Jok* Khoo Bua: Survival of an Art Form, *Hotel Information News* 1(8):48–52 (in Thai and English).

Luche, Th. 1969 'Annex A: BPR/RAS Report Area V and VI', *Contractors Semi-Annual Report*, DEVCON (Development Consultants in Support of Border Patrol Police, Remote Area Security) August 1968 – January 1969.

Mabry, M.C. and B.D. Mabry 1981 'The Role of the Arts in Developing Countries: Thailand, A Case Study', *Ekistics*, 48(288):247–250.

MacCannell, D. 1973 'Staged Authenticity: Arrangements of Social Space in Tourist Settings', *American Journal of Sociology*, 79(3):589–603.

MacDowell, M. 1989 *Stories in Thread*, East Lansing: Michigan State University Museum, Folk Art Division.

Manager 1991 'On the Road Again [and successive stories]', *Manager*, No. 34:40–44.

Manibhandu, A. 1988 'The Greening of Isan', *Bangkok Post,* April 21:6.

Marks, T. 1973 'The Meo Hill Tribe Problem in North Thailand', *Asian Survey*, 13(10):929–944.

Marks F. 1994 *Making Revolution: The Insurgency of the Communist Party of Thailand in Structural Perspective*, Bangkok: White Lotus.

Marshall, D. 1981 'The Hmong: Dying of Culture Shock?', *Science*, 212:1008.

McCaskill, D. 1997 'From Tribal Peoples to Ethnic Minorities: The Transformation of Indigenous Peoples: A Theoretical Discussion', in D. McCaskill and K.Kampe (eds.) *Development or Domestication? Indigenous Peoples of Southeast Asia*, Chiang Mai: Silkworm Books, pp. 26–60.

McClain, J. 1985 'Time in the Visual Arts: Lessing and Modern Criticism', *Journal for Aesthetics and Art Criticism*, 44(1):41–58.

McCoy, A.W. 1972 *The Politics of Heroin in Southeast Asia*, New York: Harper.

McIntosh R.W. and C.R. Goeldner 1990 *Tourism: Principles, Practices, Philisophies* (6th edition), New York: Wiley.

McKinnon J. and W. Bhruksasri (eds.) 1983 *Highlanders of Thailand*, Kuala Lumpur: Oxford University Press.

McKinnon J. and B. Vienne 1989 *Hill Tribes Today: Problems in Change*, Bangkok: White Lotus-Orstom.

Meo Handbook 1969 *Meo Handbook,* Bangkok: Joined Thai-U.S. Military Research and Development Center.

Miles, D. 1974 'Marriage, Agriculture and Ancestor Worship among the Pulanka Yao' Chiang Mai: Tribal Research Center (mimeo).

Mitchell, W.J.T. 1986 'Space and Time: Lessing's Laocoon and the Politics of Genre' *in* W.J.T. Mitchell (ed.) *Iconology*, Chicago: University of Chicago Press pp. 95–115.

Moderne Kunst 1979 *Moderne Kunst in Africa* Berlin: Kunsthalle [An Exhibition Catalogue].

Morechand, G. 1968 'Le chamanisme Hmong', *Bulletin de l'École Francaise d'Éxtreme-Orient*, No. 64:53–294.

Morell, D. and Ch. Samudavanija 1981 *Political Conflict in Thailand*, Cambridge MA: Oelgeschlager, Gunn and Hain.

Morphy, H. 1977 'Too Many Meanings', Ph.D. Thesis, Canberra: Australian National University.

Mottin, J. 1979 *Fête du Nouvel An chez les Hmong Blanc de Thaïlande*, Bangkok: Don Bosco.

Mottin, J. 1981 *Allons faire le tour du ciel et de la terre: le chamanisme des Hmong vu dans les texts*, Bangkok: Don Bosco.

Na Renunakhon, D. 1993 '"Mae Chaem" *Teen Jok* and Hand-Woven Textile', *Silk Magazine*, 1(9):81–85 (in Thai and English).

New York Times 1981 'Laotian Needlework from Rhode Island', *New York Times*, March 26.

New York Times 1984 'Hmong in U.S. Find Little Profit in Ancient Arts', *New York Times*, Nov. 18:50

New York Times 1985 'Project Aims to Preserve Folkways of the Hmong', *New York Times*, Aug. 11:47.

Ngamsit, P. 1982 'Baskets', *Sawaddi*, Sept.-Oct.:14–17.

Nildej, S. 1986 'Thai Goldware', *Muang Boran*, 12(4):10–17 (in Thai and English).

Nutcherinphon, N. B.E. 2515 *Laisan* [Weaving Patterns], Bangkok (in Thai).

Pächt, O. 1962 *The Rise of Pictorial Narration in Twelfth-Century England*. Oxford: Clarendon Press.

Pan, Ch. 1991 Yao Dailectology, *in* J. Lemoine and Ch. Chien (eds.): *The Yao of Southern China*, Paris: Pangu, pp. 47–70.

Pandit, V. 1991 'Nielloware in Thailand', *Lookeast*, 22(8):33–36.

Parker, J.E. 1997 *Code Name Mule: Fighting the Secret War in Laos for the C.I.A.*, Bangkok: White Lotus.

Parnwell, M.J.G. and S. Khamanarong 1990 'Rural Industrialization and Development Planning in Thailand', *Southeast Asian Journal of Social Science*, 18(2):1–28.

Peetathawatchai, V. B.E. 2519 *Folk Crafts of the South*, n.l.: Housewives Voluntary Foundation (in Thai and English).

Penth, H. 1994 *A Brief History of Lān Nā: Civilization of North Thailand*, Chiang Mai: Silkworm Books.

Perczel, Cs.F. 1978 'The Queen of Sheba Legend in Ethiopian Art', *Art International*, 22(5/6):6–11.

Peterson, S. 1988 'Translating Experience and the Reading of A Story Cloth', *Journal of American Folklore*, 101(1):6–22.

Phelan, B. 1975 'Plight of the Meo', *Far Eastern Economic Review*, 89(35):20–22.

Phondee, U. 1993: 'The Thai Yuan Fabric Designs of Ratchaburi', *Silk Magazine*, 2(13):91–97 (in Thai and English).

Phondee, U. 1994 'The Original Design of Thai Yuan Fabrics', *Silk Magazine*, 2(17):104–109 (in Thai and English).

Pollard, D. 1987 'The Potters of Pak Kret', *Bangkok Post*, July 30:7.

Pongpaichit, P. and Ch. Baker 1996 *Thailand's Boom!*, Chiang Mai: Silkworm Books.

Popelka, Ch. A. and M.A. Littrell 1991 'Influence of Tourism on Handcraft Evolution', *Annals of Tourism Research*, 18:392–413.

Porter, D.G. 1970 'After Geneva: Subverting Laotian Neutrality', in N.S. Adams and A.W. McCoy (eds.) *Laos: War and Revolution*, New York: Harper & Row, pp. 179–212.

Prangwatthanakun, S. and P. Cheesman 1987 *Lan Na Textiles: Yuan Lue Lao*, Chiang Mai: Center for Promotion of Arts and Culture (in Thai and English).

305

LOWLAND VILLAGE CRAFTS

Preechakul, R. 1987 'Problem of the Illegal Hmong', *Bangkok Post*, March 28:4.
Pringle, J. 1979 'End of the Hmong', *Newsweek*, Aug. 27:8–9.
Pruess, J.B. 1992 'Sanctification Overland: the Creation of a Thai Buddhist Pilgrimage Center' in A. Morinis (ed.) *Sacred Journeys*, Westport: Greenwood Press pp. 211–231.
Quain, A. 1983 'Pottery Making in Darn Kwen (sic!), Thailand', *Ceramics Review*, No. 79:10.
Raksakul, S. 1993 'The Politics and Economics of Art', *Bangkok Post*, Oct. 3:17,20–21.
Raksakul, S. 1995 'Fleeing the War Zone', *Bangkok Post*, Feb. 12:20–21.
Randall, J. (ed.) 1984 *Art of the Hmong-Americans*, Davis, CA: University of California, C.N. Gorman Museum.
Redfield, R. and M. Singer 1969 'The Cultural Role of Cities' in R. Sennett (ed.) *Classic Essays in the Culture of Cities*, New York: Appleton-Century-Crofts pp. 206–233.
Resnick, S. 1970 'The Decline of Rural Industry Under Export Expansion: A Comparison Among Burma, Philippines and Thailand, 1870–1938', *Journal of Economic History* 30(1):51–73.
Ressler, Ph. 1981 'Umbrellas', *Sawaddi*, March-April:17–20.
Richter, D. 1978 'The Tourist Art Market as a Factor in Social Change', *Annals of Tourism Research*, 5(3):323–338.
Ronk, D. 1973 'Building from Ashes of War: Hill Tribesmen in Laos Must Reshape Shattered Lives', *Asia Magazine,* Nov. 18:3–11.
Rosenfeld, C.S. and M.C. Mabry 1982 'Discovering the Art of *Teenjok*', *Sawaddi*, Sept.-Oct.:23–25.
Roux, H. 1954 'Queques minorités ethniques du Nord-Indochine', *France-Asïe*, 9:387–413.
Rush, B. 1983 'The Art of a People in Transition', *Needle Arts*, 14(2):4–8.
Saen Sanuk 1988a 'Thai Handicrafts: A Legacy of Grace', *Saen Sanuk*, 8(8):6–31.
Saen Sanuk 1988b '1988: Reaping the Profit of Visit Thailand Year', *Saen Sanuk*, 8(1)8–17.
Samosorn, A. 1989 'Saengda Bansidh: Thailand's National Artist in Visual Art (Textile), *Kinnaree*, 6(2):19–24.
Savanya 1992 'A Sculpture form the Mountain, *Holiday Diary*, 1(2):62–78 (In English an Thai).
Savina, F.M. 1930 *Histoire des Miao*. Hong Kong: Impr. de la Société de Missions-Etrangères.
Sawaddi 1982 'Crafts of Thailand', *Sawaddi*, Sept.-Oct.:8–39 (Special Issue).
Sawaddi 1985 'Chiang Mai', *Sawaddi*, Sept.-Oct. (Special Issue).
Sawaddi 1993 'Umbrella Making', *Sawaddi*, 39(1):34–37.
Schliesinger, J. 1998 *Hill Tribes of Vietnam: Vol 2: Profile of the Existing Hill Tribe Groups*, Bangkok: White Lotus.
Schrock, L. et al. 1970 *Minority Groups in Thailand*, Washington, D.C.: Department of the Army, Pamphlet No. 550–107
Scott, G.M. 1982 'The Hmong Refugee Community in San Diego: Theoretical and Practical Implications of Its Continuing Ethnic Solidarity', *Anthropological Quarterly*, 55(3):146–160.

306

REFERENCES

Scott, P. 1970 *Geography and Retailing*. London: Hutchinson.

Seidenfaden, E. 1967 *The Thai Peoples*, Book 1. Bangkok: The Siam Society.

Sherman, S. 1988 'The Hmong: Laotion Refugees in the "Land of the Giants"', *National Geographic*, 174(4):586–610.

Shiloah, A. and E. Cohen 1983 'The Dynamics of Change in Jewish Oriental Ethnic Music in Israel', *Ethnomusicology*, 27(2):227–251.

Shitamara 1991 'Thai Silverware', *Kinnaree*, 8(7):40–49.

Shiratori, Y. (ed.) 1978 *Visual Ethnography: The Hill Tribes of South East Asia: Yao and Its Neighbors*, Tokyo: Kodansha (in Japanese with English summaries).

Siamwalla, A. 1997 'Why Are We in This Mess?', *Bangkok Post*, Nov. 12:12–13.

Silver, H.R. 1979 'Beauty and the "I" of the Beholder: Identity, Aesthetics and Social Change among the Ashanti', *Journal of Anthropological Research*, 35(2):191–208.

Sintujarivatr, A. 1972 '*Teenjok*: The New Old Art', *Impact*, June 24:16–18.

Siriphan, S. 1992 'Destination Anywhere', *Bangkok Post*, Dec. 31:5.

Smithies, M. and F. Kerdchouay 1975 '*Nang Talung*: The Shadow Theatre of Southern Thailand' *in* M. Rutnin (ed.) *The Siamese Theatre*, Bangkok: [The Siam Society], pp. 129–138.

Smuckarn, S. and K. Breazeale 1988 *A Culture in Search of Survival: The Phuan of Thailand and Laos*, Yale University Southeast Asia Studies, Monograph Series, No. 31.

Der Spiegel 1979 Auftrag vom Friseur, *Der Spiegel*, 33(28):156–157

Sricharatchanya, P. and T. Atkinson 1979 'Vang Pao Rekindles the Flames of Resistance', *Business Times Weekly*, [Bangkok], Aug.16:10–15.

Srisongmuang, B. 1987 'U.S. Accusation Does Little to Help Refugee Problem', *Bangkok Post*, March 23:4.

Stromberg, G. 1976 'The Amate Bark Painting of Xalitla' *in* Graburn (ed.) pp. 149–162.

Sukphisit, S. 1988 'A Showcase of Antique *Teen Chok*', *Bangkok Post*, Dec. 12:31.

Sukphisit, S. 1990a 'Industry Arrives in the Potters' Village', *Bangkok Post*, June 29:27,32.

Sukphisit, S. 1990b 'The Wondrous Weavers of Phrae', *Bangkok Post*, July 14:21.

Sukphisit, S. 1991a 'The Village of Antique Hunters', *Bangkok Post*, June 6:29.

Sukphisit, S. 1991b 'Sticking with Tradition', *Bangkok Post, Outlook*, Nov. 5:4.

Sukphisit, S. 1991c 'A Family Business that is Bold as Brass', *Bangkok Post*, Dec. 17:27.

Sukphisit, S. 1993 'The Cutting Edge, *Bangkok Post*, May 10:33.

Suksamrarn, N. 1988 'Phrae Laments its Vanishing Forests', *Business Review*, 16(196):13–16.

Sun watthanatham B.E. 2538 [1995] *Pha tho tin jok muang Long, changwat Phrae* [*Tin jok* Weaving of Long District, Phrae Province], [Phrae]: Sun watthanatham, chagwat Phrae, rongrien Narirath [in Thai].

Supho, Ph. 1989 'Yan Li Pao', *Lookeast* 20(8):16–19.

SUPPORT, 1985 *SUPPORT, The Royal Project of Thai Folk Arts and Crafts for Farmers*, Bangkok: Office of Her Majesty's Private Secretary.

SUPPORT 1992: *SUPPORT Foundation* [Bangkok: Bank of Asia, Ltd.].

Suvapiromchote, P. 1987 'Pottery Village: The North's New Tourist Paradise', *Bangkok Post*, Nov. 7: 26–27.

Suvapiromchote, P. 1988 'Bringing the Umbrella Village Back to Life', *Bangkok Post*, May 3:30.

Suwanachat, K. 1990 'Nam Ton Village', *Kinnaree*, 7(2):84–89.

Szombati-Fabian, I. and J. Fabian 1976 'Art, History and Society: Popular Painting in Shaba Zaire', *Studies in the Anthropology of Visual Communication,* 3(1):1–21.

Tambiah, S.J. 1976 *World Conqueror and World Renouncer.* Cambridge, Mass.: Cambridge University Press.

Tapp, N. 1982 'The Relevance of Telephone Directories to a Lineage-Based Society: A Consideration of Some Messianic Myths among the Hmong', *Journal of the Siam Society*, 70(1–2):114–127.

Tapp, N. 1986 *The Hmong of Thailand*, London: Anti-Slavery Society.

Tapp, N. 1989 *Sovereignty and Rebellion*, Singapore: Oxford University Press.

Tasanapradet, P., U. Perngparn, and V. Poshyachinda 1986 *Hill Tribe Population and Family Planning*, Bangkok: Chulalongkorn University, Institute of Health Research, Technical Report No. 02.

Teerakhamsri, N. 1996 'Playing in the Shadows', *Bangkok Post, Outlook*, March 8:27,34.

Tettoni, L.I. 1992 *Chiang Mai and Northern Thailand*. Bangkok: Asia Books.

Textile Art 1981 *The Textile Art of the Hmong*. Decorah, Iowa: Luther College.

Thai Life 1988 'Thai Folk Arts and Crafts', *Thai Life*, 6(1):1–118.

Thai Life 1994 'Thai Textiles: Threads of a Cultural Heritage', *Thai Life*, 8(1):1–127.

Thanya, W. 1997 'Amazing Thailand 1998–1999', *Thaiways*, 14(10):41–48.

The Nation 1988 'The Queen's Birthday Launches Crafts Year', *The Nation*, Aug.12:31.

The Nation 1992 'Country Korat', *The Nation*, Jan. 1:14.

Theptong, Ph. 1991 'Phrae – All Set for Tourism Boom', *Bangkok Post, Horizons*, Dec. 5:1,3.

Thomson, J.R. 1968a 'The Mountains Are Steeper', *Far Eastern Economic Review*, 60(15), April 11:139–141.

Thomson, J.R. 1968b 'The Burning Mountain', *Far Eastern Economic Review*, 60(17), April 25:218–220.

Thomson, J.R. 1968c 'Kang Haw: The Ghost Town of a Northern Province', *Bangkok World Magazine*, April 28:2–4.

Thomson, M. 1986 'The Elusive Promise', *Far Eastern Economic Review*, 134(42), Oct. 10:46–47.

Townsend, L. 1985 'The Art of Yan Lipao', *Living in Thailand*, 18(8):54–56.

Tribal Research Center 1977 Tribal Population Summary in Thailand, Chiang Mai: Tribal Research Center (mimeo).

TTC [1978] *Thai Tribal Crafts Catalogue* [commercial catalogue] [Chiang Mai: Thai Tribal Crafts].

Tuntirattanakul, A. 1987 'Dan Kwien Potteries: The Pride of Korat', *Saen Sanuk*, 7(10):58.

Turner, V. 1977 'Process, System and Symbol: A New Anthropological Synthesis', *Daedalus*, 106:61–79.

REFERENCES

Vaananen, P. 1993 'A Matter of Faith', *Manager*, No. 60:18–22.

Van-es-Beeck, B.J. 1982 'Refugees from Laos, 1975–1979' *in* M. Stuart-Fox (ed.) *Contemporary Laos*. St. Lucia, Queensland: University of Queensland Press, pp. 324–334.

Vang, T.F. 1979 'The Hmong of Laos, *in* J. Whitmore (ed.) *An Introduction to Indochinese History, Culture, Language and Life*. Ann Arbor, MI: University of Michigan, Center of South and Southeast Asian Studies, pp. 93–102.

Vienne, B. 1989 'Facing Development in the Highlands: A Challenge for Thai Society', *in* McKinnon and Vienne (eds.), pp. 33–60.

Viviano, F. 1986 'From the Asian Hills to a U.S. Valley', *Far Eastern Economic Review*, 134(42), Oct. 16:47–48.

Walker, A.R. (ed.) 1975 *Farmers in the Hills: Upland Peoples of North Thailand*. Georgetown: Pinang Universiti Sains Malaysia.

Walker, W. and D. Moffat 1986 'Hmong Children: A Changing World in Ban Vinai', *Cultural Survival Quarterly*, 10(4):54–56.

Ward, J.L. 'A piece of the Action: Moving Figures in Still Pictures' *in* C.F. Nordine and D.F. Fisher (eds.) *Perception and Pictorial Representation*, New York: Praeger, pp. 246–259.

Warner, R. 1996 *Shooting at the Moon: The Story of America's Clandestine War in Laos*, South Royalton, Vt.: Steerforth Press.

Warren, W. and L.I. Tettoni 1994 *Arts and Crafts of Thailand*, Bangkok: Asia Books.

Wedel, Y. and P. Wedel 1987 *Radical Thought, Thai Mind: The Development of Revolutionary Ideas in Thailand*. Bangkok: Assumption Business Administrative College.

Wenk, K. 1980 *Perlmutter Kunst in Thailand: The Art of Mother of Pearl in Thailand*. Zurich: Iñigo von Oppersdorff Verlag.

Westermeyer, J. 1981 'Hmong Deaths', *Science*, 213:952.

Westing, A.H. and L.G. Williams 1983 '"Yellow Rain" and the Chemical Warfare Threat', *Southeast Asian Chronicle*, 91:19–23.

White, V, 1982a 'Hmong Textiles', *The Flying Needle*, 11(3).10–11, 21.

White, V, 1982b Pa Ndau: *The Needlework of the Hmong*, Washington, D.C.: Cheney Free Press.

Whitington, G.L. 1987 'Hmong Tapestries Tell of War in Laos', *Bangkok Post*, Aug. 13:33.

Williams, C.A.S. 1960 *Encyclopedia of Chinese Symbolism and Art Motives*. New York: Julian Press.

Windsor, A. 1991 'The Pottery of Koh Kred', *Sawasdee*, 20(7):14–20.

Wisudthiluck, S. 1992 'Changes in Fabric Design and Weaving at Ban Had Siew', *Muang Boran*, 18(3/4):63–74.

Wright, M. 1978 'Gift Lacquer Cabinets of Siam', *Arts of Asia*, 8(3):41–45.

Yang Dao 1976 *The Hmong of Laos in the Vanguard of Development*, Vientiane: Siasarath Publishers.

Yang Dao, 1982 'Why did the Hmong Leave Laos?', *in* Downing and Olney (eds.) pp. 3–18.

Yawaprapas, T. 1996: Chitralada Shop, the Embodiment of Thai Art, *Kinnaree*, 13(8):78–84 (in Thai and English).

Yee, K. 1988 'Pleasures at Phrae', *Saen Sanuk*, 8(9):48–52.

Yee, K. 1992 'Banh Tawai: Handicraft Village', *Smile-A-While*, Jan.-March:20–25.

Yin, M. 1989 *China's Minority Nationalities*, Beijing: Foreign Language Press.

Young, G. 1962 *The Hill Tribes of Northern Thailand*. Bangkok: The Siam Society.

Zeitlin, A. 1992 'Who Cares: Zoua Vang Lov, A Laotian Refugee Keeps Her History Alive Through Story Cloths', *Art and Antiques*, Oct. 95.

INDEX

Buddha images 221, 223, 225–226, 229–230, 232–233, 246–247, 287
Buddhist 177, 197, 200, 203, 217, 232, 267
Buriram 172, 185
Burma 11, 14, 29, 52, 229, 269
Burmese 224–226, 230, 232–233, 244, 287

California 43
CAMA 69, 72, 80
Camacrafts 113, 121, 124, 132
Cambodia 208
Cambodian (Khmer) 172, 185, 187, 193, 195, 203, 217, 232
Catalogue 43, 45–46, 99, 121, 124, 132, 148n, 155, 205, 213
Celadon 181
Ceramics 181, 194–195, 208, 212
chao khao (hill tribes) 10
Chaos 119, 121
Chatuchak weekend market 263
Chiang Mai 2, 7, 10, 13–15, 18, 38, 65, 74–75, 77, 79, 83–84, 90, 92–95, 120, 138, 167, 169, 172, 174, 176–181, 183, 188, 194, 197, 206, 208, 213, 222, 225, 227, 229, 231, 236, 238, 240, 245–248, 249n, 253, 256–257, 263, 266, 276, 287, 289, 292
Chiang Rai 171
China 14, 29, 56, 104, 108, 216
Chinese 29, 31, 39, 56, 104, 125, 125n, 129, 136, 171, 179, 198, 232
Chitralada 19
Chokchai (district town) 212
Chonnabot (district town) 15, 269
Chuan Miao 104
Chulalongkorn University 190
CIA 33
Commercialization 1–10, 13–14, 16–19, 21–22, 27–28, 30–31, 34–35, 47, 49n, 50, 54, 56–58, 60, 64, 68, 70, 76, 82–83, 85, 87, 90, 98n, 121, 125n, 126, 130, 132, 148n, 166, 190, 206, 214, 216, 220n, 221–222, 249n, 250–253, 256, 264–266, 271, 274n, 287, 292–293

Contact arts 152
Cooperatives 45, 47
Cosmolgy 106, 125
Cosmos 106, 108, 121, 130, 153
Costumes 12, 30, 56, 91, 94, 99, 108, 110, 112, 124, 130, 135, 140, 148n, 263
Court arts 7–9
Craft ribbons 23, 165–184, 212, 239–240, 242, 245, 249n, 262
Craft villages 3, 7, 14–15, 23–24, 222, 225, 230, 248, 253, 272, 275, 282

Dan Kwien 15, 18–19, 21–22, 172–173, 176, 185–220, 234, 238, 244–245, 253, 264–265, 269, 284, 291, 193
Dan Kwien antique (style) 202
Dan Kwien glaze 201, 214, 216, 219
Deculturation 9, 12
Designs 10, 17, 32, 39–41, 43–44, 46, 48, 56–57, 60, 63–64, 66, 68, 76, 82, 84, 88–89, 99–103, 111–112, 114–119, 121–126, 128–132, 134, 136–137, 139–140, 143–144, 146–147, 148n, 149, 152–153, 198–199, 203–204, 222, 231–232, 235, 256, 259–260, 263, 265–274, 277, 280, 283, 285, 292
Disassociation 22, 219, 221–222, 224, 229, 236, 241, 244–248, 292–293
Doi Saket (Chiang Mai province) 179
Don Keo village (Saraphi district) 277–278
Don Muang airport 157, 159

Egyptian 203
Embroidery 54–56, 89, 129, 135–140, 143, 205, 268, 270
English (language) 140, 148n
Eskimos 46, 145
Ethiopia 145
Europe 35, 43, 186, 215
European 203, 275
Exhibitions 45–46
Expatriates 38, 50–51, 62, 74 90
Exports 18–20, 24, 32, 38, 43, 50, 74, 76, 188, 191–192, 197, 201,